Healthcare Value Proposition

Creating a Culture of Excellence
in Patient Experience

Healthcare Value Proposition

Creating a Culture of Excellence in Patient Experience

By
Vincent K. Omachonu, PhD

Routledge
Taylor & Francis Group
New York London

First edition published in 2019
by Routledge/Productivity Press
605 Third Avenue, New York, NY 10017
2 Park Square, Milton Park, Abingdon, Oxon OX14 4RN, UK

First issued in paperback 2021

Routledge is an imprint of the Taylor & Francis Group, an informa business

ISBN 13: 978-1-03-209432-8 (pbk)
ISBN 13: 978-1-138-49969-0 (hbk)

Contents

About the Author..xi

Introduction xiii

1 The Healthcare Industry: Challenges and Opportunities 1

Healthcare Cost and Sustainability..1

The Aging Population in the United States..3

The Growing Trend of Retail Healthcare..4

Telemedicine and Virtual Healthcare...6

Population Health Management 7

Price Transparency in Healthcare 8

Behavioral Healthcare...10

Data Security..12

Healthcare Technology and Electronic Medical Records System...........13

Data and Insights in Healthcare..16

Preventive Care 17

Empathy and Compassion 19

Transition from Volume-Based Healthcare to Value-Based Healthcare 22

Questions for Discussion 23

References 23

2 Determinants of Value: Patients' Perspective 27

Privacy, Confidentiality, and Security...30

Timeliness..31

Patient Safety...32

Care for the "Whole Person"..33

The Hassle Factor in Healthcare 34

Chief Complaint 35

Empathy, Sensitivity, and Compassion 36

Post-Discharge Follow-Up..37

Care Coordination...37
Attention to Detail (ATD) 39
Availability of Information..39
True Cost and Value...40
Clinical Outcomes as a Measure of Value...41
Value Proposition: Health Outcomes Divided by Costs 42
The Patient Experience Value Manifesto..43
Questions for Discussion 46
References 47

3 The Patient Experience...51
Measuring Patient Experience: HCAHPS Surveys.................................54
Tactics and Strategies for Improving HCAHPS Scores.........................57
HCAHPS and Health Plans...66
Questions for Discussion 66
References 67

4 Value Is in the Attention to Detail..71
Attentiveness—The Gold Standard...76
The Power of Details 79
Culture of Attention to Detail 80
Today's Culture of Distraction 81
Core Value Principles of ATD...83
Questions for Discussion 85
References 85
Additional Reading..85

5 Data and Information 87
Why Collect Data?...88
Data Collection Methods 89
Observation...90
Focus Groups and Interviews...91
    Conducting Focus Groups: Group Composition and Size.................91
Surveys 93
Documents and Records..94
Experiments 94
Stratifying Data...94
Data Variations...95
Types of Data 96
    Attribute or Discrete Data...96
    Variable or Continuous Data...97

Distinguishing Data Types...97
Summary 98
Questions for Discussion 98
References 99

6 Lean Management System..101
The Lean Process..104
Lean Tools and Their Applications..107
Value Stream Mapping...107
What Is Value Stream Mapping?..108
Defining Waste...110
The Process 111
Poka-Yoke 113
Kaizen..115
Kaizen Events..116
    Day 1—Current State Documentation..117
    Day 2—Current State Evaluation...117
    Day 3—Characterize the Future State; Plan Its Implementation.......118
    Day 4—Implement the Future State...118
    Day 5—Operationalize the Future State and Debrief 119
The 5S Method...119
Planning for 5S..121
The Steps for Implementing 5S Methodology..................................122
Benefits of 5S 125
SMED..125
Examples of SMED Healthcare Applications 127
Five Whys...129
Kanban...130
Steps for the Implementation of a Two-Bin Kanban System 132
Benefits of Kanban in Hospitals and Clinics 134
Standardized and Standard Work...134
The Process 135
Benefits of Standardized Work...136
Questions for Discussion 137
References 137
Additional Readings 138

7 Six Sigma 139
Key Concepts of Six Sigma..142
Examples of Defects 142

Control Charts 143

Control Charts for Attribute Data 143

Attribute Data Chart Categories 146

Attribute Charts for Non-Conforming Items 146

Attribute Charts for Non-Conformities 146

P-Chart Example 147

Procedure for Constructing a P-Chart 147

Results 150

An NP-Chart Example 150

Results 153

Variable Sample Size 153

Results 153

A C-Chart Example 154

Results 156

A U-Chart Example 156

Results 159

Bringing the Process Under Control 159

Evidence of an Unstable Process 159

The Meaning of a Stable Process 160

Control Charts for Variable Data 160

　Variable Data 160

Judging Process Stability 162

Example of an $\overline{X}$ – R-Chart 162

Procedure for Constructing an R-Chart 162

Results 166

Procedure for Constructing an X-Bar Chart 167

Results 167

An $\overline{X}$ - S-Chart 167

Process Improvement Tools 168

Tools for Managing Ideas 170

Brainstorming 171

　The Creativity Phase 173

　The Clarification Phase 173

　The Assessment Phase 174

Multi-Voting 174

Tools for Gathering and Analyzing Data 175

Flow Charts 175

　Process for Creating Flow Charts 175

Pareto Analysis 177

An Example 177
Cause and Effect Diagrams (Ishikawa or Fishbone Diagrams) 178
    Process for Creating a Cause and Effect Diagram 179
        Scatter Diagrams 179
        An Example 180
        Coefficient of Correlation (R) 181
Discussion Questions and Problems 183
References 187
Additional Readings 187

8 Creating Value Through Digital Transformation 189
The Meaning of Digital 190
Digital Health Applications 191
Impact on Employees 193
Role of Leadership 194
Important First Steps in Implementing a Digital Strategy 195
Questions for Discussion 196
References 196

9 Telemedicine: The Quest for Quality and Value 199
What Is Telemedicine? 199
Structure-Related Measures of Quality 204
Process of Care Measures 204
    The Institute of Medicine (IOM) Model 205
    Dimensions of Quality Measurement in Telemedicine 206
        Effectiveness and Process 211
        Patient-Centeredness and Structure 212
        Patient-Centeredness and Process 213
        Timeliness and Structure 213
        Timeliness and Process 214
        Efficiency and Structure 214
        Efficiency and Process 215
        Equitability and Structure 216
        Equitability and Process 216
Implications for Outcomes 217
Questions for Discussions 219
References 219

Index 223

About the Author

Dr. Vincent K. Omachonu is a professor of Industrial Engineering at the University of Miami and holds a secondary appointment as professor in the Department of Health Sector & Policy at the University of Miami, Florida. He received his PhD in Industrial Engineering from the New York University Tandon School of Engineering, New York. He has two masters' degrees one in Operations Research from Columbia University, New York, and the other in Industrial Engineering from the University of Miami, Florida. His BS degree is also in Industrial Engineering from the University of Miami, Florida. Dr. Omachonu was one of the early contributors to the field of healthcare quality management. His seminal book titled *Total Quality and Productivity Management in Health Care Organizations* received the Institute of Industrial Engineers Joint Publishers Book-of-the-Year Award in 1993. Dr. Omachonu is a Master Black Belt in Lean Sigma.

Dr. Omachonu's other books include *Principles of Total Quality* (co-authored with J. Ross [2004]), *Healthcare Performance Improvement* (1999). His most recent book is titled *Access to Health Care and Patient Safety* (co-authored with M. Taveras Ponce [2013]) His book titled *Principles of Total Quality* was translated into the Spanish language (*Principios de Calidad Total*) in 2014. Dr. Omachonu has published several papers in technical and professional journals and has given hundreds of seminars and presentations to professional and management groups all over the United States and South/Central America.

He has supervised the implementation of the quality management process in several service organizations. He has successfully conducted industrial engineering efficiency and customer flow studies. Dr. Omachonu has served as the evaluator for federal and state funded projects (Substance Abuse and Mental Health Services Administration [SAMHSA], Office of

Mental Health [OMH], Department of Health, Ryan White, etc.) He has been featured twice on CNN Business. He has served on the boards of a number of organizations including Interim Healthcare Services, Fort Lauderdale, Florida; Coral Gables Hospital, Coral Gables, Florida; and Palmetto General Hospital, Miami, Florida. His clients include Humana, Louisville, Kentucky; Leon Medical Centers, Miami, Florida; CAC Medical Centers, Miami, Florida; Peoples Health, New Orleans, Louisiana; Methodist Health System, Memphis, Tennessee; Holy Cross Hospital, Fort Lauderdale, Florida; Baptist Health Systems, Miami, Florida; Bascom Palmer Eye Institute, Miami, Florida; Miami Children's Hospital, Miami, Florida; Memorial Hospital System, Hollywood, Florida; Hospital Corporation of America (HCA), Nashville, Tennessee; and Tenet Hospitals, Dallas, Texas. Other clients include Florida Power & Light, Juno Beach, Florida, as well as some Fortune 500 companies. He has conducted educational and training sessions for physicians all over the United States in the areas of Physician–Patient Communication, Improving the Patient Experience, and Improving the Hospital Consumer Assessment of Healthcare Providers and Systems (HCAPH) scores.

Dr. Omachonu has facilitated several strategic planning initiatives and senior management retreats for major organizations. He has worked with several Black Belts in Lean Six Sigma. He has served as the evaluator for all primary care projects funded by the Health Foundation of South Florida. He is a renowned speaker/trainer in the areas of Management, organizational development, process re-engineering, and methods improvement. He has published research papers in *Health Services Research Journal*, *European Journal of Operational Research*, and *Journal of Healthcare Management Science*.

Dr. Omachonu has been the recipient of the University of Miami school-wide teaching awards and multiple awards for teaching excellence in the School of Business (MBA Healthcare Sector) program. He is one of 100 world-wide recipients of the IBM 2012 Faculty Award for his work in the field of healthcare. He was recently named the recipient of the Alexander Orr Teacher of the Year Award for the College of Engineering (2013).

Introduction

After decades of retooling and resets of the healthcare system in the United States, patients are left wondering if they were ever at the center of the decisions and choices driving the evolutionary journey. After half a century of several iterations of good and bad ideas, there are signs that some aspects of the patients' experience are better and some are worse. Some of the policies seem arbitrary and poorly conceived, while others died in the vineyard of execution. And still, many more seem misaligned with the goals they were intended to achieve. Because the healthcare industry has so many stakeholders with different needs, wants, and expectations, it is always a challenge trying to balance the needs of the stakeholders with the constraints of the industry. Rather than give up in the face of the mountains of challenges facing the healthcare industry, I decided to write this book in an attempt to refocus the bright lights on the patient and his/her interpretation of value. Although the healthcare value creation process largely occurs on a person-to-person basis and often within the confines of an organization, a facility, an office, or clinic, it is still subject to a whimsical pattern of laws and public policies. An awareness of the macro-level factors will deepen our understanding of the challenges facing the industry, while the micro-level factors will help us focus on the daily encounters. Any attempts to understand the healthcare value creating process must be informed by the national and even global perspectives.

According to The Commonwealth Fund's most recent study of 11 different countries' healthcare systems, the United States comes in dead last. This study measures overall industry performance and each country is ranked by five factors that contribute to their score: care process (in which the United States placed 5th), access (11th), administrative efficiency (10th), equity (11th), and outcomes (11th) (Schneider et al., 2017). According to Robert Pearl, former chief executive officer (CEO) of The Permanente Medical Group (1999–2017), "When independent researchers crunch the numbers, American health care ranks nowhere near the top of the list. Among developed countries, the United States has the highest infant mortality rate, the lowest life expectancy and the most preventable deaths per capita." After centuries of experimentation with the healthcare system, it is a perplexing irony that one of the richest countries in the world has not been able to solve the healthcare conundrum. There is a paucity of useful solutions to the problems facing the healthcare industry, and perhaps more importantly, there is little consensus about the causes of the problems. The average American sees "19 different doctors in their lifetime" (Pearl, 2017). This explains some of the challenges posed by paper records—which are still relied on by "about 50 percent of all doctors" according to Pearl (2017). "If you are like most patients, this amounts to 19 different physicians asking you about your allergies, medications and test results. Only one needs to get the information wrong to spell disaster" (Pearl, 2017).

David Rook notes that the best path to fixing the American healthcare system is by broadening access to healthcare through reductions in cost rather than government-mandated access and insurance subsidies, as they do not address the underlying price structure (Rook, 2017). This can only happen when we eliminate the perverse incentives in place at nearly every rung on the healthcare system ladder and empower consumers to shop for value, increase care options, and stimulate competition (Rook, 2017).

"Health-care providers who make prevention a priority are able to lower hypertensive disease, stroke and heart-attack rates anywhere from 10 to 30 percent below national averages" (Pearl, 2017). "If every insured American received care from these higher performers, as many as 200,000 heart attacks and strokes could be prevented each year" (Pearl, 2017).

While the pockets of success stories provide a ray of hope to the industry, they leave us wondering if this is the most we can achieve in an industry that is as complex as any in existence. Is a comprehensive reform of the industry dead or are we closer to the bull's eye than ever before? What lessons have we learned from the mistakes of the past decades?

1. The problems of the healthcare industry cannot be solved by any one discipline; it requires a multi-faceted, interdisciplinary approach involving subject matter experts and stakeholders from different sectors of the economy and society.
2. The industry cannot legislate itself out of the quagmire of inefficiency and poor quality. Policy makers represent one component of the healthcare transformation, but they should not be allowed to drive the debate.

3. Ideas organized around the patients' experience will develop wings, but only if they are balanced against the realistic constraints of the delivery system and the needs of other key stakeholders such as physicians.

4. The patient experience challenge cannot be solved in isolation. The industry has to take a comprehensive view of the patient experience and such a view must take into account the multitude of touch points in the life of a patient and/or his condition.

5. The industry must rethink the concept of "value" and define it in the context of the patients' experience.

6. The ability to focus on population health gives the industry a new level of legitimacy.

7. Digital transformation is indispensable to the current and future state of the healthcare industry.

8. The healthcare industry has been painfully slow at adopting ideas from other industries even when the evidence shows that such ideas would have merit in healthcare. In some cases, it takes decades to adopt proven methodologies and ideas.

In Chapter 1, I highlight some of the key factors and opportunities driving change in the healthcare industry. In Chapter 2, I examine the determinants of value from the patients' perspective. Chapter 3 looks more deeply at the patient experience and how to improve it. Chapter 4 deals with how an organization's attention to detail conveys the perception of value to the patients. In Chapter 5, I emphasize the significance of data, information, and insight and how organizations can use them to drive the patients' experience. In Chapters 6 and 7, I introduce the concepts of Lean Management and Six Sigma respectively. Chapter 8 addresses the implications of digital transformation in the healthcare industry. In Chapter 9, I address the role of telemedicine and how it can profoundly change the healthcare landscape.

References

Pearl, R., 2017. *Mistreated: Why We Think We're Getting Good Health Care and Why We're Usually Wrong.* New York: PublicAffairs.

Rook, D., 2017. "Why America's Healthcare System Is Broken." JP Griffin Group. https://www.griffinbenefits.com/employeebenefitsblog/why-americas-healthcare-system-is-broken

Schneider, E.C., Sarnak, D.O., Squires, D., Shah, A., and Doty, M.M., 2017. "Mirror, Mirror 2017: International Comparison Reflects Flaws and Opportunities for Better U.S. Health Care." The Commonwealth Fund. https://interactives.comm onwealthfund.org/2017/july/mirror-mirror/assets/Schneider_mirror_mirror_ 2017.pdf

Chapter 1

The Healthcare Industry: Challenges and Opportunities

National health expenditure growth is expected to average 5.6 percent annually from 2016 to 2025, according to a report published by *Health Affairs* and authored by the Centers for Medicare & Medicaid Services' (CMS) Office of the Actuary (OACT). These projections do not assume potential legislative changes over the projection period. What continues to be shocking to most healthcare observers is the fact that, despite the growth rate, there is no evidence that the overall patient experience has improved. The report also projects the healthcare share of gross domestic product (GDP) to rise from 17.8 percent in 2015 to 19.9 percent by 2025. According to the report, for 2016, total health spending was projected to have reached nearly $3.4 trillion, a 4.8 percent increase from 2015. The report also found that, by 2025, federal, state, and local governments are projected to finance 47 percent of national health spending, a slight increase from 46 percent in 2015. The challenges and opportunities facing the healthcare industry include the following:

Healthcare Cost and Sustainability

The calls for reform grow increasingly louder as the global healthcare sector continues to be besieged by unprecedented change. Providers, payers, governments, and other stakeholders experiment with various business and operating models in efforts to deliver effective, efficient, and equitable care. These responses are fueled by many factors, including aging and growing populations; the proliferation of chronic diseases; an increasing focus on patient experience, quality of care, and value; informed and empowered consumers; and innovative treatments and technologies—all of which are leading to rising costs and an increase in spending for care delivery. In addition, the trend toward universal healthcare is likely to accelerate growth in numerous markets. However, the pressure to reduce costs, increase efficiency and effectiveness, and demonstrate value will continue to mount.

On average, other wealthy countries spend about half as much per person on health than the United States spends. As would be expected, wealthy countries like the United States tend to spend more per person on healthcare and related expenses than lower-income countries. However, even as a high-income country, the United States spends more per person on health than comparable countries. Health spending per person in the United States was $9,451 in 2015—2022 percent higher than Switzerland, the next highest per capita spender (Sawyer and Cox, 2017). While the United States has much higher total spending as a share of its economy, its public expenditures alone are in line with other countries. In 2015, the United States spent about 8.4 percent of its GDP on health out of public funds—essentially equivalent to the average of other comparable countries. However, private spending in the United States is much higher than any comparable country: 8.6 percent of the U.S.'s GDP, compared to 2.4 percent on average for other nations (Figure 1.1). According to the Centers for Medicare & Medicaid Services, U.S. healthcare spending grew 4.3 percent in 2016, reaching $3.3 trillion or $10,348 per person. As a share of the nation's GDP, health spending accounted for 17.9 percent.

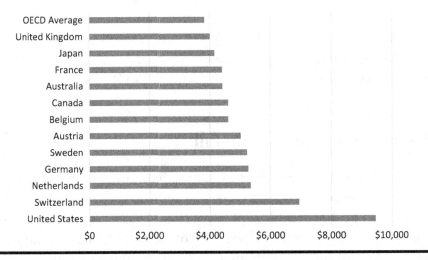

Figure 1.1   Total health expenditures per capita, U.S. dollars, PPP adjusted, 2015.

The expenditure for Australia was estimated.*

Because health spending is closely associated with a country's wealth, Figure 1.1 compares the United States to similar OECD countries—those that have above-median national incomes (as measured by GDP) and above-median income per person. The average amount spent on health per person in comparable countries ($4,908) is just over half that of the United States ($9,451). The average per capita health expense in the OECD overall (including smaller and lower-income countries) is significantly lower at $3,814 per person, or 40 percent of that spent in the United States.

The Aging Population in the United States

The two main variables shaping the healthcare landscape in the next few decades are the age structure of the overall population and the composition of the older population (age, gender, race, and ethnicity). The change in these characteristics over the next three to four decades will dramatically shape the healthcare landscape. Between 2010 and 2050, the United States is projected to experience rapid growth in its older population. In 2050, the number of Americans aged 65 and older is projected to be 88.5 million, more than double its projected population of 40.2 million in 2010. The Baby Boomers are largely responsible for this increase in the older population, as they began crossing into this category in 2011 (Vincent and Velko, 2010).

As the U.S. population ages, the older demographic's racial and ethnic makeup is also expected to change. Many experts expect an increase in the proportion of the older population that is Hispanic and an increase in the proportion that is a race other than White. As 2050 approaches, it is believed that the oldest age categories will grow concerning numbers and proportions. This changing age structure will significantly affect families, patient-provider encounters, patient experiences, and society as a whole. Here are some of the ways the patient experience might be affected:

■ Younger physicians (providers) would have to rethink how best to interact with an older population. The amount of time allowed per patient may also need to be reexamined. The norm of 15 minutes per

---

* Source: Kaiser Family Foundation analysis of data from the Organisation for Economic Co-operation and Development (OECD) (OECD, 2017), "OECD Health Data, Health Expenditure and Financing: Health Expenditure Indicators," OECD Health Statistics.

follow-up patient and 30–45 minutes per new patient may no longer work. Today, it might take as much as three to five minutes for an elderly patient to make his/her way into a doctor's office and get settled. A seemingly simple request from a provider like, "Can I see all the medications you're currently taking?" may take six to seven minutes to address with an elderly patient. Providers usually count on a comfortable mix of younger and older patients to achieve their average visit duration. However, when most of one's patients are 65 and older, that becomes unrealistic.

■ With the current projections indicating a growing Hispanic population in the United States, healthcare providers would have to be more bilingual, more culturally sensitive, and reflect a more diversified staff. How provider offices communicate with patients could become a vital part of their business strategy. Other far-reaching implications include an examination of the number of Hispanic or Spanish-speaking providers produced.

■ Often, significant growth in the aging population implies an increase in chronic conditions and the need to address end-of-life issues.

The Growing Trend of Retail Healthcare

Between 2000 and 2006, when the first retail clinics emerged and quickly proliferated, traditional healthcare providers raised concerns about quality and protecting their market share. Meanwhile, the ability to get affordable and convenient treatment for minor illnesses such as coughs and sore throats became a welcome change with patients. The majority (91 percent) of patients who recently used a retail clinic reported that they were "satisfied" or "very satisfied" with their visit, according to an April 17, 2017, retail clinic survey from healthcare market researcher Kalorama Information.

Given the growing popularity and convenience of these retail healthcare delivery systems, many healthcare organizations have embraced that concept through partnerships with or the creation of storefront clinics, standalone walk-in and urgent care clinics, and supplemental telemedicine services. Retail giants like CVS and Walgreens are pushing further into care delivery, continuing to pressure traditional providers to increase access to care. The real question is: how will shifting the spectrum of care from hospitals to lower-cost sites affect the patient experience?

While the scope of services and delivery methods continue to evolve, what these on-demand healthcare services consistently have in common are convenience, affordability, and access. All three are vital to the patient experience. Doctors will be required to step up their efforts to optimize the patient experience, beyond measuring patient satisfaction.

Although some organizations were reluctant to embrace the retail movement, this disposition is changing. Since 2009, Springfield, Missouri-based CoxHealth has maintained a presence at numerous Walmart Supercenters. To date, CoxHealth runs five Walmart walk-in clinics and one clinic at a Hy-Vee grocery store. While Medicare and Medicaid also reimburse services provided at retail clinics, self-pay patients are expected to pay at the time of service. All prices are provided up front.

For the medium ground between assessing bug bites and performing surgery, urgent care centers provide relief without the wait or expense of going to the emergency department (ED). As they have become more widespread, so has their popularity. According to a study by Accenture, visits to urgent care centers rose 19 percent from 2010 to 2015. There are nearly 7,400 urgent care centers and counting in the United States, according to the Urgent Care Association of America.

One of the chief concerns of the opponents of retail healthcare is the quality of services offered. In the early retail clinic days, physicians' organizations, including the American Medical Association (AMA) and American College of Physicians (ACP), were especially vocal about the trend's potential downsides, including patient safety risks, damage to the physician-patient relationship, and the business threat to physician practices. In June 2017, the AMA House of Delegates adopted a policy that states that any individual, company, or other entity that establishes or operates retail health clinics should follow certain guidelines.

Among other things, delegates said that retail clinics should help patients without primary care providers (PCPs) obtain one; use electronic health records (EHRs) to transfer records to PCPs, with patient consent; and use local physicians as medical directors or supervisors of retail clinics. AMA delegates also stated that retail clinics should not "expand their scope of services beyond minor acute illnesses" such as a sore throat, common cold, flu symptoms, cough, or sinus infection. Similarly, the ACP released a position paper in 2015 that reflected an evolved marketplace in which the largely nurse practitioner (NP)-staffed clinics and primary care offices could coexist and even collaborate. The thrust of the new recommendations urged that retail clinics serve only as a backup alternative to primary care.

Nonetheless, many retail clinics that originally handled a short list of minor illnesses and injuries now play a role in chronic care management and more. CVS Health, for example, announced new MinuteClinic services for women's health, skin care, and travel health assessments. Walgreens, in the meantime, has begun tackling mental health through an online screening questionnaire.

Retailers and grocery chains alike are expanding their operations to capture the value that the changing healthcare industry is creating. Adapting to the needs and wants of their customers, more pharmacy operations are demonstrating an increased focus within the health and wellness space. These companies' evolution is assisting them in gaining a competitive advantage over their customers.

Telemedicine and Virtual Healthcare

Telemedicine and virtual healthcare are very quickly becoming a mainstay in the healthcare field. When it comes to short-term, self-limited needs, telemedicine and virtual medicine offer viable options for meeting consumers' demands. They help consumers avoid having to call a medical office to make an acute care appointment; they obviate the need to drive to the office, sit in a crowded waiting room, and eventually be seen. This convenience can be especially appealing to a generation accustomed to doing everything with mobile devices, from texting to booking and checking in for flights. Patients needn't take time off work or school to visit the clinic for consultations, follow-up appointments, lab results, or post-operative guidance. Physicians have more time in their schedules for new patients and those who must be seen in person.

Telemedicine can meet many different needs for both patients and physicians. Technology compliant with the Health Insurance Portability and Accountability Act (HIPAA) has evolved to where it is helping providers offer continuity of care and a seamless experience for patients while enabling practices to generate more revenue. Telemedicine also enables physicians and other providers to take care of urgent patient calls. Time savings and convenience are the benefits of telemedicine most often cited by physicians. In addition, sometimes patients are too frail or sick to visit the office. Some systems enable the provider to make diagnoses, do follow-ups, and discuss lab results on these calls. Providers also feel the system helps them get a good visualization of problems and informs them which insurances are billable.

The idea of a doctor seeing patients via a computer screen may no longer be new, but the doctors' adoption of telemedicine services with their own patients is still a struggle. The Information Technology and Innovation Foundation shares a vision of how telemedicine can reduce patient backlogs:

> Imagine a world where patients in rural areas far from a nearby doctor can easily find a healthcare provider to consult with online from the comfort of their own homes; where doctors living in Pennsylvania can help reduce the backlog of patients waiting to see doctors in Mississippi; and where patients can connect to a doctor over the Internet for routine medical purposes with a few clicks of the mouse—like they do when ordering a book on Amazon.

Balancing in-person visits and telemedicine will require doctors to adjust their approach to care. Learning to diagnose remotely also requires new skills and detailed reporting.

Population Health Management

Population health refers to the most important determinants of populations' health. Population health has been defined as "the health outcomes of a group of individuals, including the distribution of such outcomes within the group." This approach aims to improve the health of an entire human population. The healthcare landscape has shifted, moving toward consumer-centric care and overall population health management. Adapting to the needs and wants of the consumer (i.e., convenience, timeliness, quality) has created opportunities for the improved coordination of care, which has increased quality and decreased healthcare delivery costs. According to the Population Health Forum, the following indicators measure population health:

■ Life expectancy
■ Infant mortality
■ Death rates
■ Disability
■ Quality of life
■ Self-assessed health
■ Happiness and well-being

Population Health Management is the aggregation of patient data across multiple health information technology resources, the analysis of that data into a single, actionable patient record, and the actions through which care providers can improve both clinical and financial outcomes. The Centers for Disease Control and Prevention (CDC) identified the 10 most important public health problems and concerns as follows:

- Alcohol-related harm and food safety
- Healthcare-associated infections
- Heart disease and stroke
- HIV- and AIDS-related illnesses
- Motor vehicle injury
- Nutrition, physical activity, and obesity
- Prescription drug overdose
- Teen pregnancy
- Tobacco use

For primary and preventive care, value should be measured for defined patient groups with similar needs. Patient populations requiring different bundles of primary and preventive care services might include, for example, healthy children and adults, patients with a single chronic disease, frail elderly people, and patients with multiple chronic conditions. Care for a medical condition (or a patient population) usually involves multiple specialties and numerous interventions. Value for the patient is created by providers' combined efforts over the full cycle of care. The benefits of any one intervention for ultimate outcomes will depend on the effectiveness of other interventions throughout the care cycle.

Accountability for value should be shared among the providers involved. Thus, rather than "focused factories" concentrating on narrow groups of interventions, integrated practice units that are accountable for the total care of a medical condition and its complications are needed.

Price Transparency in Healthcare

One tactic for reducing spending is to increase price transparency in healthcare—to publish the prices that providers charge or those that a patient would pay for medical care—with the aim of lowering prices overall (Sinaiko and Rosenthal, 2011). State progress on healthcare pricing transparency has slowed around the country, and some states have even stepped backward in providing clearer information to consumers about their healthcare costs. Altarum's Center for Payment Innovation, along with Catalyst for Payment Reform, has published state report cards on healthcare price transparency since 2013. In Altarum's latest rendition, the center examined how readily consumers can access healthcare prices across all 50 states. According to the report, 43 states received an "F" for healthcare price transparency. High grades were given to states that required providers to report prices or mandate an all-payer claims repository; offered data denoting paid amounts as opposed to charged amounts; provided inpatient and outpatient procedure information; and had an accessible website.

Most experts agree that that the U.S. healthcare market is unlike any other market. Patients rarely know what they'll pay for services until they've received them. Healthcare providers bill payers pay different prices for the same services, and privately insured patients pay more to subsidize the shortfalls left by uninsured patients (Sinaiko and Rosenthal, 2011). According to Sinaiko and Rosenthal, "prices" refers to consumers' out-of-pocket costs and the amount paid by an insurer on their behalf. Understandably, consumers are mainly interested in what they will have to pay. Therefore, most price transparency efforts attempt to distinguish between total prices (the actual charges by hospitals and other providers) and consumers' out-of-pocket costs.

In a report by the National Conference of State Legislators (NCSL, 2017) prices for health services vary significantly among providers, even for common procedures such as laboratory tests or mammograms, although there's no consistent evidence showing that higher prices are linked to higher duality. One analysis found considerable price variation for common preventive services: a 755 percent cost variation for diabetes screenings (from $51 to $437), 264 percent variation for Pap smears (from $131 to $476), and 132 percent cost variation for colonoscopies (from $786 to $1,819) over a 12-month period. Since the Affordable Care Act mandates these preventive screenings be free for individuals, plan sponsors bear the costs. Another analysis found that hospital charges for appendicitis in California hospitals ranged from $1,529 to a high of $182,955 (Hsia et al., 2012). One analysis found that U.S. spending on healthcare could be reduced by $36 billion a year if the 108 million Americans with employer-sponsored coverage comparison-shopped for 300 common medical procedures (Coluni, 2012).

Indeed, according to the U.S. Government Accountability Office (2011), "Meaningful price information is difficult for consumers to obtain before receiving care." Consumer advocates, as well as employers and health plans, are pushing for greater price transparency. They argue that, if consumers realized they could receive high-quality services from lower-cost providers, they would seek them out. This, in turn, could encourage competition among providers based on the value of care—not just reputation and market share (Hostetter and Klein, 2012).

There are many challenges to making comparative pricing information available. A September 2011 report from the U.S. Government Accountability Office outlined some of the most significant, including the difficulty of determining in advance the health services any given patient will need. The wide variety of insurance benefit structures, a lack of standard formatting for reporting prices, and the difficulty of determining prices when charges originate from multiple providers further complicate these efforts. Consumers have been slow to use healthcare quality reports; it remains to be seen if price information will be a sufficient hook to engage them in comparison shopping for care.

Behavioral Healthcare

The United States spent an estimated $201 billion on mental disorders like anxiety and depression in 2013, according to an analysis published in the journal *Health Affairs* (Roehrig, 2016). That makes it the costliest medical condition in the country. Researcher Charles Roehrig, founding director of the Michigan-based Center for Sustainable Health Spending, examined approximately 10 categories of conditions using the most recent estimates available from the National Health Expenditure Accounts, provided by the U.S. Centers for Medicare and Medicaid Services. Heart conditions were the second-costliest condition, falling far behind mental disorders at $147 billion. Trauma and injury were third at $143 billion.

The study is the most comprehensive look at the cost of mental healthcare issues in the United States because it includes both the general population and those in institutions like prisons (Holmes, 2017). The healthcare industry is starting to recognize that mental health is important to the well-being of employees and consumers, according to a report from Price Waterhouse Coopers (PWC). The report notes that one out of five American adults experiences a mental illness every year. These conditions cost businesses more than $440 billion each year. Healthcare organizations and employers will look at behavioral care as "key to keeping costs down, productivity up, and consumers healthy," the report said.

One of the biggest challenges facing the healthcare industry is how to create and improve access to care for people with mental illness. Mental Health America has established nine measures for ranking access to care for people with any mental illness (AMI) as follows:

The nine measures that make up the access ranking are:

1. Adults with AMI who did not receive treatment
2. Adults with AMI reporting unmet need
3. Adults with AMI who are uninsured
4. Adults with a disability who could not see a doctor due to costs
5. Youth with major depressive episodes (MDEs) who did not receive mental health services
6. Youth with severe MDEs who received some consistent treatment
7. Children with private insurance that did not cover mental or emotional problems
8. Students identified with emotional disturbance for an individualized education program
9. Mental health workforce availability

According to Mental Health America (MHA), 14.7 percent (over 6.3 million) of adults with a mental illness remain uninsured. Missouri (7.7 percent), South Carolina (2.7 percent), and Kansas (2.4 percent) had the largest increase in adults with AMI who are uninsured. With a national focus on healthcare access, the uninsured rate is improving (3 percent reduction).

Unfortunately, MHA notes that having insurance coverage does not mean access to needed treatment. Nearly 57 percent of adults with mental illness received no past-year treatment, and for those seeking treatment, 20.1 percent continue to report unmet treatment needs. The state prevalence of uninsured adults with mental illness ranges from 3.3 percent in Massachusetts to 23.8 percent in South Carolina (MHA, 2017).

People with mental health problems are more likely to have no insurance or to be on public insurance (43 percent). The inability to pay for treatment due to high treatment costs and/or inadequate insurance coverage remains a barrier for those individuals despite being insured (MHA, 2017). One out of five (20.1 percent) adults with a mental illness report they cannot obtain the treatment they need. Unlike the number of people with mental illness who did not receive treatment, the individuals who are reporting unmet need are seeking treatment and facing barriers to getting the help they need.

Data also suggests that not addressing mental illness can affect a company's bottom line. Serious mental illnesses result in approximately $193 billion in lost earnings per year, according to the National Alliance on Mental illness (Holmes, 2017).

Data Security

Patient privacy issues, including concerns about data breaches, continue to be a challenge for providers, payers, and consumers. Providers and payers must be aware of the best practices for data security to avoid the type of HIPAA violations that can harm an organization. According to Cocchi, nearly 40 percent of consumers "would abandon or hesitate using a health organization" if it was hacked, and more than 50 percent of consumers would avoid or be wary of using a connected medical device if a breach were reported (Cocchi, 2016). Regarding cybersecurity concerns over medical devices, according to Cocchi, internet-connected healthcare products are estimated to be worth $285 billion by 2020. This is good because it helps provide virtual care. However, with this connectivity of mobile apps and medical devices comes the concern of hacks and breaches. The news is already full of security breaches, and the situation will only worsen as increasingly more medical devices require cyber security. Hackers have made healthcare data a major target, a particularly worrisome development given the sensitivity of this information.

For individuals to feel comfortable sharing their data, everyone in the healthcare ecosystem must constantly remain vigilant about protecting data and information privacy. Data privacy and interoperability must be addressed by government legislative bodies to create a regulatory environment that encourages research and innovation while protecting patients.

Aetna has launched a new security system for its consumer mobile and web apps that, in something of a twist, makes passwords optional. Instead of a password or fingerprint being the only barrier to entry, Aetna's new behavior-based security system monitors user devices and how and where a consumer uses that machine. Consumers can add biometric protection to their devices (Siwicki, 2017).

Healthcare Technology and Electronic Medical Records System

One of the biggest challenges is to free data from the silos in which it too often remains, an issue that affects both patient care and medical research. A first step is to make electronic medical records (EMRs) interoperable, so patients can freely share their information with as many providers as they wish. The days when patients are greeted at a doctor's office by only a clipboard should be long gone. Allowing for truly portable records will lead not only to major improvements in the efficiency of the healthcare system, but also to improvements in care (Leaf and Minor, 2017).

The shift toward significant investments in technology to optimize physician data usage is quite evident across the healthcare landscape. The adoption of EHRs among non-federal acute care hospitals is nearly universal. In 2015, nearly all reported hospitals (96 percent) possessed certified EHR technology. This rate is similar to 2014, suggesting the adoption of certified EHR systems may be plateauing. In 2015, over eight in ten non-federal acute care hospitals adopted all the functionalities associated with a basic EHR; this represents a nine-fold increase since 2008, before the Health Information Technology for Economic and Clinical Health (HITECH) Act of 2009. Basic EHRs, a historical measure of EHR adoption, includes functionalities, such as viewing imaging results, which are not included in certified EHRs. The hospital adoption of EHRs with more advanced functionality is also increasing while the adoption of EHRs with less advanced functionality is declining. Although EHR adoption rates differ depending on the specific measure, both key measures of EHR adoption—certified EHRs and basic EHRs—consistently show their widespread adoption (Henry et al., 2016).

Although the technology is generally viewed favorably, there are significant challenges, and the technological implementation has not been as successful as expected. While some medical systems are already realizing the cost efficiencies of EMRs, a recent study found that physicians spend more time on desk work than with patients. This suggests that, in fact, EMR technology is not reducing paperwork and providing more time with patients, merely changing the type of desk work that physicians are responsible for (Sinsky et al., 2016).

Healthcare is ripe for other advanced technologies. The emergence of artificial intelligence (AI) has caught the attention of leading healthcare organizations. This technology is already beginning to permeate our everyday lives in very real and practical ways, whether automated checkouts, social media algorithms, or artificially intelligent lawyers. Incrementally, "robots"—by which we mean a machine with digital automation or AI technology—are taking over or contributing to tasks humans previously handled. However, the grand visions of automated cities and personal assistants are still a long way from being commercially available. The utility of the technology must be consolidated—in terms of efficiency, technology, and social acceptability—before it becomes the new paradigm.

The adoption of AI in healthcare is on the rise, and so is its use for solving various problems for patients, hospitals, and the healthcare industry overall (*Healthcare IT News*, 2017). The following are examples of AI applications in solving many of the persistent problems facing healthcare organizations and their patients (*Healthcare IT News*, 2017):

- Insurance verification: At the doctor's office, coverage information is digitally verified to reduce the manual calls typically needed to ensure a patient's insurance information is accurate and valid. The medical appointment booking app Zocdoc has launched Insurance Checker, a new feature powered by AI for its iOS and Android mobile apps and for its mobile website. Seeking to ease a process pain point common for both patients and providers, Insurance Checker targets deciphering, understanding, and verifying health insurance. For healthcare provider organizations, getting insurance information from patients can be a time-consuming process. Administrative costs make up about 15 percent of all healthcare expenditures, according to the *2016 CAQH Index Report*, and Zocdoc internal data reveals that office managers spend nearly a quarter of their time dealing with insurance (*Healthcare IT News*, 2017).

- Healthcare provider organizations spend a great deal of money on customer service representatives taking patient inquiries via phone, email, or live chat. Technological advances in the form of automated chatbots infused with AI are showing promise. Healthcare providers will benefit from the increased use of chatbots, which are becoming more adept at their work because of AI advances. Healthcare providers are using healthcare bots to tackle challenges in the customer service aspects of medicine. Patients can now interact with AI through phones or a website for all their medical queries and requests. Virtual assistants are replacing humans in booking appointments, scheduling visits, medication, and even billing requirements. They offer 24/7 medical assistance and improve service for basic requests. Moreover, they decrease administrative costs for healthcare providers (*Insights Success*, 2017). Most chatbots use multiple technologies: natural language processing, knowledge management, and sentiment analysis (Siwicki, 2017). First, natural language processing tries to understand what a user is asking about. Second, technological provides conversational flow and responses, either directly or through guidance. Typically, natural language processing will identify the intent of a question with some level of confidence. Then, based on the confidence level, the chatbot will either ask a follow-up or disambiguate the question for the user. Once the confidence level is acceptable for the use case, the chatbot will present the proper response based on an intent taxonomy that associates the intent of the question with the desired response. More advanced chatbots will try to anticipate the next question or guide the user to relevant resources or responses based on the previous intent (Siwicki, 2017). According to AI experts, knowledge management systems are the necessary tools that allow the documentation of common questions and answers as well as problem-solving tips accumulated over the life of a product or a solution.

■ One of the major advantages of AI is the ability to assist people in staying healthy. Mobile applications are already encouraging the instilling of healthy habits in individuals and assisting with the proactive management of a healthier lifestyle. It also increases the ability of healthcare professionals to understand the needs of the people they serve and enables them to provide better directions and assistance for maintaining patients' health (*Insights Success*, 2017).

■ AI chatbots are addressing cases like helping customers select a benefit plan, providing customer service, and guiding consumers to resources.

■ Recently developed AI software in Houston, Texas, claims to detect a cancer risk 30 times faster than any doctor, with 99 percent accuracy. Moreover, researchers are training AI to detect tuberculosis (TB) on chest X-rays, which could help with screening and evaluation in TB-susceptible zones that lack access to radiologists (*Insights Success*, 2017).

■ The increase of wearable and other medical devices used with AI are assisting in detecting early stage heart diseases and enabling doctors to monitor potentially life-threatening events at an early, treatable stage (*Insights Success*, 2017).

■ AI is receiving attention in medical diagnosis as well. Numerous healthcare organizations are applying cognitive technology to unlock enormous amounts of data and promote diagnosis. The ability to store more medical information containing journals, treatments, and symptoms is much faster than any human competency. Earlier, diagnostic programs regarding disease-specific features were written using predefined assumptions. Now, with the development of AI, a wider variety of conditions and diseases can be easily handled (*Insights Success*, 2017).

■ AI is particularly used to improve imaging modalities that include reading X-rays, CT scans, and suspicious nodules and lesions in cancer patients. This technology combines machine learning and neuroscience to generate powerful learning algorithms into a neural network that mimics a human brain (*Insights Success*, 2017).

■ AI has shown tremendous value in treatment. Beyond scanning records, AI can help take a more comprehensive approach toward disease management, assist with the better coordination of healthcare programs, and help patients manage their long-term treatment plans. Using AI, doctors can gather collective information on patients' visits and analyze which treatment works best for them.

■ For decades, robots have been used in medicine, from simple laboratory robots to highly advanced surgical robots that can help a human surgeon or execute procedures themselves. Furthermore, they are used in labs and healthcare organizations for repetitive tasks and to support those with long-term conditions.

Chatbots could save organizations $8 billion annually world-wide by 2022, up from $20 million this year, according to one forecast (Siwicki, 2017; Juniper Research, 2017). The annual cost savings from the adoption of chatbots in healthcare will reach $3.6 billion globally by 2022, up from an estimated $2.8 million in 2017. This growth will average 320 percent per annum, as AI-powered chatbots will drive improved customer experiences for patients (Juniper Research, 2017).

Data and Insights in Healthcare

In the era of big data and advanced data analytics, there is no doubt that the healthcare industry has unprecedented access to vast amounts of data that was previously unavailable, including socioeconomic, biomedical, environmental, molecular and genetic information, health status, and prevalence of disease. Questions about value, patient experience, population health, and overall improvement in care cannot be addressed adequately unless we can bring together diverse data sets. The Stanford Medicine 2017 Health Trends Report identified five areas in which "Data is permeating every component of the healthcare ecosystem," as follows:

■ Medical research: Access to new, diverse data and open datasets are fueling drug discovery and making clinical trials and research more efficient.
■ Daily life: Wearable devices, online diagnostic tools, and genetic sequencing services hold the promise of better informed and engaged patients.
■ The patient experience: Health systems are investing heavily in technology, including machine learning, which is proving as effective or more effective than human diagnosticians.
■ Ongoing care: Telemedicine and health apps make it possible for physicians to see patients virtually, outside of traditional facilities for increased access and tailored care.
■ Prediction and prevention: Health data is allowing doctors to build better patient profiles and predictive models to anticipate more effectively, diagnose, and treat disease.

Preventive Care

Any serious consideration of value must include preventive care. Preventable diseases in adults present a significant economic burden. In the United States alone, the cost burden for four vaccine-preventable diseases among adults over the age of 65 is $15.3 billion per year; the cost burden soars to $26.3 billion when including adults ages 50 to 65. Although vaccinations are integral to promoting patient wellness, hospitals face several obstacles when implementing adult immunization initiatives. Challenges include shifting away from the historic fee-for-service (FFS) model, changing physician attitudes toward recommending vaccines, and overcoming a lack of education about the importance of preventive medicine in adults (Paavola, 2017). One way to bolster support for immunization initiatives is to educate providers on the importance of adult immunizations.

Another area in which we are seeing a shift toward encouraging preventive care is through an increased focus on nutrition, exercise, and wellness, as well as a pivot toward value-based payment models. This shift opens the door for the participation of nutritionists and dieticians in a myriad of multi-disciplinary programs involving primary care practices regarding the federal government. Registered dietitian nutritionists (RDNs) now have the opportunity to demonstrate their value as specialists in prevention and wellness, as research continues to reveal links between diet and chronic illness (Edwards et al., 2014; Jortberg and Fleming, 2014). The patient-centered approach to preventing disease through nutrition is squarely within the domain of RDNs. The RDN's role in a primary care setting affords him/her the opportunity to demystify many of the unsubstantiated claims about fad diets and unregu-lated supplements. Although Americans have traditionally been more willing to spend money on nutritional supplements and medications than consulta-tions with an RDN, the decision-making process changes significantly when RDNs are embedded in patients' primary care office and their services come as part of the care delivery process.

With the push to reduce and penalize readmissions and reward improved outcomes, the RDN is receiving new attention from primary care practices. RDNs with a background in diabetes education are especially well-suited for roles in a whole-person model addressing chronic illness. In terms of reim-bursement, these models emphasize wellness and prevention, and encour-age providers to treat whole-patient issues, as opposed to the traditional FFS model that attached bills to each individual point (Boyce, 2015). The RDNs speak to the concept of the whole patient and payment for value. The con-cept of patient-centeredness was defined as such by authors of the Institute of Medicine's 2001 report *Crossing the Quality Chasm: A New Health System for the 21st Century*, as "providing care that is respectful and responsive to individual patient preferences, needs, and values, and ensuring that patient values guide all clinical decisions" (Burton et al., 2015).

Patients generally consider their physician to be a highly credible source of health and dietary information (Hiddink et al., 1997). However, the debate over whether physicians have the time or the skills to provide nutri-tion counseling has been a long one. In a 1994 Connecticut Behavioral Risk Factor Surveillance System survey, only 29 percent of all overweight adults and fewer than half with additional cardiovascular risk factors reported receiving counseling from physicians about weight loss (Nawaz et al., 1999). A survey of 1,030 physicians reported that they felt a lack of time for nutri-tion counseling. This survey suggests that multiple barriers exist that prevent the primary care practitioner from providing dietary counseling. A multi-faceted approach will be needed to change physician counseling behavior.

(Kushner, 1995). This study, however, noted that dietitians had the knowledge and skills to complement the physician and proposed a physician dietitian team. Many years later, the same gaps exist regarding the effectiveness of primary care physicians in this arena.

Empathy and Compassion

In an era of digital transformation and technological innovation, there is overwhelming evidence to support the value of technology in healthcare. Equally compelling is the fact that the best technology in the world cannot substitute for the empathetic care of nurses. In fact, of all the characteristics that make a great nurse, empathy may be the most essential (Aubin, 2017).

Value-based healthcare requires that healthcare organizations get the best talent possible, because better talent will deliver better patient care, including clinical and non-clinical talent. For today's healthcare industry, finding and keeping top-notch physicians, nurses, and other providers is key to patients' well-being and high patient satisfaction scores. However, competition for higher quality talent is fierce, and turnover can be high.

According to Nursing Solutions' 2016 Healthcare Staffing Survey, there are 78 million Baby Boomers. Since 2011, every 7.6 seconds another individual turns 65 years old. This segment represents 12 percent of the population, but that segment consumes 34 percent of healthcare services. However, there might be a shortage of nurses to deal with the increasing demand for services.

The American Nursing Association (ANA) estimates that 23 percent, or 187,200, of registered nurses (RNs) plan to retire in the next two to three years, and an additional 81,900 will switch to part-time status. In total, it is estimated that 269,100 RNs will exit the work force or reduce their hours. In addition, the rising demand for advance practice nurses (APNs) can draw another 198,000 RNs from the bedside. About 67 percent of hospitals report rising turnover rates. The 2015 average turnover rate for bedside RNs was 16.4 percent, which is projected to increase. In 2015, the average time to fill an RN vacancy was 85 days, ranging from 53 to 110 days, given the specialty. According to the American Society for Healthcare Human Resources Administration, 20.4 percent of healthcare employees—one in every five—quit their jobs each year.

When it comes to taking care of the sick and the elderly, we are not all gifted with the capacity to show empathy and compassion. The labor involved in caring for the sick, the poor, the disadvantaged, and the frail is mostly emotional, not physical. Unfortunately, the healthcare industry has not always attracted people with the right temperament and disposition. Some of the people attracted to the field of nursing and medicine today are motivated by the opportunity to easily find employment and make money. Although inadequate staffing levels can be blamed for some of a nurse's rudeness and lack of empathy, it is equally true that a person with a psychotic temperament should never be allowed to practice nursing in the first place. A similar argument can be made for physicians and other providers. It is disheartening to see a clinically influential physician with poor bedside manner.

In no other profession is the need for empathy graver than in healthcare. A patient's complex life circumstances coupled with the tyranny of disease make empathy a necessity in patient care. Studies have shown that empathy is an important skill for healthcare providers and is significantly associated with improved clinical outcomes. Social determinants of health, which include environmental factors, have a larger impact on health than medical intervention. Social determinants of health such as income, education, food and housing access, and racial and ethnic inequality affect one's health from birth to death and can be difficult to understand and control for within a healthcare visit (Hill, 2014). Some patients cannot fully comply with treatment plans, follow provider instructions, return for a follow-up visit, and ultimately, experience good health outcomes because of lack of access to resources. A few specific examples include: problems accessing care without insurance, finding funds to cover needed services or prescriptions, securing transportation to get to and from appointments on time, finding a babysitter to keep an appointment, inability to read, inadequate housing, lack of access to mobile phone, lack of Internet access, or a language barrier.

Unfortunately, very few medical schools and residency programs incorporate the subject of empathy into their curriculum. These healthcare professionals are then expected to function within a healthcare system that does not reward empathy. Whether breaking bad news to a young patient or comforting a grieving mother who just lost a child to cancer, the health profession needs people who are skilled in understanding what the other person is experiencing and can respond with empathy and compassion. Empathy is a prerequisite to a caring response.

Empathy should not be confused with sympathy, which is described as feeling sorry for another person. Sympathy does not require an understanding of the other person's point of view. Instead, it is an emotional response. In healthcare, feeling sympathy for a patient can overwhelm the caregiver with sorrow and may even inhibit proper care. There are many factors responsible for the erosion of empathy, including a lack of time, technology, and the hiring of people with empathy deficits to take care of patients.

The power of distal touch (touch to the hand, shoulder, etc.) has long been recognized as an effective healing tool. Touch has historically been a large part of a nurse's work. When nurses hold a patient's hand or arm to take his/her pulse, for instance, it contributes to the kind of connection shown to release the feel-good hormone oxytocin (Dean, 2017). When applied correctly, distal touching can be an effective tool in the relationship between a care giver and a patient.

Empathy is hardly ever communicated without the clinician's understanding and acknowledgment of the patient's background (Choe et al., 2010). For example, knowledge of the patient, level of education, emotional state, social network, where he/she lives, patient's feelings, patient's understanding of the disease and options, relationships, and nature of his/her work and home life are all indispensable in the journey toward empathy.

One of the unintended consequences of the transition from paper-based medical record-keeping to digital and online formats (EMRs) is the potential loss of the human element that occurs during face-to-face doctor–patient interaction. Technology design can play a crucial role in addressing this problem. According to Choe et al., the interface that records health information could be designed to contain personal characteristics and narratives that help clinicians to better remember each patient, thus facilitating the ability to treat them more like "a human being," rather than as a number or an illness. Patients' distinct characteristics include personality, previous key events, background, relationships, family or guardian information, and the nature of their work and home lives. Visual cues, such as photos or past conversations, can help clinicians quickly recall the patient, even if they meet with the patient only once or twice a year.

It is realistic to assume that empathy would be naturally present in someone who makes a conscious decision to enter the field of healthcare. The reality, however, is that empathetic clinicians are often in short supply. Today, many of the young people attracted to the nursing profession enter into it devoid of the life experiences necessary to consistently engender empathetic responses. On the other hand, many of the experienced nurses are so jaded by their lifelong experience of caring for patients that they have become desensitized to the power of empathy.

Transition from Volume-Based Healthcare to Value-Based Healthcare

In today's rapidly changing healthcare landscape, payers are asking providers to shift from volume-based care (fee for service) to a value-based reimbursement structure (fee for value). This shift toward value-based reimbursement bodes well for the patient, the healthcare provider, and the payer. A reimbursement system based on value motivates healthcare providers to deliver the best care possible at the lowest cost. In return, patients receive a higher quality of care at a better value.

According to McKesson (2016), making the move to a value-based reimbursement (VBR) model aimed at population health requires the following:

- Transforming the traditional "siloed" care model into a network care model, both for increased care coordination and the ability to scale effective interventions with the patient population
- A significant increase in the need to acquire, aggregate, and analyze data across a healthcare network
- An integrated financial and clinical platform for a common view of the patient across care settings and over time
- Reorganizing the institutional structure to accommodate value-based payments; this restructuring can also help healthcare providers identify changes that could reduce operating cost and boost efficiency
- Physician engagement with common goals and an incentive structure that supports these goals
- Instituting new clinical and operational processes that foster sustained behavioral change

VBR helps healthcare providers and institutions prepare for an evolving patient population with:

- Increased access to care, which can lead to more patients and less loss of patients
- A higher number of chronic diseases that must be treated
- An aging population and sicker patients with multiple chronic conditions

- A more engaged patient population responsible for its own care. Patients, in turn, want more insight into their care and value for their dollar
- Increasing market share when patients have more choice in where they receive care

As healthcare delivery moves toward VBR, the business model and the care model become increasingly intertwined. Changes made to care processes can have a significant impact on financial performance. Organizations need tools that help them identify their revenue and cost drivers and provide insight regarding how cost, quality, and care decisions impact the network as a whole (McKesson, 2016). One of the challenges of readiness to transition to VBR involves the modernization of healthcare IT from its current FFS basis to one that can support mixed reimbursement models—that is, a complex mix of FFS and value-based models (Wukitch and Gonzales, 2016).

Of course, healthcare industry challenges are nothing new. Technology and legislation will continue to change the landscape. Doctors and their medical teams must evolve their approach and focus to meet them.

Questions for Discussion

1.1. Which of the challenges discussed in this chapter do you think is the most difficult for the industry to overcome, and why?
1.2. Which of the opportunities discussed in this chapter is most likely to be a game changer? Why?
1.3. What other challenges and opportunities do you believe are most vital to the healthcare industry?
1.4. Select two of the opportunities discussed in the chapter and explain their impact on hospitals and Medicare Advantage Plans.

References

Aubin, B., 2017. "The Importance of Empathy in Nurses and Caregivers." Amplio. https://blog.amplionalert.com/importance-of-empathy-nurses-caregivers.

Boyce, B., 2015, November. "Emerging Paradigms in Dietetics Practice and Health Care: Patient-Centered Medical Homes and Accountable Care Organizations." *Journal of the Academy of Nutrition and Dietetics* 115(11): 1756–1770.

Burton, R., Devers, K., and Berenson, R., 2015. "Patient-Centered Medical Home Recognition Tools: A Comparison of Ten Surveys' Content and Operational Details." Centers for Medicare and Medicaid Services website. http://www.cms.gov/Research-Statistics- Data-andSystems/Statistics-Trends-and-Reports/Reports/downloads/Burton PCMH Re Cognition Tools May 2011.pdf. Published May 2011.

Choe, E.K., Duarte, M.E. and Kientz, J.A., 2010. "Empathy in Health Technologies." WISH 2010, Atlanta, GA. https://terpconnect.umd.edu/~choe/download/WISH-10-Choe.pdf

Cocchi, R., 2016. "Top 10 Issues Impacting Healthcare Industry in 2016." Healthcare News & Insights. January 19, 2016. http://www.healthcarebusinesstech.com/issues-impacting-hospitals-2016/

Coluni, B., 2012. "Save $36 Billion in U.S. Healthcare Spending Through Price Transparency." White Paper. http://64.64.16.103/wp-content/uploads/2012/09/thomsonreuters_savings_from_price_transparency.pdf.

Dean, S., 2017. "Are Our Busy Doctors and Nurses Losing Empathy for Patients?" The Conversation, Health + Medicine. http://theconversation.com/are-our-busy-doctors and-nurses-losing-empathy-for-patients-68228

Debra Shute, 2017, September 29. "What's Next for Retail Healthcare?" HealthLeaders Media. https://www.healthleadersmedia.com/strategy/whats-next-retail-healthcare

Edwards, S., Bitton, A., Hong, J., and Landon, B., 2014. "Patient-Centered Medical Home Initiatives Expanded in 2009–13: Providers, Patients, and Payment Incentives Increased." *Health Affairs* 33(10): 1823–1831.

Healthcare IT News, November 2017. http://www.healthcareitnews.com/slideshow/how-ai-transforming-healthcare-and solving-problems-2017

Henry, J., Pylypchuk, Y., Searcy T., and Patel V., 2016, May. "Adoption of Electronic Health Record Systems among U.S. Non-Federal Acute Care Hospitals: 2008–2015." ONC Data Brief, No. 35. Office of the National Coordinator for Health Information Technology, Washington, DC.

Hiddink, G.J., Hautvast, J.G.A.J., van Woerkum, C.M.J., Fieren, C.J., and van't Hof, M.A., 1997. "Consumers' Expectations About Nutrition Guidance: The Importance of Primary Care Physicians." *Am J Clin Nutr* 65: 1974S–1979S.

Hill, A., 2014. "Empathy: The First Step to Improving Health Outcomes." *Health Affairs Blog*, February 25, 2014.

Holmes, L., 2017. "The Highest Health Care Cost in America? Mental Disorders." *Huff Post. Healthy Living.* https://www.huffingtonpost.ca/entry/highest-health-costs-mental_us_574302b8e4b045cc9a716371

Hostetter, M. and Klein, S., 2012. "Health Care Price Transparency: Can It Promote High Value Care?" *Quality Matters*, The Commonwealth Fund. https://www.commonwealthfund.org/publications/newsletter/health-care-price-transparency-can-it-promote-high-value-care

Hsia, R.Y., Kothari, A.H., Srebotnjak, T., and Maselli, J. 2012. "Health Care as a 'Market Good'? Appendicitis as a Case Study." Archives of Internal Medicine, published online April 23, 2012.

Insights Success, 2017. "Artificial Intelligence: A Game Changer for Healthcare." http://www.insightssuccess.com/artificial-intelligence-a-game-changer-for-h ealthcare/

Jortberg, B. and Fleming, M., 2014. "Registered Dietitian Nutritionists Bring Value to Emerging Healthcare Delivery Models." *J Acad Nutr Diet* 114(12): 2017–2022.

Juniper Research, 2017. "These AI Startups Are Disrupting Healthcare in a Big Way." *Juniper Research White Paper.* https://www.juniperresearch.com/docu-ment library/white-papers/these-ai-startups-are-disrupting-healthcare.

Kushner, R.F., 1995. "Barriers to Providing Nutrition Counseling by physicians: A Survey of Primary Care Practitioners." *Prev Med* 24: 546–552.

Leaf, C. and Minor, L., 2017. "Brainstorm Health: The Biggest Challenges in Health Care Data." *Fortune.* http://fortune.com/2017/09/01/brainstorm-health-the-big gest-challenges-in-health-care-data/

McKesson Health, 2016. "Journey to Value: The State of Value-Based Reimbursement in 2016." A New National Study of 465 Payers and Hospitals Conducted by ORC International and Commissioned by McKesson. Las Vegas, Nev., June 13, 2016-AHIP Institute & Expo. http://www.mckessonhs.com

Mental Health America, 2017. "Mental Health in America—Access to Care Data." http://www.Mentalhealthamerica.net.

National Conference of State Legislators (NCSL), 2017. http://www.ncsl.org/issues research/health/transparency-and-disclosure-health-costs.aspx#Table 1

Nawaz, H., Adams, M.L. and Katz, D.L., 1999. "Weight Loss Counseling by Healthcare Providers." *Am J Pub. Health* 89: 764–767.

"OECD Health Data: Health expenditure and financing: Health expenditure indica-tors", OECD Health Statistics (database). DOI: 10.1787/health-data-en (Accessed on March 19, 2017)

Paavola, A., 2017. "The Importance of Preventive Care Strategies in a Changing Healthcare Environment." *Becker's Hospital Review.* https://www.beckershospit alreview.com/population-health/the-importance-of-preventive-care-strategies -in-a-changing-healthcare-environment.html

PWC, 2014. "Creating a Mentally Healthy Workplace – Return on Investment Analysis." https://www.headsup.org.au/docs/default-source/resources/beyondbl ue_workplaceroi_finalreport_may-2014.pdf

Roehrig, C., 2016. "Mental Disorders Top the List of the Most Costly Conditions in the United States: $201 Billion." *Health Affairs* 35(6): 1130–1135.

Sawyer, B. and Cox, Cynthia, 2017. "How Does Health Spending in the U.S. Compare to Other Countries?" Peterson-Kaiser Health System Tracker. https://www.hea lthsystemtracker.org/chart-collection/health-spending-u-s-compare-countries/#ite m-average-wealthy-countries-spend-half-much-per-person-health-u-s-spends.

Sinaiko, A.D. and Rosenthal, M.B., 2011. "Increased Price Transparency in Health Care—Challenges and Potential Effects." *N Engl J Med* 364: 891–894.

Sinsky, C., Colligan, L., Li, L., Prgomet, M., Reynolds, S., Goeders, L., Westbrook, J., Tutty, M., and Blike, G., 2016. "Allocation of Physician Time in Ambulatory Practice: A Time and Motion Study in 4 Specialties." *Annals of Internal Medicine* 165(11): 753–761, December 2016.

Siwicki, B., 2017. "Aetna Replacing Security Passwords with Machine Learning Tools." *Healthcare It News*, July 14, 2017. http://www.healthcareitnews.com/news/aetnareplacing-security-passwords-machine-learning-tools.

Siwicki, B., 2017. "AI Chatbots Might Be the Money-Savers Hospitals Are Looking for." *Healthcare IT News*. http://www.healthcareitnews.com/news/ai-chatbots-might-be money-savers-hospitals-are-looking.

The OACT Report. http://www.cms.gov/Research-Statistics-Data-and Systems/Statistics-Trends-and-Reports/NationalHealthExpendData/NationalHealthAccounts Projected.html

U.S. Government Accountability Office, 2011. "Meaningful Price Information Is Difficult for Consumers to Obtain Before Receiving Care." September 23, 2011 http://www.gao.gov/products/GAO-11-791

Vincent, Grayson K. and Victoria A. Velko, 2010. *The Next Four Decades, The Older Population in the United States: 2010 to 2050, Current Population Reports*: P25–1138, U.S. Census Bureau, Washington, DC.

Wukitch, C.J. and Gonzales, A., 2016. "Value-Based Reimbursement in Healthcare." McKesson Health Solutions. https://www.mckesson.com/blog/payer-provider-value-based-reimbursement/

Chapter 2

Determinants of Value: Patients' Perspective

Regardless of the product or services being purchased, one thing is clear—no one likes to pay for something that doesn't work. The industry can no longer hide behind its "uniqueness" to deflect attention from the important debate regarding the value of its services. The traditional arguments offered about the complexity of healthcare services can no longer insulate the industry from scrutiny. The rising cost of healthcare services coupled with increasing copays is causing patients to question the value of what they are getting. The patient perspective of value is particularly important now, as patients are responsible for more and more of the costs of their care.

Today, more than one in four Americans report challenges paying for their medical bills, and about 79 percent of cancer patients report moderate to catastrophic financial burden related to their care. Low-income families often spend more than 20 percent of their after-tax income on out-of-pocket healthcare spending, even when enrolled in low- or no-deductible plans (Seidman et al., 2017). Patients typically ponder the following aspects of their encounter to determine the value of the healthcare services they receive:

- The extent to which the chief complaint was addressed or resolved
- The extent to which their symptoms were effectively addressed
- The patient's perception of whether he/she was treated like a "whole person"
- The true cost of the service received
- How much of a hassle it was to access and receive the service

- Whether the service was delivered with empathy and compassion
- The extent to which the staff and clinicians enhanced the patient's understanding and knowledge of his/her condition/symptoms to take better care of themselves or prevent a recurrence
- The extent to which other knowledgeable people would confirm the scientific validity of the treatment option provided

In certain cases, it is very difficult to measure value in the context of a short or sporadic patient encounter, that is, what a patient might express is the perception of value-as-you-go. In some cases, these assessments of value can only be made over a long time; however, patients continue to assess their experience for as long as it takes. The healthcare market behaves differently from other markets. Value in the context of clinical outcomes may require a longer assessment via a longitudinal study. The value of a healthcare service is informed by the time horizon over which its value is determined. Ideally, value should be measured over the patient's lifetime. In practice, measurement is limited to shorter time frames due to various market factors (e.g., patients switch insurers multiple times throughout their lives, other co-morbidities, fragmented care, etc.).

Healthcare consumers lack the information necessary to make the best purchasing decisions when confronted with a health condition or crisis. Most healthcare practitioners would admit that the healthcare system is simply too complex. Healthcare decisions sometimes carry with them enormous consequences, with irremediable effects. In this regard, the healthcare marketplace does not behave like other markets. One of the profoundly enduring requirements of a functioning healthcare market is the provision that the purchasers of services will understand what they are getting.

There are several reasons why healthcare organizations need a clear definition of value. If the concept of value is to be taken seriously, the rewards, reimbursements, and incentives applied to the systems that deliver care would have to be aligned with value creation. The concept of value is meaningless unless we can accurately measure it. Some organizations erroneously measure value in terms of quantity or volume of activities performed or the process of care. Patients may not appreciate the fact that a healthcare facility or practitioner has performed so many unnecessary procedures on them. Real value should be measured in terms of clinical and service outcomes relative to costs in the context of the customers' total, complete experience.

Another real challenge with the value proposition is that some providers tend to define and measure value in terms of the aspects of care they directly control or affect. These providers argue that the particular aspects of the services they control worked out well, stating that they do not control what the other providers do. While this might be true in certain cases, it does not address the patients' perception of value. This is analogous to a basketball team in which a star player scores 50 points but for a losing cause. There can be no winners on a losing team! This explains why some physicians fail to accept joint responsibility for outcomes, blaming lack of control over "outside" providers involved in care, even when those providers work for the same hospital.

When organizations focus on cost reduction without regard for the associated outcomes, they make a mockery of the concept of value. According to Porter and Teisberg (2006), The proper unit for measuring value should encompass all services or activities that jointly determine success in meeting a set of patient needs. These needs are determined by the patient's medical condition, defined as an interrelated set of medical circumstances that are best addressed in an integrated way. The definition of a medical condition includes the most common associated conditions—meaning that care for diabetes, for example, must integrate care for conditions such as hypertension, renal disease, retinal disease, and vascular disease and that value should be measured for everything included in that care.

Keckley (2015) notes that, in most industries, value as defined by consumers is associated with four attributes:

■ Accessibility: "Can I get what I need or want from you?"
■ Service: "Is dealing with you a pleasant experience?"
■ Effectiveness: "Is what you're providing going to satisfy my need or want?"
■ Costs: "What's the cost to me and my family, and is it worth it?"

The healthcare industry continues to offer a myriad of reasons why it cannot adopt these dimensions of value. Knowing what a test, procedure, drug, or visit costs before the service is rendered would be an important factor in the patient's ability to assess value. If the healthcare industry is serious about its value proposition, it can make such information available to patients. Healthcare organizations can take this concept to the next level by delivering the information through the consumer's smartphone with comparison pricing readily accessible. Most providers struggle with the concept of value because the current structure and information systems of healthcare delivery make it difficult to measure and deliver real value. Because patients have a limited knowledge and understanding of clinical outcomes, they tend to define value mainly in the context of their personal experience. That is not to say that patients do not care about clinical outcomes.

The value is expressed as what we gain relative to what we give up—the benefit relative to the cost. In this chapter, we examine the factors that would influence the patient's perception regarding the value of the services he/she receives. Value in healthcare is expressed as the physical health and sense of well-being achieved relative to the cost. Therefore, high value in healthcare means getting the right care, at the right time, to the right patient, for the right price, and the right patient experience level.

Some physicians do not believe that patient satisfaction is a goal worth pursuing. They believe that the only thing a patient should care about is a correct diagnosis, a proper treatment plan, and the doctor's medical knowledge. While it is true that patients value these things, patients also value whether the doctor treats them with respect and courtesy, listens to them, displays empathy and compassion, and takes the time to explain what is being done and why.

There are many factors that influence the patients' perception of value. In the instances in which patients reflect on the value of the services they received, the focus of their reflections tends to include both the tangible and intangible aspects of their experience. Below is a discussion of the factors that could alter or reinforce patients' perception of value.

Privacy, Confidentiality, and Security

The absence of service elements such as privacy, confidentiality, and security would in most cases create the perception of less value. There are various reasons for placing a high value on protecting the privacy, confidentiality, and security of health information (Pritts, 2008). Some theorists depict privacy as a basic human good or right with intrinsic value (Fried, 1968; Moore, 2005; NRC, 2007; Terry and Francis, 2007). They see privacy as being objectively valuable in itself, as an essential component of human well-being. They believe that respecting privacy and autonomy is a form of recognizing the attributes that give humans their moral uniqueness.

The more common view is that privacy is valuable because it facilitates or promotes other fundamental values, including ideals of personhood

(Bloustein, 1967; Gavison, 1980; Post, 2006; Solove, 2006; Taylor, 1989; Westin, 1966), such as:

- Personal autonomy (the ability to make personal decisions)
- Individuality
- Respect
- Dignity and worth as human beings

Patients place a high value on breaches of privacy and confidentiality not only because they may affect a person's dignity, but can also cause harm. When personally identifiable health information, for example, is disclosed to an employer, insurer, or family member, patients worry that it can result in stigma, embarrassment, and discrimination. Thus, without some assurance of privacy, patients may be reluctant to provide candid and complete disclosures of sensitive information even to their physicians. Confidentiality is particularly important to adolescents who seek healthcare. When adolescents perceive that health services are not confidential, they report that they are less likely to seek care, particularly for reproductive health matters or substance abuse (Weddle and Kokotailo, 2005). In addition, the willingness of a person to make self-disclosures necessary to mental health and substance abuse treatment may decrease as the perceived negative consequences of a breach of confidentiality increase (Petrila, 1999; Roback and Shelton, 1995; Taube and Elwork, 1990).

Timeliness

Timeliness is another important characteristic required for the patients' perception of value. Timeliness in healthcare is the system's capacity to provide care quickly after a need is identified. It is one of the six dimensions of quality the Institute of Medicine (IOM) established as a priority for improving the healthcare system (AHRQ, 2014). Measures of timeliness include the following:

- Time spent waiting in doctors' offices
- Waiting time in the emergency department
- Time to obtain an appointment (for non-routine care)
- The interval between identifying a need for specific tests and treatments and actually receiving services

- Time to receive a call back from a provider or physician
- Waiting time for pain medication

The consequences of lack of timeliness are quite extensive and grave. Timeliness has a tremendous impact on morbidity and mortality, as follows:

- Lack of timeliness can result in emotional distress, physical harm, and higher treatment costs (Boudreau et al., 2004).
- Stroke patients' mortality and long-term disability are largely influenced by the timeliness of therapy (Kwan et al., 2004).
- Timely delivery of appropriate care also can help reduce mortality and morbidity for chronic conditions such as kidney disease (Kinchen et al., 2002).
- Timely delivery of childhood immunizations helps maximize protection from vaccine-preventable diseases while minimizing risks to the child and reducing the chance of disease outbreaks (Luman et al., 2005).
- Timely antibiotic treatments are associated with improved clinical outcomes (Houck and Bratzler, 2005).

The patient has a sense of urgency (real or imagined) about the state of his/her condition. The patient's assessment of the value of the care received is a function of the caregiver's response to the patient's notion of urgency. Healthcare should happen promptly, for the sake of both patients and healthcare providers. Today, most patients must wait on the telephone, wait for appointments, wait in the doctor's office, and wait for test results. Waiting can take an emotional toll on patients and their family members. In the worst-case scenario, waiting can be medically harmful. Anxiety and unexplained delays create a lethal mix of emotions that can derail any notion of value in the service received.

Patient Safety

Patient safety is a critical component of the value proposition. Without patient safety, it is impossible for a patient to entertain the notion of value in a healthcare service encounter. The IOM defines patient safety as "freedom from accidental injury due to medical care or medical errors" (Kohn et al., 2000). In 1999, the IOM published *To Err Is Human: Building a Safer Health System*, which called for a national effort to reduce medical errors and improve patient safety (Kohn et al., 2000). The absence of patient safety is a non-starter in any attempt to measure value. Patient safety refers to how hospitals and other healthcare organizations protect their patients from errors, injuries, accidents, and infections. While many hospitals are good at keeping their patients safe, some hospitals are not. According to Leapfrog Hospital Safety Grade, many hospitals in the United States have safety records that would not be tolerated in any other industry. The statistics are alarming:

■ As many as 440,000 people die every year from hospital errors, injuries, accidents, and infections
■ Every year, one out of every twenty-five patients develops an infection while in the hospital—an infection that did not have to happen
■ A Medicare patient has a one in four chance of experiencing injury, harm, or death when admitted to a hospital
■ Today alone, more than 1,000 people will die because of a preventable hospital error

Of all the members of the healthcare team, nurses play a critical role in ensuring patient safety by monitoring patients for clinical deterioration, remaining vigilant in detecting errors and near misses, and performing other life-saving acts to ensure patients receive safe care. An excellent patient safety program requires the involvement of all staff—clinical and non-clinical, as well as great leadership.

Care for the "Whole Person"

While a clinician's focus should be on the outcomes associated with a patient's condition, there are several other factors that affect the "whole person." A 2008 IOM report accurately describes the fears and worries that accompany most life-threatening illnesses, regardless of the diagnosis. These include basics like:

■ The physical pain and exhaustion of the condition and its treatment
■ Not understanding the diagnosis, treatment options, and how to manage one's illness and overall health
■ Not having family members or other people who can provide emotional support and practical day-to-day help, such as performing important household tasks

- Not having transportation to medical appointments, pharmacies, or other health services
- Financial problems, ranging from concerns about health insurance to payments for treatments, or problems paying household bills during and after treatment
- Concern for how family members and loved ones are coping
- The challenges of changing behaviors to minimize the impact of the disease (smoking, exercise, dietary changes, etc.).

Below is an excerpt from an interview with a patient:

> Each interaction I have with your office has either left me feeling like a whole person or like a catalogue of individual and separate issues. There are times when I feel that I am being bounced around from person-to-person with no one willing to take responsibility for addressing all of my needs. Each person seems to pick and choose which of my issues they prefer to address at any given time. I am passed from one provider to the other, with each provider remaining detached from my core problem. No one seems to remember or know anything about me; no one seems to really care.

The Hassle Factor in Healthcare

The American Society of Internal Medicine defined the hassle factor as follows (ASIM, 1990):

> The increasingly intrusive and often irrational administrative, regulatory review, and paperwork burdens being placed on patients and physicians by the Medicare program and other insurers.

Hassles represent the challenges encountered by patients in navigating their health and life circumstances. Here's a typical scenario encountered by a patient with a medical need. The patient calls the doctor's office to make an appointment, keeps the appointment by visiting the doctor's office, runs across town to a lab for a blood test or diagnostic procedure, and then gets an appointment for an MRI. There's a good chance all this will require several agonizing phone calls and much back and forth with the patient's insurance company. In some cases, the doctor believes the patient actually needs an MRI, but would not authorize it because the health insurance company requires the patient first to have an unnecessary X-ray. No matter the perspective, the process is a hassle and time-consuming. Each appointment requires the patient to take time off from work or other matters. About a third of working adults say their jobs do not come with paid sick leave, according to a poll by National Public Radio, The Robert Wood Johnson Foundation, and the Harvard T.H. Chan School of Public Health (Kodjak, 2016). However, many doctors say it is not just the system they created that is complicated. It is also complex rules imposed by Medicare and insurance companies that make being a patient very difficult. In addition, the hassle factor is by no means limited to patients and their family members. Physicians experience more than their fair share of hassles, and patients feel the effects.

Such annoyances can have the following direct consequences for patients:

■ Medical students may be discouraged from certain fields of medicine
■ Patients may find physicians less accessible or willing to add to their patient caseloads
■ Administrative costs increase—leading to higher premiums and physicians' fees
■ Patients are denied insurance benefits for necessary and appropriate services
■ Physicians find their roles changing from patient advocate to cost-containment watchdog for the insurance company (ASIM, 1990)

Patients generally expect some challenges when visiting a facility. What patients do not expect is a reckless indifference to the irritations of navigating such a complex system. Worse, patients are often unaware of resources that could help them overcome or manage these obstacles. Even when they are aware, limitations in mobility, fatigue, pain, transportation, or cost often prevent them from taking advantage of resources that could actually help them (Jerant et al., 2005).

Chief Complaint

When asked to assess the value of a medical care service, a patient's first inclination is to answer the question in the context of his/her chief complaint. A chief complaint is the medical term to describe the patient's primary problem that led him/her to seek medical attention and about which he/she is most concerned. The chief complaint is a patient's self-reported primary reason for presenting for medical care. The physician obtains this chief complaint in the initial part of the visit when the medical history is taken. It will be elicited by asking the patient what brings him/her to be seen and what major symptoms or problems he/she is experiencing. Even when a physician determines the chief complaint must take a backseat to a more urgent or critical issue, the necessary communication is still vital to the patient's notion of value.

Empathy, Sensitivity, and Compassion

Empathy is defined as "the ability to understand and share the feelings of another." It is the capacity to put oneself in another's shoes, feel what that person is enduring, and share his/her emotions. Empathy is the recognition and validation of a patient's fear, anxiety, pain, and worry. Moreover, it is the ability to facilitate more accurate diagnoses and more caring treatment (MedicalGPS, 2016). Research presented at the 2016 Annual Meeting of the American Academy of Orthopaedic Surgeons (AAOS) linked patient-perceived physician empathy with improved outcomes and medical care satisfaction. According to the study, 65 percent of patient satisfaction was attributed to physician empathy. Many other studies have recognized empathy's impact on improving health outcomes and its significance to patient care. Empathy extends far beyond a patient's medical history, signs, and symptoms. It is more than a clinical diagnosis and treatment. Empathy encompasses a connection and an understanding that includes the mind, body, and soul. It is a highly effective and powerful communication tool that can help build patient trust, calm anxiety, and improve health outcomes (MedicalGPS, 2016). Research conducted at Massachusetts General Hospital and published in the *Journal of General Internal Medicine* in 2012 revealed that empathy in healthcare was essential to the formation of strong patient-physician relationships, positive patient outcomes, and overall satisfaction with the experience (Riess et al., 2012). The following excerpt from a patient interview illustrates the point of empathy, sensitivity, and compassion:

> After checking in, I returned to the crowded waiting area to wait until I am called. One of the ladies from the back called out my

name. I stood up, and before I could walk towards her, she said, "Ms. Jones, was your number disconnected? We tried to contact you twice and was told your number was disconnected." Feeling thoroughly embarrassed, I said, "No! my number was never disconnected." She then said, "Can you please confirm your telephone number?" At that time, I decided not to publicize my phone number in a waiting room filled with strangers. I walked up to her and provided her with the information she needed. As she walked away, she turned around and said, "Be sure this is a good number, now."

Post-Discharge Follow-Up

Patients face tremendous anxiety over what happens to them after they leave a healthcare facility's care and supervision. Consequently, the value proposition must include what a healthcare facility does to mitigate that fear and anxiety on the patient's part. The healthcare system's high readmission rates are generally attributed to inadequate communication with the patient and his/her doctors at discharge, including physicians' failure to follow-up after discharge (Epstein, 2009; Weissman et al., 1999).

Care Coordination

When viewed through the eyes of the patient, the value of healthcare services is significantly diminished if there is a failure in care coordination. Patients get frustrated when they believe the care they have received is highly fragmented, and no one person or entity is responsible for their entire experience. Patients often feel that healthcare facilities pick and choose which aspects of their problems to address, and it is up to each facility to do what needs to be done. The IOM identifies care coordination as a key strategy with the potential to improve the effectiveness, safety, and efficiency of the U.S. healthcare system. Well-designed, targeted care coordination delivered to the right people can improve outcomes for everyone: patients, providers, and payers. Care coordination involves deliberately organizing patient care activities and sharing information among all the participants concerned with a patient's care to achieve safer, more effective care. This means that the patient's needs and preferences are known ahead of time and communicated at the right time to the right people, and that this information is used to provide safe, appropriate, and effective patient care (Agency for Healthcare Research and Quality (AHRQ), 2016). The continuity and coordination of care between medical and behavioral health services is a major issue facing the healthcare delivery system.

The main goal of care coordination is to meet patients' needs and preferences in the delivery of high-quality, high-value healthcare. Examples of specific care coordination activities include (AHRQ, 2016):

■ Establishing accountability and agreeing on responsibility
■ Communicating and sharing knowledge
■ Helping with transitions of care
■ Assessing patient needs and goals
■ Creating a proactive care plan
■ Monitoring and follow-up, including responding to changes in patients' needs
■ Supporting patients' self-management goals
■ Linking to community resources
■ Working to align resources with patient and population needs

The value the patient ascribes to care coordination cannot be overstated. While everyone recognizes the importance of care coordination, the U.S. healthcare system faces significant challenges in addressing it. The following exemplify the problems:

■ Current healthcare systems are often disjointed, and processes vary among primary care and specialty sites
■ Patients are often unclear why they are being referred from primary care to a specialist, how to make appointments, and what to do after seeing a specialist
■ Specialists do not consistently receive clear reasons for the referral or adequate information on tests already performed. Primary care physicians often do not receive information about what happened in a referral visit
■ Referral staff deal with many processes and lost information, meaning care is less efficient
■ There is rarely one entity willing to take responsibility for the outcomes of the entire process

The following voice of the customer (patient) interview illustrates the point:

> Each interaction I've had with your hospital has either left me feeling like a whole person or like a catalog of individual and separate issues. There are times when I feel that I am being bounced around from person to person, with no one willing to take responsibility for addressing all of my needs. Each person seems to pick and choose which of my issues he/she prefers to address at any given time. I am passed from one provider to the other, with each provider remaining detached from my chief complaint. No one seems to remember or know anything about me; no one seems to really care.

Attention to Detail (ATD)

When seemingly routine activities and procedures are handled in a manner that suggests a lack of ATD, it leaves the patient wondering about the value of the service received. The time constraints under which caregivers work is also partly to blame for the lack of ATD. Concerns about small and big issues falling through the cracks are exacerbated by the many distractions caused partially by our addiction to social media and mobile devices. When there is evidence of a lack of ATD, trust in the service is broken, altering the perception of value.

Availability of Information

Healthcare practitioners have routinely underestimated patients' need for information. Several studies show that, even when patients do not ask questions, their desire for information is quite high. Highly educated patients and patients from a high socioeconomic background receive more information from physicians than patients with less education or a lower socioeconomic background. Studies also demonstrate no difference in both groups' desire for information. Patients' questions often go unstated and, consequently, unanswered. When a visit produces no or only partial answers, patients' perception of value is diminished. Figure 2.1 illustrates the qualitative relationships between patients' typical questions and a hospital's functions.

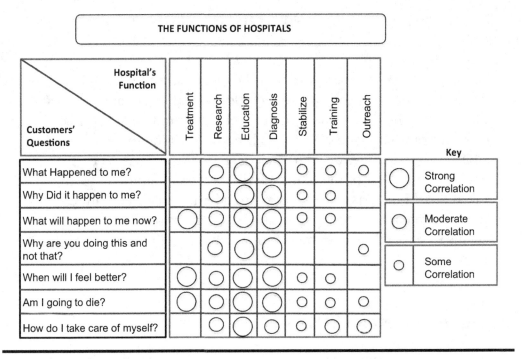

Figure 2.1 Hospitals vs. patients' questions.

This figure underscores the significance of three powerful aspects of hospitals' functions: education, diagnosis, and treatment.

True Cost and Value

An article by Michael E. Porter (2010) in the *New England Journal of Medicine* suggests that achieving high value for patients must become the overarching goal of healthcare delivery, with value defined as the health outcomes achieved per dollar spent. One of the challenges of healthcare lies in the fact that this goal, although extremely important to patients, is not shared by all stakeholders in the healthcare system. Metaphorically speaking, this amounts to one music conductor trying to lead a large orchestra of talented musicians, each reading from a different score. The modern symphony orchestra is made up of four groups of instruments—strings, woodwinds, brass, and percussion. The challenge is exacerbated by the lack of agreement among the members of each group of instruments. Moreover, imagine that the strings are the largest family of instruments in the orchestra and they come in four sizes: the violin, which is the smallest; the viola; the cello;

and the biggest, the double bass, sometimes called the contrabass. Now, picture a scenario in which the violinists have conflicting interpretations of the music piece's goal. In this case, the result is a cacophony. Without a shared goal, it is impossible to reach a harmonious convergence of all stakeholders' interests and efforts. One would be hard pressed to find another industry with this many conflicting goals and priorities—everything from access to care, exceptional patient experience, safety, cost containment, more pricing transparency, high quality, convenience, coordination of care, patient satisfaction, better outcomes, patient-centeredness, etc.

The short-term nature of the patient–payee relationship creates a significant challenge for the measurement of value. Healthcare activities are interdependent; therefore, value for patients is often revealed only over time and is manifested in longer-term outcomes such as sustainable recovery, the need for ongoing interventions, or treatment-induced illnesses (IOM, 2006). For patients with multiple medical conditions, value should be measured for each condition, with the presence of the other conditions used for risk adjustment. This approach allows relevant comparisons among patients' results, including comparisons of providers' ability to care for patients with complex conditions (Porter, 2010).

With the growing debate about value, the way a patient or consumer perceives value in pharmaceuticals is transforming. According to McKesson, traditionally, value to a patient was based heavily on convenience, as measured by location, cost, and speed (McKesson, 2017). However, as more of the healthcare spending burden shifts to the patient, value is taking on new meaning. Going forward, value is becoming all about the quality of care. An early indication that quality was becoming a key influence in pharmacy choice came in a study published in 2013. The study, published in the *Journal of the American Medical Association (JAMA)*, showed new beneficiaries in Medicare Advantage plans were making enrollment decisions based on Medicare's Five-Star Quality Rating program. The study found that the likelihood of enrolling increased by 9.5 percentage points for every one-star rating increase.

Clinical Outcomes as a Measure of Value

Determining the relevant outcomes to measure for any medical condition (or patient population in the primary care context) is never easy. Outcomes should include the health circumstances most relevant to patients.

They should cover both near-term and longer-term health, addressing a period long enough to encompass the ultimate results of care. Additionally, outcome measurements should include the sufficient assessment of risk factors or initial conditions to allow risk adjustments (Porter, 2010).

Value Proposition: Health Outcomes Divided by Costs

Where:

Health Outcomes = outcome(s) important to the patient or realistic outcome (or achievable under the circumstances) + patient experience (access to care, being bounced around, ease of using the delivery system, lack of empathy and compassion, etc.).

Costs = total cost of delivering these outcome(s) and experiences over the cycle of care for the condition in question.

What constitutes "value" can be nuanced and vary from person to person. Patients value qualities of care depending on their health needs. Other barriers to value delivery include the misalignment of incentives, trust issues between stakeholders, regulations that discourage collaborations between organizations, and a lack of data standardization, interoperability, and transparency. According to Feeley (2016), it is critically important that doctors and patients understand that outcomes of care concern more than basic questions, such as will the patient survive an operation? or how long will a patient live with cancer?

Outcomes also involve the patient experience—questions such as Will there be pain with treatment? How long will the patient miss work? and What will the impact on the family be? In a value-based system, both doctors and patients should know what outcomes to expect and demand that outcomes be measured and publicly reported. When outcomes of care are reported, doctors can improve their results, and patients can make meaningful choices about where to receive care. Feeley notes that the costs of care delivery—the other part of the value equation—also need to be measured and made transparent to doctors and patients (Feeley, 2016). High medical bills have been linked to bankruptcy, yet most doctors do not know how much the care they outline will cost the patient, and most patients do not know how much their care will cost. It is time that patients know this information and that providers be transparent about their costs. The expectation that the government alone can fix the healthcare system is misguided. In fact, the system cannot be fixed by any single stakeholder group alone.

Only with all parties focusing on value for the patient will the industry make progress on this front. The challenges facing the healthcare system cannot be solved by any one discipline or entity. The federal and state governments cannot legislate their way out of the healthcare quagmire, and the private sector will also have a key role in this transformation.

The Patient Experience Value Manifesto

The following principles address aspects of the patient's experience that might cause patients to question or reaffirm an organization's value proposition:

1. *Chief Complaint Principle*: Understand the chief complaint and display a laser-like focus toward addressing it. Patients expect to be provided with the best-known (evidence-based) options for addressing their chief complaint. In other words, deliver clinical quality care in accordance with the best-known scientific guidelines, affordably and sustainably. It is difficult to acknowledge value if a patient's chief complaint is not resolved satisfactorily. The clinical outcome associated with the patient's primary health concern must be satisfactory to the patient, the patient's family, or other significant representative of the patient.
2. *Hassle Factor Principle*: Be sensitive to the inconvenience imposed on the patient by the system of care delivery, whether or not you are responsible for the inconvenience. Inconveniences may take the forms of waiting room temperature, scheduling error, staff error, physician running late, machine or equipment breakdown or malfunction, inadequate staffing, long wait times, delays in responding to call lights, excessive noise, etc. Ideally, there should be one place to go for all things healthcare. Hassles suck the life out of providers and patients and reinforce the perception of diminished value.
3. *Safety Principle*: Do no harm. Avoid anything that could make matters worse, unless the patient consents. Disclose all risks fully. Demonstrate how much premium you and your organization place on patient and staff safety. Negligence of any kind, real or imagined, makes the perception of value impossible. Make a commitment to safety, as demonstrated through things like hand hygiene, hospital-acquired infections, patient falls, mislabeled specimens, medication errors, etc. Each safety

concern weakens the patient's trust in the quality of the service and psychologically devalues it.

4. *Empathy, Sensitivity, and Compassion Principle*: Demonstrate empathy, sensitivity, and compassion in your decisions, choices, attitudes, and communications with patients and their family members. A lack of empathy could erode trust, create patient dissatisfaction, and impede clinical outcomes—the cornerstones of a value proposition.

5. *Post-Discharge Principle*: Be genuinely interested in how the patient will care for himself/herself after leaving your facility. Provide tools for self-care, and offer the patient and patient's family information that would help prevent a recurrence. Post-discharge calls and other follow-up calls reaffirm the notion of value.

6. *Respect and Dignity Principle*: Patients also value whether the doctor treats them with respect and dignity, as manifested in how the doctor listens and cares, and treats them. A patient, by the very nature of his/her complaint, is vulnerable. Any display of condescension or failure to make eye contact can leave the patient feeling disrespected. In most cases, when a patient feels disrespected, the psychological impact leaves that person unwilling to entertain any idea of a value proposition.

7. *Attention to Detail Principle*: Pay attention to detail, especially toward the noticeable and unnoticeable, the visible and invisible, the spoken and unspoken, the consequential and the seemingly inconsequential. Obsess over the so-called "small stuff." Failure to handle the details can cause anxiety in patients and may lead to the perception of inferior service.

8. *Price Transparency Principle*: Be transparent about price, costs, and charges. Hidden charges and billing errors destroy your credibility as an organization. A perceived lack of transparency erodes the acknowledgment of value.

9. *Whole Person Principle*: Show interest in the whole person, even though medicine requires that you address the primary complaint. Handoffs that do not include the management of care across the continuum of care diminish the perception of value. Every patient has unique needs and characteristics. Address the whole patient, by considering everything from therapy's effect on functional and cognitive status, as well as a regimen's complexity, to mental health and nutritionists, etc. Go the extra mile. Show interest in the unspoken or peripheral issues or problems, even if the patient is not focused on them. When a patient

feels that you are only concerned about your piece of the puzzle and nothing more, they develop a fragmented view of value. When aggregated, that view leaves much to be desired.

10. *Trust Principle*: When trust is broken, any sense of a service's value is highly compromised. Trust is vital to the perception of value. When trust is absent, the patient is forced into high levels of vigilance or the readiness to assert his/her autonomy. Trust animates the patient's belief in the services, which can dramatically influence the perception of value.

11. *Information Principle*: Never underestimate patients' desire for information. Even if a patient does not ask questions or seems incurious, he/she is still hungry for information regarding his/her condition and prognosis. The provider's ability to elicit questions and address even unasked questions is a plus. In the end, information is an important piece of the question, "What did I get out of the experience?"

12. *Communication Principle*: It is difficult to acknowledge value in healthcare if communication barriers are not addressed. Barriers could be cultural, educational, psychological, etc. Effective communication requires that the provider communicates at a level and style that the patient would understand. It is important to patients and their family members to be invited to participate in decisions regarding the patient's health. This level of communication makes it possible for the patient to acknowledge value in the services provided. First, seek to understand patients by finding what and how much they know about their condition. When patients believe that you understand them, they tell you everything, and when this happens, the value of your service is boosted massively. One way to reach an understanding is to listen actively. Listening is perhaps one of the greatest tools with which you must increase your value with your patients. Communication can address many unspoken needs that could potentially make the patient and his/her family members feel at ease.

13. *True Cost Principle*: To accurately assess value, one must consider costs that accrue to patients and their families. It is imperative to consider out-of-pocket costs to the patient and family, non-medical costs and burdens to the patient and family, and the impact of a treatment on future costs. Other cost factors include deductibles, copayments, the cost of associated supportive care, costs due to lost productivity, the cost of travel, and the level of burden on family and caregivers.

Throughout the process of care delivery, the patient is subconsciously trying to balance what he/she received against the true cost.

14. *Timeliness Principle*: Most patients believe that their condition(s) is urgent and needs to be addressed quickly. They worry about the effect of delays and long wait times. Reducing waits and sometimes harmful delays for both those who receive and those who give care is vital to the patient's perception of value.

15. *Privacy, Security, and Confidentiality Principle*: In the context of personal information, concepts of privacy are closely intertwined with those of confidentiality and security. Privacy addresses the question of who has access to personal information and under what conditions. Confidentiality safeguards information gathered in the context of an intimate relationship. Security helps keep health records safe from unauthorized use. Healthcare organizations involved in the collection, use, and disclosure of personally identifiable health information should take strong measures to safeguard the security of health data. Patients often assume that healthcare organizations are taking care of these dimensions of service delivery. Any time patients must worry about these aspects of the healthcare delivery system, they are reminded of one more serious defect in the system.

16. *Care Coordination Principle*: This means that the patient's needs and preferences are known beforehand and communicated at the right time to the right people, and that this information is used to provide safe, appropriate, and effective care to the patient. It calls for a highly coordinated series of activities involving hospitals, nursing homes, primary care physicians, specialists, emergency rooms, etc.

Questions for Discussion

2.1. Should the concept of value be extended to a patient's family? Why or why not?

2.2. Discuss the ethical dilemmas inherent in the definition of *value* from the perspectives of healthcare delivery systems and organizations.

2.3. Which of the principles discussed in the Patient Experience Manifesto is the most controversial? Why?

2.4. Provide an example of the "hassle factor" inherent in a patient's interaction with a hospital? A health insurance company? Nursing home? Home health organization? Pharmacy?

References

AHRQ, 2014, October. "Timeliness: National Healthcare Disparities Report, 2011." Agency for Healthcare Research and Quality, Rockville, MD. http://archive. ahrg.gov/research/findings/nhgrdr/nhdr11/chap4.html

Agency for Healthcare Research and Quality, AHRQ, 2016, July. "Care Coordination." Agency for Healthcare Research and Quality, Rockville, MD. http://www.ahrd.gov/professionals/prevention-chroniccare/improve/coordinati on/index.html

Annual Meeting of the American Academy of Orthopaedic Surgeons (AAOS), 2016. "Physician Empathy a Key Driver of Patient Satisfaction." Orlando, FL, 41.

American Society of Internal Medicine (ASIM), 1990. America's Health Care System Strangling in Red Tape. https://www.acponline.org/acp_policy/policies/hass le_factor_americas_health_care_system_in_red_tape_1990.pdf ASIMhhh

Bloustein, E., 1967. "Privacy as an Aspect of Human Dignity: An Answer to Dean Prosser." *New York Law Review* 39:34.

Boudreau, R.M., McNally, C., Rensing, E.M., and Campbell, M.K., 2004, January– February. "Improving the Timeliness of Written Patient Notification of Mammography Results by Mammography Centers." *The Breast Journal* 10(1): 10–19.

Epstein, A. M., 2009. "Revisiting Readmissions—Changing the Incentives for Shared Accountability." *The New England Journal of Medicine* 360: 1457–1459.

Feeley, T. W., 2016. "Why Value in Health Care Is the Target." *NEJM Catalyst.* https:// catalyst.nejm.org/why-value-in-health-care-is-the-target/

Fried, C., 1968. "Privacy." *Yale Law Journal* 77: 475–493.

Gavison, R., 1980. "Privacy and the Limits of the Law." *Yale Law Journal* 89: 421–471.

Houck, P.M. and Bratzler, D., 2005, April. "Administration of First Hospital Antibiotics for Community Acquired Pneumonia: Does Timeliness Affect Outcomes?" *Current Opinion in Infectious Diseases* 18(2): 151–156.

Institute of Medicine., 2006. *Performance Measurement: Accelerating Improvement.* Washington, DC: National Academies Press.

Jerant, A.F., von Friederichs-Fitzwater, M.M. and Moore, M., 2005. "Patients' Perceived Barriers to Active Self-management of Chronic Conditions." *Patient Education and Counseling* 57: 300–307.

Keckley, P., 2015. "The Meaning of 'Value' in Health Care." *The Health Care Blog.* http://thehealthcareblog.com/blog/2015/12/03/the-meaning-of-value-in-health -care/

Kinchen, K.S., Sadler, J., Fink, N., Brookmeyer, R., Klag, M.J., Levey, A.S., and Powe, N.R., 2002, September 17. "The Timing of Specialist Evaluation in Chronic Kidney Disease and Mortality." *Annals of Internal Medicine* 137(6): 479–486.

Kodjak, A., 2016. "Hassle of Being a Patient Can Turn into a Crisis Without Sick Leave." Shots—Health News from NPR. https://www.npr.org/sections/health shots/2016/07/11/484960907/hassle-of-being-a-patient-can-turn-into-a-crisis Without-sick-leave

Kohn, L., Corrigan, J., Donaldson, M., eds., 2000. *To Err Is Human: Building a Safer Health System*. Washington, DC: Institute of Medicine, Committee on Quality of Health Care in America.

Kwan, J., Hand, P., and Sandercock, P., 2004, May. "Improving the Efficiency of Delivery of Thrombolysis for Acute Stroke: A Systematic Review." *QJM* 97(5): 273–9.

Luman, E.T., Barker, L.E., Shaw, K.M., McCauley, M.M., Buehler, J.W., and Pickering, L.K., 2005, March 9. "Timeliness of Childhood Vaccinations in the United States: Days Undervaccinated and Number of Vaccines Delayed." *JAMA* 293(10): 1204–1211.

McKesson, 2017. "Health Care Value Is Changing." McKesson.com. https://www.mck esson.com/blog/health-care-value-is-changing/

MedicalGPS, 2016. The Importance of Empathy in Healthcare. http://blog.medicalq ps.com/the-importance-of-empathy-in-healthcare

Moore, A., 2005. "Intangible Property: Privacy, Power and Information Control." In: Moore, A., ed. *Information Ethics: Privacy, Property, and Power*. Seattle, WA: University of Washington Press.

NRC, 2007. *Engaging Privacy and Information Technology in a Digital Age*. Washington, DC: The National Academies Press.

Petrila, J., 1999. "Medical Records Confidentiality: Issues Affecting the Mental Health and Substance Abuse Systems." *Drug Benefit Trends* 11: 6–10.

Porter, M.E., 2010. "What Is Value in Health Care?" *The New England Journal of Medicine* 363: 2477–2481, December 23, 2010.

Porter, M.E. and Teisberg, E.O., 2006. *Redefining Healthcare: Creating Value-Based Competition on Results*. Boston: Harvard Business School Press .

Post, R., 2006. "Three Concepts of Privacy." *Georgetown Law Journal* 89: 2087–2089.

Pritts, J., 2008. "The Importance and Value of Protecting the Privacy of Health Information: Roles of HIPAA Privacy Rule and the Common Rule in Health Research." http://www.iom.edu/CMS/3740/43729/53160.aspx

Riess, H., Kelly, J.M., Bailey, R.W., Dunn, E.J. and Phillips, M., 2012. "Empathy Training for Resident Physicians: A Randomized Controlled Trial of a Neuroscience-Informed Curriculum." *Journal of General Internal Medicine* 27(10): 1280–1286.

Roback, H. and Shelton, M., 1995. "Effects of Confidentiality Limitations on the Psychotherapeutic Process." *Journal of Psychotherapy Practice and Research* 4: 185–193.

Seidman, J., Anderson, M., Masi, D., Atkins, M. and Japha, M., 2017, May 23. "Measuring Value Based on What Matters to Patients: A New Value Assessment Framework." *Health Affairs Blog*. DOI:10.1377/hblog20170523.060220

Solove, D.J., 2006. "A Taxonomy of Privacy." *University of Pennsylvania Law Review* 154: 516–518.

Taube, D.O. and Elwork, A., 1990. "Researching the Effects of Confidentiality Law on Patients' Self-Disclosures." *Professional Psychology: Research and Practice* 21: 72–75.

Taylor, C., 1989. *Sources of the Self: The Making of Modern Identity.* Cambridge, MA: Harvard University Press.

Terry, N.P. and Francis, L.P., 2007. "Ensuring the Privacy and Confidentiality of Electronic Health Records." *University of Illinois Law Review* 2007(2): 681–736.

Weddle, M. and Kokotailo, P., 2005. "Confidentiality and Consent in Adolescent Substance Abuse: An Update." Virtual Mentor, *American Medical Association Journal of Ethics.* http://virtualmentor.ama assn.org/2005/03/pdf/pfor1-0503.pdf

Weissman, J.S., Ayanian, J.Z., Chasan-Taber, S., Sherwood, M.J., Roth, C. and Epstein, A.M., 1999. "Hospital Readmissions and Quality of Care." *Medical Care* 37: 490–501.

Westin, A., 1966. "Science, Privacy and Freedom." *Columbia Law Review* 66(7): 1205–1253.

Chapter 3

The Patient Experience

The battle line in the quest for excellence in healthcare goes through the patients' experience. The patient experience is no longer an afterthought but the very essence of healthcare organizations' existence. Excellence in patients' experience is inextricably linked to excellence in employee experience, and patient experience suffers when staff morale is low. Of the many factors responsible for low staff morale, the most compelling have to do with management's failure to strike the right balance between the workload demand and the organization's capacity. When the staff is visibly overwhelmed, it is unrealistic to expect them to care much about the patient experience. Without careful monitoring of the available resources and staff's capacity (in terms of time, equipment, processes, competencies, and skills), the patient experience will remain a distant concern for employees.

There will always be employees who give of themselves regardless of the morale in the unit or department. However, they are the exception. Unless there is a wholesale retooling of the employee experience, employees that are unengaged can only produce sporadic evidence of successes. Patient experience survey results are up for two months, then down for three, then up for one, etc. These organizations are perpetually in pursuit of the elusive top box score, and the employees are forever confounded by their lack of sustainable progress. Many of these survey "warriors" are unwilling cast members in a theatre of anguish fueled by a recalcitrant organizational culture.

The Beryl Institute defines the patient experience as the sum of all interactions shaped by an organization's culture that influence patient perceptions across the continuum of care (Beryl Institute, 2013). There are two key components of the patient experience—clinical excellence and service excellence. Most patients do not understand the clinical aspects of the services they receive; however, there are certain experiences that would cause them to lose trust in clinical services. The most significant determinants of patients' erosion of trust is a failure in patient safety, failure to reduce patient suffering, and failure to show caring, empathy, and compassion. If a patient falls ill from a hospital-acquired infection or does not receive effective care that follows proven protocol, trust is eroded, and patients' experience will suffer. Ensuring patient safety and quality care is the first step to creating a positive patient experience.

Providers can reduce patient suffering by being more attentive to the latter's needs. Checking in on call buttons or determining if a patient needs help reaching an item or using the bathroom can help protect patients from falls or other harms, reducing preventable suffering. As patients have more choice and healthcare decisions impact their wallets more, they will increasingly compare their healthcare experience to their expectations in other aspects of their lives. As patients bear more out-of-pocket healthcare expenses, they will become choosier and more critical in their evaluation of services. Healthcare organizations will need to live up to the realities of a new service expectation to continue to win the business of their service-savvy customers.

While critical acclaim and business accolades such as "the Best Hospitals," or the "Number One Hospital" are essential to business success, the greatest measure of leadership success is the degree to which excellence in non-clinical aspects of the service match or exceed the excellence in clinical outcomes. Neither by itself is sufficient. There are four critical areas of concern for patients, as follows:

1. *Engaged Staff with a Pleasant Disposition*: A patient in a vulnerable state would prefer to deal with a healthcare provider (nurse, physician, or other staff) with an overall pleasant disposition. Patients often perceive a person with a pleasant disposition as being more approachable. A provider who seems overwhelmed, in a hurry, or otherwise frustrated sends out signals that suggest he/she does not want to be bothered or, worse, does not want to be there. The message to the patient is: Limit the number of questions you might have, speak fast, and get straight to the point. A patient's nightmare scenario is to deal with an angry nurse

or physician. In that situation, the patient's concern is that he/she might exacerbate whatever is causing the provider to be angry. Some patients might even wonder if they are the target of the anger. Management must ensure that workload and staffing ratios allow providers sufficient time to provide the needed services. While the goal of a "happy staff" may be unrealistic, it is within the purview of good management to ensure providers have a reasonable chance of being successful at their responsibilities.

2. *Connection with the Patient*: When a caregiver connects with the patient, it speaks to how much respect he/she has for the patient. When a provider connects personally with the patient, it acknowledges the patient is an individual worthy of respect and courtesy. This goes against conventional thinking about the need for providers to remain objective and unemotional. By connecting with the patient, a provider builds trust and increases the likelihood of a successful encounter.

3. *Teamwork Among Caregivers*: When patients perceive a lack of teamwork among providers, it shatters their trust in the process. The best evidence of a lack of teamwork is in communication breakdowns or failures. The perceived lack of communication between the doctor and the nurse leads some patients to conclude that they are receiving an inferior level of care.

4. *Empathy Deficit*: It takes a gifted clinician to demonstrate the ability to put themselves in the shoes of patients (and their family members) while providing a service to them. Most patients can perceive a caregiver's indifference. Empathy enables providers to listen to the concerns of patients, understand their feelings and fears, and explain the choices and options caregivers are making and why. Patients value displays of concern and caring, especially in the emergency room.

5. *Keeping Patients Informed*: Providers often underestimate patients' desire for information. Patients seek information about any and everything connected to their condition or the process for addressing it. This includes information about delays, options, and self-care at home.

By focusing on care quality and safety as parts of the patient experience, as well as using patient-centered care approaches to drive patient satisfaction and access, healthcare leaders can achieve a better patient experience. To reduce negative patient experiences, healthcare providers must focus on better patient-provider communications. If health systems want to improve the patient experience, they must put patients first and at the center of everything they do. Because patients do not fully understand the clinical aspects of their care, they will continue to measure their experience based on their own proxy measures, like being treated respectfully, being listened to, receiving a good explanation, etc.

Measuring Patient Experience: HCAHPS Surveys

The Centers for Medicare & Medicaid Services (CMS), along with the Agency for Healthcare Research and Quality (AHRQ), developed the HCAHPS (Hospital Consumer Assessment of Healthcare Providers and Systems) Survey, also known as Hospital CAHPS®, to provide a standardized survey instrument and data collection methodology for measuring patients' perspectives of hospital care. HCAHPS is the first national, standardized, publicly reported survey of patients' perspectives of hospital care. The HCAHPS Survey (pronounced "H-caps") is a 32-item instrument and data collection method for measuring patients' perceptions of their hospital experience. HCAHPS allows valid comparisons across hospitals—locally, regionally, and nationally. The survey was nationally implemented in 2006, and public reporting of hospital scores began in 2008. Since 2012, HCAHPS scores have played a role in hospital payment through the Hospital Value-Based Purchasing program.

The original HCAHPS Survey captures the patient's experience of communication with doctors and nurses, responsiveness of hospital staff, pain management, communication about medicines, cleanliness and quietness of the hospital, discharge information, transition to post-hospital care, and the overall rating of the hospital. The survey is administered between two and forty-two days after discharge to a random sample of adult patients. There are four approved modes of administration: mail, telephone, mixed (mail with telephone follow-up), and interactive voice response. The survey is officially available in Spanish, Chinese, Russian, Vietnamese, and Portuguese translations. About 4,000 hospitals participate in HCAHPS, and over three million patients complete the survey each year.

The HCAHPS survey is 32 questions in length—21 substantive items that encompass critical aspects of the hospital experience, four screening questions to skip patients to appropriate questions, and seven demographic items for adjusting the mix of patients across hospitals for analytical purposes.

Hospital Compare currently reports results for seven composite topics, two individual topics, and two global topics, as follows:

Composite topics

■ Nurse communication (questions 1, 2, 3)
■ Doctor communication (questions 5, 6, 7)
■ Responsiveness of hospital staff (questions 4, 11)
■ Pain management (questions 13, 14)
■ Communication about medicines (questions 16, 17)
■ Discharge information (questions 19, 20)
■ Care transition (questions 23, 24, 25)

Individual topics

■ Cleanliness of hospital environment (question 8)
■ Quietness of hospital environment (question 9)

Global topics

■ Hospital rating (question 21)
■ Willingness to recommend hospital (question 22)

Hospital-level results are publicly reported on the Hospital Compare web-site four times a year. HCAHPS results are based on four quarters of data on a rolling basis. The HCAHPS survey is administered to a random sample of adult patients across medical conditions between forty-eight hours and six weeks after discharge; the survey is not restricted to Medicare beneficiaries.

According to CMS, the HCAHPS survey was shaped by three broad goals, as follows*:

1. To produce data about patients' perspectives of care that allow objective and meaningful comparisons of hospitals on topics that are important to consumers
2. To create incentives for hospitals to improve their quality of care
3. To enhance accountability in healthcare by increasing the transparency of the quality of hospital care provided in return for the public's investment

---

* Source: "HCAHPS: Patients' Perspectives of Care Survey." https://www.cms.gov/Medicare/Qualit y-Initiatives-Patient-Assessment-Instruments/Hospital QualityInits/HospitalHCAHPS.html

Unfortunately, the financial incentives associated with HCAHPS, coupled with the growing focus on value-based care, have given rise to the tendency to equate the patient experience with HCAHPS. However, the patient experience spans a wider range of emotions about the services provided to patients. The "hassle factor" is an essential component of the service encounter, and HCAHPS fails to accurately measure the difficulties patients encounter in trying to navigate the system of care delivery.

The HCAHPS survey was originally designed to produce data about patients' perspectives to enhance safety and accountability in healthcare. While HCAHPS does not measure the entire patient experience, it does measure key aspects of care such as pain management, responsiveness of the hospital staff, discharge information, and so forth. Measuring the true patient experience and care value is more complex. Metrics must also include the assessment of teamwork, communication, and the connection between patients and caregivers. The quality of the relationships creates the environment and culture of the workplace, which permeate all aspects of the patient experience.

Many hospitals have seen their scores rise and fall and are confounded by their inability to achieve their desired target. Just when the staff believe that they have found the answer to the patient experience puzzle with high scores for three to four consecutive months, their hopes are shattered when the scores plummet in the following three months. Without a culture of devotion to the patient experience or patient-centeredness, these wild, confounding patterns in HCAHPs scores will continue.

Some hospitals resort to focusing on improving one variable at a time. They do so in the hope that their overall score will improve if they address the variable with the lowest score. This strategy works only under certain conditions. A hospital with some culture of patient-centeredness can have some success with this tactic. However, a hospital lacking that basic culture does not stand a chance of achieving success by focusing on one variable at a time. The basic culture is like the foundation of a building and represents a predisposition to improving the patient experience across all functional areas. Put another way, a hospital whose scores are mostly "Usually" and a sprinkling of "Always" would have more success with the tactics of focusing on the weakest link—one variable at a time. Conversely, a hospital whose scores are mostly a combination of "Sometimes" and "Never" need a comprehensive retooling of its culture across all functional areas before it can benefit from the one-variable-at-a-time tactic.

What patients experience in the emergency department invariably carries over to the inpatient floors. Everything is related and connected. Physicians' influence on the patient experience debate cannot be overstated. What is also clear is that patients want doctors who listen and treat them with respect, which is easier said than done. According to a *Wall Street Journal Online*/Harris Interactive healthcare poll in 2004, "People place more importance on doctors' interpersonal skills than their medical judgment or experience," and doctors' failings in these areas are the overwhelming factor that drives patients to switch doctors. Eighty-five percent of those polled said that treating a patient with dignity and respect is an extremely important quality in a doctor, and 84 percent cited listening carefully and being easy to talk to as important qualities.

Tactics and Strategies for Improving HCAHPS Scores

1. *Leadership Rounding*: Leadership rounding is a process where leaders (e.g., administrators, department heads, and nurse managers) walk around the building with staff and residents, talking with them directly about the care and services provided in the organization. Rounding with staff and residents is an effective method for leaders to hear firsthand what is going well and what issues should be addressed. Leadership rounding has become a key to successful management over the years. Tom Peters coined the term "management by walking around" in the late 1970s; the Japanese know it as the "Gemba Walk." It goes beyond visibility and serves as an important signal of leadership's commitment to performance improvement. It is a good time to acknowledge the work done by staff, physicians, and other clinical personnel. Leader rounding provides a great opportunity for bridging the divide between administration and clinicians. Studies have shown that senior leader rounds provide a way for patients to access and provide feedback to an organization's C-suite (Dempsey et al., 2014). Senior leader rounds give leaders an opportunity to express their appreciation to the patients who chose the hospital for their care (Dempsey et al., 2014). Patients visited by a nurse leader during their hospital stay are more likely to give top box ratings across all HCAHPS measures. A visit from a nurse leader improves the way a patient perceives nursing care in general and the areas of nurse communication, information regarding medication, and preparation for discharge and the transition to the

patient's home. Indeed, patients perceive responses to concerns and complaints more favorably when a nurse leader has visited them during their hospital stay (Institute for Innovation, 2014).

Rounds are positively associated with the patient experience, employee and physician engagement, and clinical quality indicators. Rounds are also linked with decreases in the overall trend for falls, pressure ulcers, and catheter-associated urinary tract infections. Patients who experience rounds perceive attention to personal needs and patient safety more favorably (Reimer and Herbener, 2014). A Cleveland Clinic study found that leader rounds help the executive team to understand caregiver concerns, get needed resources, remove roadblocks, and solve problems. Leader rounds give leaders the opportunity to speak to patients and families about how well their needs are being met. Leader rounds build trust with patients and families and promote confidence that safe and reliable care is being provided (Cleveland Clinic, 2012). Rounding in the emergency department (ED) reception and treatment areas is effective and improves outcomes (Meade et al., 2010). According to Meade et al., three rounding protocols combined reduced Leaving Without Being Seen (LWBS) by 23.4 percent, leaving Against Medical Advice (AMA) by 22.6 percent, falls by 58.8 percent, call light use by 34.7 percent, and approaches to the nursing station by 39.5 percent (2010).

According to Nash et al. (2010), effectively implementing two high-impact tactics (nurse leader rounds and post-discharge phone calls) results in higher levels of the patient experience. Sharing meaningful data with leaders on whether nurse leader rounds and post-discharge phone calls are being executed effectively promotes leader engagement and hardwires accountability for performance improvement. The quantitative evidence about the strategy execution provided by nurse leader rounds and discharge call tracking tools helps maintain efforts to improve the patient experience (Nash et al., 2010). Other studies have concluded that nurse leader rounds improve clinical quality, the patient experience, and staff engagement. The combination of nurse leader rounds and discharge phone calls produces improved patient perceptions of overall care. Implementing nurse leader rounds and discharge phone calls can make the difference in being at the top or bottom of the Press Ganey national inpatient database (Setia and Meade, 2009).

Employees want leaders who share the same goals and are willing to roll up their sleeves to overcome organizational challenges. Committing to rounding as a daily necessity is a crucial first step in facilitating a strong connection between a leader and his/her organization. Leader rounding closes the social distance between the leader and the patients. There is no substitute for observing firsthand the fact that the clock in the patient's room has not been adjusted to reflect daylight savings time or that the portable X-ray machines have been broken for several weeks, or that the garbage can in the hallway is full and overflowing. It also provides the administrator with the opportunity to address observed problems on the spot. Employees respond positively to a leader with an approachable demeanor.

Leaders should round with the intention of making a difference. It is difficult for an executive to truly understand the needs of patients, physicians, and nurses without interacting with them daily. To maximize the benefits from rounding, leaders must insist on maintaining a consistent rounding schedule. Some directors and managers eventually abandon rounding due to time constraints. In some cases, even when rounding activities are scheduled, they are frequently bumped because of last-minute meeting changes and other emergencies. It is also important for leaders to round on nights, weekends, and holidays. In so doing, an executive demonstrates his/her appreciation for the staff's sacrifices. The symbolic power of seeing an executive scrub up for the operating room and observe a surgery is unmatched. One way to demonstrate support for physicians is to visit them in their offices.

2. *Purposeful (Hourly) Rounding*: According to Stanford Health Care (SHC), Purposeful Rounding seeks to improve the patient experience through a structured hourly rounding routine. SHC's Purposeful Rounding protocol was developed in 2012 and has widely proven to improve patient outcomes and satisfaction. The process begins when the Purposeful Rounding concept is introduced to the patient and family members upon admission to set expectations for the hospital stay. SHC has identified eight specific behaviors that inform the success of Purposeful Rounding. They are as follows:
   - Use opening key words (C-I-CARE) with PRESENCE. This reduces anxiety and contributes to efficiency.
   - Accomplish scheduled tasks.
   - Address the 4 Ps (Pain, Potty (toileting), Positioning, fall Prevention).
   - Address additional personal needs and questions.
   - Conduct an environmental assessment (bed alarms, IV pumps, hats, urinals).

- Ask, "Is there anything else I can do for you before I go? I have time."
- Tell each patient when you will be back.
- Document the round.

Research on hourly rounding in 14 hospitals revealed impressive improvements (Meade et al., 2006; Leighty, 2006):

- 12 percent increase in patient satisfaction scores.
- 52 percent reduction in patient falls.
- 37 percent reduction in light use.
- 14 percent decline in skin breakdowns.
- In addition, one hospital measured a 20 percent reduction in the distance walked each day by the nursing staff.

It is vital to ensure that frontline staff, nurse leaders, and senior managers understand the role of rounding in enhancing patient care and increasing staff engagement. The staff's initial reaction to rounding is based on the belief that rounding will simply add one more activity to an otherwise overburdened nursing staff. In fact, studies have shown that rounding actually gives time back to nurses, because it reduces call light presses and, depending upon the type of rounding, reduces time spent on paperwork. It is also important to note that rounding involves much more than popping in to say hi to patients and fluffing their pillows. In reality, rounding is an intentional, dedicated moment with a patient or staff member with the goal of accomplishing specified objectives.

There are many rounding scripts and templates available for use today, and their implementation requires careful consideration and planning. A thoughtful rounding script should include a list of patient questions and staff discussion points and should serve as a guide for frontline staff who do the daily or even hourly rounding. All types of rounds should include standardized rounding templates to ensure consistency in the data collection and actionable items.

In many cases, rounding will uncover unpleasant experiences. Some patients and/or family members will offer negative feedback regarding their care. Some may demand immediate action. The rounding staff should be trained on how to develop a proactive plan to address problems, record issues, close the loop, and/or perform service recovery. Purposeful nurse rounding has emerged as one of the best proactive tools to improve patient satisfaction, safety, and the quality of care. Nurse leader rounding provides a structured process to ensure that quality, as well as safe and compassionate care, is always delivered to every patient.

3. *Target the Emergency Department (ED)*: The ED represents the first point of entry to the hospital by most patients. The ED's first impression sets the stage for the patients' perception of everything else. Nationally, the ED accounts for over 50 percent of inpatient admissions. The experience of several hospitals reveals the fact that patients admitted through the ED were more likely to rate their experience across all composites more negatively than those patients admitted through other channels. The strategy, therefore, should be to create as good a first impression as possible with the patients that come to the ED with the understanding that a great first impression would go a long way. The negative perceptions of ED patients have centered on the following:
   - Providing information about delays
   - Waiting time to be seen by the physician
   - Pain management
   - Waiting to be discharged
   - Waiting for bed availability
   - Rudeness of staff

   Although the HCAHPS survey is the top method to track and measure the patient experience, ED-CAHPS is becoming an increasingly popular measuring tool. This indicates the continuing importance of the ED as the front door to the hospital and the first impression of the patient experience. One approach that has received a great deal of success is inpatient rounding by ED nurses and physicians. ED providers rarely experience that level of patient connection or feedback. Traditionally, ED providers take care of the patient in the ED in times of crisis and chaos. They stabilize patients and then handle admission or discharge. Despite the intensive nature of the interaction, most ED physicians rarely see those patients after they leave the ED. However, with inpatient rounding, ED providers have the opportunity to let patients know they are still thinking about them. It is also an opportunity to ask patients how their care could have improved their experience. Patients have a chance to provide immediate feedback, and they see a truly integrated team caring for them. This approach requires ED physicians to come in 30 minutes early to make inpatient rounds before resuming their work in the ED. The rounding team typically consists of one ED physician and one ED nurse manager.

4. *Post-Discharge Follow-Up Calls*: At discharge, many patients are so anxious to leave the hospital and get home to their familiar environment that they do not absorb all of the information given to them at the time of discharge. Once at home, they often have questions. Patients may not appreciate the instructions they receive in the hospital as they have not encountered the challenges that are the reasons for the instructions. The instructions take on new meaning once the patient encounters a new set of realities in his/her home environment. Discharge phone calls give patients an added opportunity to double-check instructions, possibly minimizing unnecessary calls to providers and visits to the ER.

   Examples of post-discharge follow-up questions include the following:
   - Did you understand your discharge instructions?
   - Were you able to get your prescriptions filled?
   - Do you have any questions about your medications?
   - Are you having any pain related to your condition?
   - Have you been able to make follow-up appointments with your doctors?
   - May I ask how your care was?
   - What could we have done differently?

   Follow-up from every call is documented in the system using a telephone encounter. If patients have clinical questions or are experiencing a medical problem, the nurse refers them to their physician or care provider as appropriate. The nurse will also circle back to the physician team to let them know there was a finding from the call.

5. *Patient Whiteboards as a Communication Tool*: Patient whiteboards can serve as a communication tool between hospital providers and as a mechanism to engage patients in their care. Communication is a major component of the patient experience, and communication failures are a frequent cause of adverse events (Arora et al., 2005; Gawande et al., 2003; Greenberg et al., 2007; and Sutcliffe et al., 2004). The Joint Commission (TJC) reports that such failures contributed to 65% of reported sentinel events (Sutcliffe, et al., 2009). Strategies to improve communication have focused on implementing formal teamwork training programs and/or teaching specific communication skills (Awad et al., 2005; Morey et al., 2002; Clancy and Tornberg, 2007; Dunn et al., 2007; Barrett et al., 2001; Leonard et al., 2004; Haig et al., 2006; Sehgal et al., 2008). While these strategies largely address communication between healthcare providers, there is a growing emphasis on developing strategies to engage patients in their care and improving

communication with them and their families. The placement of whiteboards in patient rooms is an increasingly common strategy to improve communication. These boards, typically placed on a wall near a patient's hospital bed, allow any number of providers to communicate a wide range of information to the patient, his/her family members, and other providers (Sehgal et al., 2010). Both Kaiser Permanente's Nurse Knowledge Exchange program and the Institute for Healthcare Improvement's Transforming Care at the Bedside promote whiteboard use, though with little specific guidance about practical implementation (Rutherford et al., 2004; Fahey and Schilling, 2007). Sehgal et al. (2010) offer the following guidelines regarding the use of whiteboards in hospitals:

- Whiteboards should be placed in clear view of patients from their hospital bed.
- Buy and fasten erasable pens to the whiteboards themselves.
- Create a whiteboard with template information to standardize the information.
- Whiteboard templates should include the following items: day and date; patient's name (or initials); bedside nurse; primary physician(s), including attending, resident, and intern, if applicable; goal for the day; anticipated discharge date; family member's contact information (phone number); and questions for providers.
- Bedside nurses should facilitate writing and updating information on the whiteboard.
- Create a system for auditing whiteboards' utilization and providing feedback early during their rollout.
- Finally, it is important to comment on the confidentiality of all patient information.

6. *Staff Training*: Training is one of the most powerful tools in any service organization. The right training will have a positive effect on staff behavior and the overall patient experience. Thus, it is important to provide regular and targeted customer service training to staff. The initial training could be for one day, followed by mandatory half-day refresher training once a year. The focus of the training should be to remind the staff about patient-centeredness, define what patient experience means to the organization, and the need for improving the patients' experience throughout the organization. A shorter version of the training should be offered at new employee orientation. Children's National Medical Center designed a one-day learning program for faculty, staff, patients, and

families called the Patient Experience Day. From 7 a.m. to 6 p.m., participants could attend eleven fifty-minute sessions, according to an article from the Association for Patient Experience (2014). Topics were selected based directly on key drivers of patient satisfaction in the hospital's key settings (i.e., inpatient, NICU, outpatient specialty clinics, and ED).

7. *Reacting to Survey Results*: Share the results of the survey with staff and ask for suggestions for mitigating the performance gaps identified. Search for additional insight in the HCAHPS scores by digging deeper into the results for each area. In addition to traditional, formal patient satisfaction surveys, develop your own internal data system to track down the real-time experience of patients so bad experiences can be quickly corrected. This could be in the form of instant surveys to inpatients via the TV in the patient's room. If the scores are not all optimal, staff members are notified via email, and within minutes, someone is in the patient room to discuss the issue.

8. *Share Patient Stories*: Patient stories represent one of the most effective ways to make an emotional case for patient satisfaction. Another approach is to start executive and board meetings with a patient story. This approach is advocated by the United Kingdom's National Health Service (NHS), as described in a guide assembled together by the NHS's Patient Safety First campaign (2013). These stories will help close the administrative distance between patients and the organization's executives, as well as improve accountability.

9. *Develop and Adopt a Unique Perspective of the Patient Experience*: Define what patient experience means to your organization. A 2013 survey by the Beryl Institute found that organizations with a formal definition of patient experience are 10 percent more likely to score in the 75th percentile and above on patient satisfaction surveys.

10. *Hire the Right Staff*: If an organization does not make it a priority to meticulously search for and hire the right person, it has no reasonable chance of success in improving the patient experience. Mediocre managers will continue to hire mediocre employees, and soon enough, the organization becomes a dumping ground for employees that other organizations have rejected. It is not enough to hire the right employees; it is equally important to strive to retain the best.

11. *Improve Employee Engagement and Satisfaction:* Research correlates high employee satisfaction with higher patient satisfaction scores. A 2013 study in *Health Affairs* found that the percentage of patients who reported they would "definitely recommend" a hospital to their loved

ones decreased by 2 percent for every 10 percent of the nurses who expressed dissatisfaction with their jobs.

12. *Burnout Prevention*: Workplaces are experiencing a burnout epidemic, and no profession has been hit harder than healthcare. It has been reported that up to 60 percent of healthcare professionals say they are burned out (Monegain, 2013). Burnout is defined as a process of chronic disengagement that can affect several areas of one's life. It is marked by three general dimensions:
    – Chronic exhaustion (wearing out, loss of energy, and fatigue)
    – Cynicism (irritability, loss of idealism, and withdrawal)
    – Feeling increasingly ineffective on the job (reduced productivity and low morale) (Maslach and Leiter, 2005).

    The field of nursing has traditionally attracted people with a desire to help others. They tend to be empathetic and compassionate. However, these unique and vital qualities can leave many nurses susceptible to "nurse burnout"—a term used to encompass the physical, mental, and emotional fatigue nurses can experience after hardships on the job. The *Journal of the American Medical Association* (*JAMA*) linked hospital nurse staffing to nurse burnout and job dissatisfaction in their research on the topic of high nurse turnover. "Nurses in hospitals with the highest patient-to-nurse ratios are more than twice as likely to experience job-related burn-out and almost twice as likely to be dissatisfied with their jobs compared with nurses in the hospitals with the lowest ratios" (Aiken et al., 2002).

    The more patients that nurses are expected to treat in a given shift, the less time they have per patient. This can make the usually empathetic task of caring for patients feel more robotic, stressful, and incomplete, ultimately leading to a negative patient experience. Healthcare organizations may think they are saving money by assigning more patients to a nurse, but they end up losing money when the patients' experience is less than desirable.

    Not surprisingly, the ED, intensive care, and other critical care units are characterized by high levels of work-related stress, and work-related stress is a factor known to increase the risk of burnout. Nurses are expected to act decisively, dispense medication accurately, and provide good "customer service." Doing this often requires emotional labor, which involves suppressing one's real emotions (frustration, anxiety, anger) to show interest, concern, and empathy to patients and their families. Emotional labor has been linked to job stress and burnout, yet in those units where nurses could express their emotions with their colleagues authentically (i.e., they could appropriately "let it go" without backlash or repercussion), burnout was buffered (Grandey et al., 2012). Healthcare organizations must rethink their policies regarding nurse–patient ratios, vacation schedules, staff rotations, support groups, and frequency of breaks to address the important challenge of nurse burnout. The American Nurses Association (ANA) has recommended several resources for helping nurses cope with stress and burnout (http://www.nursingworld.org/healthynurse2017-april).

13. *Other Tactics and Strategies*: Other approaches for improving HCAHPS scores include the use of key words and phrases throughout the patient encounter, following up on patients' requests, service recovery, discharge planning, and better anticipation of the patients' needs.

HCAHPS and Health Plans

In the case of health plans, the challenge continues to be about how to drive improvements at the medical group level. Many of the measures in the CAHPS ambulatory surveys address issues outside of the direct control of health plans because the locus of the care or service lies at the medical group or practice level. However, health plans can exert some influence on medical groups and individual physicians, encouraging and motivating them to improve the patient's experience in the doctor's office. The degree of influence a plan can exert depends in part on the structure of its relationship with its provider network. Health plans that own physician practices and/or employ physicians, and those that have an exclusive relationship with their contracted providers, tend to have more influence than those that account for only a small share of a medical group's patients.

Questions for Discussion

3.1. In addition to the tactics and strategies discussed in this chapter, what other tactics and strategies are being utilized in improving HCAHPS scores?

3.2. Discuss the pros and cons of each of the strategies and tactics discussed in this chapter.

3.3. In what specific ways does "nurse burnout" contribute to lower patient experience scores?

3.4. Why is a patient's experience in the emergency room such a strong predictor of their overall experience after they get transferred to the inpatient floors?

References

Aiken, L. H., Clarke, S.P., Sloane, D.M., Sochalski, J., and Silber, J.H., 2002. "Hospital nurse staffing and patient mortality, nurse burnout, and job dissatisfaction." *JAMA* 288(16): 1987–1993. doi:10.1001/jama.288.16.1987

Arora, V., Johnson, J., Lovinger, D., Humphrey, H.J., and Meltzer, D.O., 2005. "Communication Failures in Patient Sign-Out and Suggestions for Improvement: A Critical Incident Analysis." *Quality & Safety Health Care* 14(6): 401–407.

Association for Patient Experience, 2014. "7 Leadership Tactics for Improving the Patient Experience." http://www.hfma.org/Leadership/Archives/2014/Spring/7_Leadership_Tactics_for_Improving_the_Patient_Experience/

Awad, S.S., Fagan, S.P., Bellows, C., Albo, D., Green-Rashad, B., De La Garza, M., and Berger, D.H, 2005. "Bridging the Communication Gap in the Operating Room with Medical Team Training." *The American Journal of Surgery* 190(5): 770–774.

Barrett, J., Gifford, C., Morey, J., Risser, D., and Salisbury, M., 2001. "Enhancing Patient Safety through Teamwork Training." *Journal of Healthcare Risk Manageent* 21(4): 57–65.

Clancy, C.M. and Tornberg, D.N., 2007. "TeamSTEPPS: Assuring Optimal Teamwork in Clinical Settings." *American Journal of Medical Quality* 22(3): 214–217.

Cleveland Clinic, 2012. "Healthcare Management & Leadership." Retrieved from www.youtube.com.

Dempsey, C., Reilly, B. and Buhlman, N., 2014. "Improving the Patient Experience: Real-World Strategies for Engaging Nurses." *Journal of Nursing Administration*, 44(3): 142–151.

Dunn, E.J., Mills, P.D., Neily, J., Crittenden, M.D., Carmack, A.L. and Bagian, J.P., 2007. "Medical Team Training: Applying Crew Resource Management in the Veterans Health Administration." *The Joint Commission Journal on Quality and Patient Safety* 33(6): 317–325.

Fahey, L., and Schilling, L., 2007, September/October. "Nurse Knowledge Exchange: Patient Hand Offs." American Academy of Ambulatory Care Nursing (AAACN) Viewpoint. http://findarticles.com/p/articles/mi_qa4022/ is_200709/ai_n21137476

Gawande, A.A., Zinner, M.J., Studdert, D.M., and Brennan, T.A., 2003. "Analysis of Errors Reported by Surgeons at Three Teaching Hospitals." *Surgery* 133(6): 614–621.

Grandey, A., Foo, S.C., Groth, M., and Goodwin, R.E., 2012. "Free to Be You and Me: A Climate of Authenticity Alleviates Burnout from Emotional Labor." *Journal of Occupational Health Psychology* 17(1): 1–14.

Greenberg, C.C., Regenbogen, S.E., Studdert, D.M., Lipsitz, S.R., Rogers, S.O., Zinner, M.J. and Gawande, A.A, 2007. "Patterns of Communi Cation Breakdowns Resulting in Injury to Surgical Patients." *Journal of the American College of Surgeons* 204(4): 533–540.

Haig, K.M., Sutton, S., and Whittington, J., 2016. "SBAR: A Shared Mental Model for Improving Communication Between Clinicians." *The Joint Commission Journal on Quality and Patient Safety* 32(3): 167–175.

Institute for Innovation, 2014. "Inspiring Innovation: Patient Report of Nurse Leader Rounding." http://www.theinstituteforinnovation.org/docs/default-source/anno tated-bibliographies/leader-rounds-on-patients_oct-2016.pdf?sfvrsn=2

Leighty, John, 2006, December 4. Hourly Rounding Dims Call Lights. www.Nurse. com.

Leonard, M., Graham, S., and Bonacum, D. 2004. "The Human Factor: The Critical Importance of Effective Teamwork and Communication in Providing Safe Care." *Quality & Safety in Health Care* 13(suppl 1): i85–i90.

Maslach, C. and Leiter, M.P., 2005. Stress and Burnout: The Critical Research in Handbook of Stress Medicine and Health. 2nd Ed. Cary L. Cooper, Ed., 155–172.

Meade, C.M., Kennedy, J., and Kaplan, J., 2010, June. "The Effects of Emergency Department Staff Rounding on Patient Safety and Satisfaction." *The Journal of Emergency Medicine* 38(5): 666–674.

Meade, Christine M., Bursell, A.L., and Ketelsen, L., 2006, September. "Effects on Nursing Rounds on Patients' Call Light Use, Satisfaction, and Safety." *American Journal of Nursing* 106(9): 60.

Monegain, B. (April 30, 2013). "Burnout Rampant in Healthcare." http://www.heal thcareitnews.com/news/burnout-rampant-healthcare.

Morey, J.C., Simon, R., Jay, G.D., Wears, R.L., Salisbury, M., Dukes, K.A., and Berns, S.D., 2002. "Error Reduction and Performance Improvement in the Emergency Department through Formal Teamwork Training: Evaluation Results of the Med Teams Project." *Health Services Research Journal* 37(6): 1553–1581.

Nash, M., Pestrue, J., Geier, P., Sharp, K., Helder, A., and McAlearney, A.S., 2010. "Leveraging Information Technology to Drive Improvement in Patient Satisfaction." Journal of Healthcare Quality, 32(5): 30–40.

NHS Patient Safety Campaign, 2013. http://patientsafety.health.org.uk/resources/ patient-safety-first-2008-2010-campaign-review

Reimer, N. and Herbener, L., 2014. "Round and Round We Go: Rounding Strategies to Impact Exemplary Professional Practice." *Clinical Journal of Oncology Nursing* 18(6): 654–660.

Rutherford, P., Lee, B., and Greiner, A., 2004. "Transforming Care at the Bedside." IHI Innovation Series White Paper. Boston, MA: Institute for Healthcare Improvement. http://www.ihi.org

Sehgal, N.L., Fox, M., Vidyarthi, A.R. et al., 2008. "A Multidisciplinary Teamwork Training Program: The Triad for Optimal Patient Safety (TOPS) Experience." *Journal of General Internal Medicine* 23(12): 2053–2057.

Sehgal, N.L., Green, A., Vidyarthi, A.R., Blegen, M.A., and Wachter, R.M., 2010. "Patient Whiteboards as a Communication Tool in the Hospital Setting: A Survey of Practices and Recommendations." *Journal of Hospital Medicine* 5(4): 234–239.

Setia, N. and Meade, C., 2009. "Bundling the Value of Discharge Telephone Calls and Leader Rounding." *Journal of Nursing Administration* 39(3): 138–141.

Sutcliffe, K.M., Lewton, E. and Rosenthal, M.M., 2004. "Communication Failures: An In- Sidious Contributor to Medical Mishaps." *Academic Medicine* 79(2): 186–194.

The Beryl Institute, 2013. Improving the Patient Experience. http://www.theb erylinstitute.org/store/download.asp?id=C9181DC5-3C30-48EE-BDBB-E8805F 58FD0F

Chapter 4

Value Is in the Attention to Detail

If you long to accomplish great and noble tasks, you first must learn to approach every task as though it were great and noble. Even the grandest project depends on the success of the smallest components.

Gary Ryan Blair (2009)

Healthcare services are not transactions that occur in a vacuum. Patients are not widgets passed from one machine to another. Patient encounters are often anxiety-inducing interactions between patients and their caregivers. In some cases, the participants in these high-stake encounters are people whose lives have been assaulted by the tyranny of disease and fear of dying. For patients, there is nothing routine about such encounters. There is nothing routine about surgeries or doctors' visits. Every interaction awakens certain impulses and appeals to certain sensibilities of the patient. These sensibilities can engender pessimism or optimism, confidence or doubt, joy or sadness, fear or courage, etc. What the patient sees, hears, feels, perceives, and touches forms a collage that then becomes the basis of their experience. The patient's experience is often built around visual, tactile, auditory, and other multi-sensorial elements that evoke a specific kind of response.

When an organization commits to a culture of attention to detail (ATD), its service delivery apparatus is intentionally choreographed to achieve a distinctive and desirable response from the customer at every turn. Every detail, noticeable and unnoticeable, every communication, and every action is subject to the highest level of scrutiny and weighed against the highest standards possible. At every service access point, the patient feels as though he/she is entering the center of a service universe designed to handle the whole person rather than its parts. While service failures are inevitable, in successful organizations, each service failure is met with a fiercely authentic attempt at service recovery and a determination to prevent recurrence. The mantra seems to be "Obsess about every detail, and leave nothing to chance." Attention to detail requires nuanced insights that, when deployed, can awaken the right sensibilities in the patient.

The one question every patient wants to address is: how easy is it to do business with this particular organization? The ATD disposition creates the experiences and outcomes that consumers demand, and businesses need, leading to market dominance and customer loyalty. A commitment to service excellence will influence how patients experience an organization's service or brand.

Designing ATD into the patients' experience requires a critical assessment of all the engines of service delivery, including how space is used (whether the space is inviting vs. cold), what customers will feel, appearance of staff, ambiance, attentiveness of service providers, and how an organization communicates with its patients. These service imperatives give rise to various sensations, memories, and behaviors that create a mosaic of the patients' overall experience. Everything comes into focus: long lines, dead lightbulbs, coffee stains, typographic or grammatical errors, insensitivity of staff, and long and inauthentic staff communication. All are examples of factors that affect patients' sensibilities and overall experience. To be outstanding in their role, service providers are required to strike the right tone and balance between urgency and caring and between efficiency and effectiveness. They must determine when to be flexible or rigid, act with spontaneity or be more deliberate, act with precision and accuracy or embrace the benign gray area, counsel or listen, smile or be serious, and so forth. Their ability to manage these impulses would determine the outcome of the service encounter and how much value patients derive from each encounter.

The optics of a slow-moving, long line is an aspect of the patient experience that leaves an indelible mark in the minds of patients. Disney is very adept at effectively mitigating the optics of long lines. Indeed, Disney attacks the negative effect of long lines with an unmatched creativity and resolve. To minimize the demoralizing effect of the sight of long lines, every ride at Disney has a serpentine queue that winds through something like a movie set, with plenty of distractions. The Haunted Mansion has a waiting room with special effects, and Space Mountain has 87 game stations preceding the ride.

Though no one wants to see the line, people still want to know how long the wait will take, so the waiting time is advertised in front of every ride. There is even a free app, My Disney Experience, that will relay the wait times of every ride within 200 feet of the visitor, a definite advantage in a resort the size of San Francisco. However, Disney does not limit itself to managing expectations and optical illusions. Its command center beneath Cinderella Castle is always ready to act. According to *The New York Times*, if a popular ride like Pirates of the Caribbean is looking slow, the command center may give the order to release more boats or dispatch Disney characters to entertain people while they wait.

Successful organizations present their offerings as integrated wholes, fitting all the little details into a greater context that supports a positive experience and enriches patients' senses. The following excerpt from an interview with a hospital patient illustrates the point further:

> Each interaction I have with your office leaves me feeling like a catalog of individual and separate issues. There are times when I feel that I am being bounced around from person-to-person with no one willing to take responsibility for addressing all my needs. I am passed from one physician to the other, as each person seems to pick and choose which of my issues they prefer to address at any given time.

Starbucks is a pioneer at delivering service in an environment created to satisfy all the sensibilities of its customers. The company's success has significantly affected organizations like McDonald's, Dunkin Donuts, and many other coffee-serving businesses. Many competitors have tried to replicate Starbucks' success by copying isolated components of its customer experience, perhaps the great coffee made from high-quality beans or redesigned interiors of rivals' retail cafes. Nevertheless, these competitors cannot quite capture the magic of a holistic experience. Starbucks' success is largely due to its ability to design for the functional and emotional needs of its customers by creating goods and services that are not only consumed but also have become part of daily routines.

According to Kevin Stirtz (2017), a new customer will develop an impression about a business's employee (and a business) in his/her first seven seconds with the employee. In that slice of time, the customer will judge the employee in 11 different ways, all of which affect how likely customers are to continue to patronize the business. The 11 ways all employees are judged are cleanliness, knowledge, professionalism, friendliness, helpfulness, courtesy, credibility, confidence, attractiveness, responsiveness, and understanding (not necessarily in that order). During that initial interaction, customers will make judgments about the company's dependability, integrity, and ability to serve their needs. Every subsequent interaction serves only to reaffirm or invalidate that first impression. The outcome of these judgments is important. These judgments will culminate in one opinion of the business that will determine the likelihood of becoming a new or repeat customer. The decision they make is reflected in one of three conclusions:

1. Customers like the employee and the business.
2. Customers dislike the employee and the business.
3. Customers are indifferent.

While the first of these seems desirable and may even suggest customer satisfaction, it does not imply customer loyalty. There is still the goal of converting satisfied customers into disciples or loyal customers. A satisfied customer may not be actively seeking other service providers, but he/she is open to new service opportunities. A loyal customer has made a psychological commitment to remain with a product or service long-term. The other two conclusions can be a death sentence for a business. Obviously, dislike is bad. However, in the long run, so is indifference. An indifferent customer is a temporary customer who is actively seeking a product or service that would replace what the current business offers. They are with a company only until something better comes along.

A similar phenomenon happens when a customer "meets" a business for the first time. Three distinct aspects of the patient experience that are often ignored are: (1) What an organization does behind the scenes, (2) What an organization does after the patient departs or after the encounter ends, and (3) What's in the patient's line of sight. These three aspects are discussed next.

■ *What an Organization Does Behind the Scenes*: Most healthcare facilities focus only on activities that are visible to the patients, in the belief that activities that are not visible may invite less scrutiny. Sadly, this is very erroneous. Whether it is the laundry room of a hotel or the kitchen in a restaurant, the connection between what the customer sees and what they do not see is undeniable. Similarly, a patient's experience transcends the line of visibility. Activities that are invisible to patients include the storage area for hospital supplies, patient charts, specimens, laundry services, labs, etc. While Walt Disney World Resort attracts millions of visitors each year, each visitor's experience is the result of the painstaking thoroughness with which the 60,000 cast members approach their roles daily. There is as much attention given to the details behind the scenes as to what every visitor sees.

■ *What an Organization Does after the Patient Departs or the Encounter Ends*: The fact that a patient's visit ends does not mean that the organization's interaction with the patient has ended. It also does not mean that the patient has stopped evaluating his/her experience. For example, bills may be mailed, post-discharge phone calls may be scheduled, or the customer might return to pick up a lost item. The quality of these interactions may impact the patients' perception of the entire encounter. When attention to detail is on full display, the patients' experience is taken to a new level, and the patients' belief in the organization is animated to an extraordinary degree.

■ *What Is in Patients' Line of Sight*: I recall a visit to a local hospital's emergency room (ER) at night to see a friend whose son suffered a severe sports-related injury. As I walked toward the ER entrance, I noticed that the lightbulb had died on the letter "C" in the word "EMERGENCY." Accordingly, the word at the ER read "EMERGENY" instead. My first stop was at the security/information desk, which was staffed by an elderly gentleman with the disposition of a retired cop. He indicated that his machine, which took visitors' pictures for a temporary ID or visitor's badge, was not working. He asked me to write my name on what seemed like a hastily assembled log sheet. There was not enough room for both my first and last name. When he noticed that I might be going beyond the space provided, he suggested I shorten my name by writing only the first three letters. As I walked into the ER, it was hard to miss the 60-yard-long hallway. Ordinarily, my penchant for detail comes and goes, but on this day, I could not but notice everything in my line of sight during my protracted walk. The ceiling had a couple of dead lightbulbs, so the lighting was spotty in different parts of the hallway. About halfway down the hallway, there was an orange hazard cone placed in one corner to steer people away from the bucket catching the ceiling's water leak. The drips were loud enough to catch the attention of passersby, and the bucket was about two-thirds full. I did not make much of the encounter until after my visit, when I noticed that the bucket was now about three-quarters full. Instinctively, I was caught up in an internal debate. Does this matter? And if so, to whom? Who cares about the fact that the front entrance signage was missing a letter, or the name badge machine does not work, or some lightbulbs are dead, or the hallway ceiling has a leak? Perhaps most people would not care about these inadequacies, but invariably, someone might. Nevertheless, I had more questions. Who is responsible for these failures? Did someone conclude that these are "minor details"? If so, do these details matter? What other forms of details are overlooked? Does anyone else see what I see? How does an organization handle these telling images forced on the senses or the mind?

The most challenging jobs are those that not only place an employee in patients' line of sight, but also in a patient's personal space. Examples include nursing, medical assistants, therapists, physicians, dentists, dental hygienists, phlebotomists, paramedics, etc. For these jobs and professions, it is not only about appearance. It is also about personal hygiene.

Attentiveness—The Gold Standard

In 2010, I visited New Orleans and checked into a hotel a few days after my birthday. The registration clerk at the hotel asked to see my ID and method of payment. As she inspected my ID, she said, "Happy Birthday! I see you just had a birthday." She surprised me by sending a bottle of red wine to my room with a card that said, "Happy Birthday!" She was only required to check to make sure that my name matched the name on my reservation. Her action was marked by extreme care and attention to detail.

Details surround us in every aspect of what we do. Our line of sight presents us with an incredible number of details. Every encounter, every task, everyone we meet presents an opportunity to hear the unspoken and see the invisible. The following excerpt from my interview with a patient might illustrate this point further:

My medical condition has brought many things into a rather awkward focus. Please understand that something that may seem so insignificant to you may carry a lot of weight in my mind. It bothers me when you devalue the events or complaints that I report to you. I understand your need to remain objective and unemotional; what I do not understand is your insensitivity and indifference.

My fascination with the patient experience began almost 25 years ago when I started conducting patient satisfaction surveys for healthcare organizations. That experience increased my interest in patient "thank you" notes, patient reviews, and patient complaints. After reviewing thousands of notes, verbatim comments, and patient complaints, I concluded that the real genius of a service experience lies in the "little things." The expectation is that most healthcare organizations know how to take care of the "big things" that represent their core business. Over time, most businesses acquire the necessary experience required to create a better product or service. The distinguishing element tends to be their insistence on perfecting the little things beyond the core product or service. Over time, I began pondering several questions, including the following:

What is it about a customer's experience that causes the customer to escalate his/her commitment from a loyal customer to a "brand disciple"?

- At what point in the customer's experience does he/she willfully volunteer to become an advocate for a company's services or product?
- In the moment when a company drops the ball or fails to deliver as promised, why are some customers still willing to give the company the benefit of the doubt? Why are they so forgiving of an organization's imperfections?

Part of the answer to these questions lies in the extent to which a company and its employees pay attention to detail and handle all things, especially the little things. Little details do not escape the watchful eyes of those inclined to detect and notice them. Because little things are often unexpected, they communicate a sense of craft and dedication. Consequently, they tend to be the things that create the most memorable impression in the minds of your customers in general and patients in particular.

The big things (such as a successful surgery, discharge instructions, accurate diagnosis, treatment protocol) matter, and no healthcare organization can survive without paying attention to them. However, the genius is in the little things! The details! The big things bring patients to a hospital or ER doorstep, but caregivers' attention to detail is what ignites a patient's belief in them. Most patients expect healthcare providers to do the big things well. What truly delights customers is an organization's ability to handle the details. In many walks of life, inattention to detail is a prescription for failure. According to Pastor Charles R. Swindoll, 2000:

> The difference between something good and something great is attention to detail. That is true of a delicious meal, a musical presentation, a play, a clean automobile, a well-kept home, a church, our attire, a business, a lovely garden, a sermon, a teacher, a well-disciplined family.

For the most part, service experience lives or dies on the basis of the little things. In today's job market, more and more job descriptions cite "attention to detail" as a critical attribute. Yet, the lack of proper attention to detail continues to be a source of frustration for organizations and their customers. These mistakes are costly!

In our nationwide survey of 1,000 people conducted in 2016, it was confirmed that attention to detail evokes many positive reactions from customers. About 43 percent of the respondents stated that, when they experience attention to detail, "It tells me that the company offers high-quality service"; 38 percent said, "I feel that they care about me"; and 18 percent remarked, "It tells me that they can take care of the 'big' things too."

The results of our survey highlighted three levels of perception associated with attention to detail—superior service quality, a caring disposition, and a generalizable inference about the core service offered by the company.

Seventy-three percent of survey respondents commented that they have decided to stop patronizing a company because of its "lack of attention to detail," and 84 percent said that they have personally experienced a lack of attention to detail in a service transaction.

Often, the concept of detail is left to the interpretation and judgment of the employee responsible for each specific task. An organization pays attention to detail when it focuses on the following:

- The small things that some may dismiss as unimportant.
- The things that may be unnoticeable and things some may argue should be ignored.
- The things that seem peripheral to your core service and things that some may conclude are inconsequential.

■ The things that make some say, "This does not matter much, since we do so many other things well."

■ The things that make some say, "Don't spend too much time on that, because no one would notice the difference."

■ Anything that may affect a customer's perceptions, even though the customer may or may not see it, hear it, feel it, or touch it.

The Power of Details

Attention to detail provides a richer customer experience in any industry. Crime investigators, detectives, and law enforcement officials know that it is in the details of a crime scene that they find critical clues to solving a crime. Architects and engineers have been taught that the stability of the most complex structure depends on the integrity of its smallest element. Similarly, the missed details of a patient's experience carry with them something significant about the character and texture of the entire service team, personnel, or organization.

The following excerpt from a letter written by a hospital patient explains:

> As a result of my illness, some of the things I used to do I now find objectionable when others do them. I know that work is hard and we must allow moments of lightheartedness. While attending to me, when I see you chewing bubble gum or laughing hysterically or attending to a personal phone call on your cell phone or sipping a cup of coffee, I often wonder if what I am going through means anything to you. Also, this morning, when you ended your personal phone call, I noticed that your mood had changed. Even though I believed it may have had something to do with your phone call, I still worried about how I might be affected.

What were the details missed in this excerpt? What do these details say about the organization affected? What do they say about its service providers? When service organizations fail to pay attention to or manage details, they lose sight of the essence of customers' total experience.

To understand a healthcare organization's commitment to service quality, one must understand its level of attention to detail.

Consider the following examples and what they may tell you about an organization's attention to details:

- Getting the details of a patient's discharge order wrong
- A mislabeled specimen
- A coffee stain on a nurse's uniform or evidence of a blood stain on hospital sheets
- A typo on an organization's website
- A grammatical error in an organization's brochure, flyer, or posted notice
- A light out on a button of a hospital elevator
- Running out of toilet paper in a patient's restroom
- A dusty artificial plant in the waiting lounge of a doctor's office
- Clocks not adjusted to reflect daylight savings time or a clock with dead battery in the hallway
- Slow drainage in a patient's bathroom, sink, or shower tub
- A garbage can in a patient waiting area that is so full, it cannot take any more garbage, with spillover from excess garbage displayed at the foot of the garbage can
- Restroom or bathroom with no soap in the soap dispenser or no toilet paper in the toilet paper holder

We have all encountered these seemingly minor inadequacies. A lack of attention to detail chips away at an organization's "benefit of the doubt capital" over time. Eventually, the accumulation of these experiences erodes customer goodwill. When your organization no longer has "benefit of the doubt capital" from the client or customer, the customer may not be willing to defend your imperfections.

Culture of Attention to Detail

Attention to detail (ATD) is manifested through the individual actions of people—the clinical and non-clinical staff of healthcare organizations. To create a culture of ATD, what becomes important is the collective patterns of beliefs and expectations shared by the staff regarding the patient experience and what ATD brings to that experience. We define a culture of ATD as consisting of the following characteristics:

- A work environment in which all tasks (small or big) are performed carefully, accurately, and in accordance with specific standards

- The meticulous and painstaking thoroughness with which the needs of patients are attended to through what an organization does, says, or how its staff conducts itself
- The consistency of work quality and compliance with standards, requirements, and expectations
- A heightened ability to detect, anticipate, or catch inadequacies, mistakes, and/or to address areas and issues that may not even occur to the patient to ask about

Every patient encounter is a collection of details. At the heels of every triumph lies an immeasurable layer of details. In the words of Gary Ryan Blair, "Although we measure our lives in years, we live them in days, hours, minutes, and seconds."

Organizations that have mastered the science of ATD embrace a deliberate, even obsessive intolerance for mediocrity or failure, as well as a passion for completeness. By paying ATD, an organization delights, assures, reassures, clarifies, enlightens, and illuminates the many impulses invoked by the service experience. Perhaps the most significant benefits of ATD are that they build trust, customer loyalty, and an army of disciples for an organization's services. ATD reaffirms patients' belief in an organization's commitment to handle not just the seemingly inconsequential, but also the desperately vital. When you have a history of ATD, your most critical patients will passionately defend and forgive your imperfections because they happen so infrequently.

When a company demonstrates a history of ATD, the majority of its customers reach the following conclusions:

- A company that obsesses over the little things must truly care about its customers
- A company that obsesses over the little things and the seemingly inconsequential must be capable of taking care of the big things
- To obsess over the little things means that you possess good-quality products and services

Today's Culture of Distraction

Distraction is the enemy of ATD. Today's modern devices and digital conveniences—from the web and social media to smartphones and tablets—may be making society more distracted and less able to concentrate. The incessant demands of cell phones and social media, not to mention email and other forms of distraction may be making it difficult for us to connect with patients that value ATD. These distractions may be inhibiting the ability to think about anything other than the next jolt of stimulation from the devices all around us. We discount real human connections when our digital devices take precedence over the patients right in front of us. According to Bloomberg, 8 billion texts are sent each day, and a large number of them are now being sent from and received in the workplace. In a world increasingly saturated with appealing distractions, the dangers of losing focus and the resulting inattention to detail are quite real to today's healthcare customers.

Just like other workplace distractions such as chattering with coworkers, horseplay, or having one's mind on something other than the present task, being distracted by the phone also causes one to lose focus on the job at hand. Using phones to do such things as watch TV, stay updated on news and social media, and play video games affects our production level.

Hospitals, nursing homes, and clinics all face the increasing challenge of divided attention. The attention of care providers is divided between the needs of patients for undivided attention and the ubiquitous, beckoning calls of text and email alerts. Society has become increasingly dependent on technology to fill every unoccupied moment during work and relaxation. The combined effects of extensive digital multitasking and speed of interaction are creating a healthcare workforce driven by a continuously increasing need for more stimuli, a significantly decreased attention span, and the ability to focus. Restrooms and hallways of healthcare organizations are filled with employees sneaking out to read or send text messages during business hours. Look closely around any workspace, and one will promptly notice the ubiquitous presence of a mobile device waiting patiently to be consulted by its owner. The sounds of beeps and alerts interrupt the quiet of care delivery on nursing floors.

It takes a highly disciplined employee to ignore the persistent invitation of a mobile device. According to the FCC, the popularity of mobile devices has had unintended and even dangerous consequences. We now know that mobile communications are linked to a significant increase in workplace distractions as well as distracted driving, resulting in injury and loss of life. For many teens and even adults, it is particularly frightening to know that these devices stay perpetually on. From the millions of texts that often run through the night and the on-demand access to music to the obsession with

Facebook stalking, our technologies are increasingly controlling our lives instead of our controlling the technology.

A survey of more than 500 employees showed that technology accounts for about 60 percent of workplace distractions—through email, social websites, and even the time it takes to toggle between applications. About 45 percent of the respondents kept at least six items open simultaneously, and 65 percent said they used more than one device in addition to their main computer. According to the study, two out of three people communicate digitally with someone else, at least sometimes, while attending an in-person meeting. Most respondents also said that they sometimes stay connected after work hours, during vacation, and while in bed. As technology and interruption become increasingly prevalent, the negative consequences of not paying attention become more pronounced. These distractions are causing healthcare organizations to miss hundreds of opportunities to win the hearts and minds of patients who value attention—and ATD. When workplace distractions go unmanaged, an organization has a difficult time transitioning from a good company to a great one. ATD is like the glue that strengthens the bond between an organization and its patients. Every transaction carries with it the artifacts of this bond.

Core Value Principles of ATD

1. Nothing ignites the senses like an organization's ability to take care of the details, especially in an unexpected way. As patient demands become more complex and disappointments become the norm, a company's ability to obsess over details makes the patients' experience unforgettable. If a healthcare organization wishes to separate itself from its competitors, there is no better way to do so than by displaying a passion for details.
2. Abolish the distinction between what the patient might or might not notice. A company should pursue a commitment to all aspects of its services, even when such aspects of a service may not be noticeable to all or some patients. Certain details of a service may be noticeable only to a handful of an organization's patients, such as the uniquely curious, the technologically savvy, the digitally fluent, or the otherwise super gifted.
3. Excellence in communication is one of the hallmarks of ATD. A company should pursue a commitment to ATD in all aspects of its services, especially in its communication, internally and externally. Healthcare

organizations communicate with their patients, potential patients, and healthcare partners, through advertisements, websites, brochures, emails, service outreach, letters, etc.). ATD should also be on display in all these many avenues of communication between the organization and its customers.

4. Service should be personalized to reflect the unique needs, circumstances, and characteristics of each patient. Even when the service is the same, every patient is unique and should be treated as such. Each patient is a product of a series of unique and sometimes complex experiences which, in turn, inform their expectations and perspectives. This mindset demands a unique approach to ATD because it integrates the uniqueness of the patient with the uniqueness of the service provider to create a unique patient experience.

5. Manage and control workplace distractions. A company should pursue a commitment to ATD in all aspects of its services by vigorously fighting the forces of workplace distractions in the multiple ways they are manifested. Companies create or permit the practices that make ATD impossible or difficult to embrace.

6. Healthcare leaders' role in creating and sustaining a culture of ATD cannot be overstated. Every healthcare leader sends signals to subordinates that affirm and reaffirm their belief (or lack thereof) in the patient experience. These signals over time form the foundation of an organization's culture. When an organization's sensibilities are awakened to the little things that can be missed, the big things are automatically brought into focus on their radar. Conversely, when the focus is mainly on the big things, the little things may be missed. This is not necessarily the result of reckless indifference; it is often because the company's culture values and rewards mainly the big things. It is also based on how a company defines success.

7. Everything matters! Everything comes into focus! Every gesture, every touch, every smile, every word, every eye contact, every shift, every associate, every time, and every day. Our senses are constantly being fed by the myriad things and situations we encounter. We decide; we choose how we respond to what we see, hear, touch, smell, or feel. Our senses give us an opportunity to uncover layers of details in our daily encounters.

8. Empathy allows us to feel and anticipate the pain of others, to see the invisible, and to hear the unspoken. The more we feel, see, and hear, the more likely we are to value the precious details that matter to

others. Empathy calls for an awareness of the feelings and emotions of other people. It is a key element of emotional intelligence, and it establishes the link between the self and others.

Questions for Discussion

4.1. How does today's culture of distraction affect the patient experience? What should healthcare organizations do about it?
4.2. List the ways your organization can improve the details that are important to its patients.
4.3. Do a tour of the main entrance of your organization and compile a list of the unpleasant details in the patients' line of sight.
4.4. What factors explain some of the empathy deficit you have observed in healthcare facilities? What can be done to address them?

References

Blair, G.R., 2009. *Everything Counts: 52 Remarkable Ways to Inspire Excellence and Drive Results*,. John Wiley & Sons, Inc. , Hoboken, New Jersey.
Swindoll, C., 2000. *Day by Day with Charles Swindoll*, Thomas Nelson, Nashville, Tennessee.

Additional Reading

Stirtz, K., 2017. "Making a Great First Impression with Your Customers," Business.com. https://www.business.com/articles/making-a-great-first-impression-with-your-customers/

Chapter 5

Data and Information

The ability to collect, analyze, and derive insight from data is a vital component of a successful performance improvement process. Most healthcare organizations claim to be undertaking quality improvement (QI) initiatives, but only a few can demonstrate proof of sustainable success. Part of the problem lies in the failure to effectively manage data and information. The critical failure factors in the use of data and information are as follows:

- Lack of access to the right data
- Lack of in-house data analytics skills
- Analysis limited to the data available rather than the data needed
- Inability to convert the data into information
- Analysis that provides insufficient insight
- Inexperience with data collection tools and methodology
- A culture that relies excessively on "gut feel," hunches, and wild, arbitrary guesses
- Lack of accountability
- Insufficient use of technology to harness the right data

The term "analytics" refers to the systems, tools, and techniques that help healthcare organizations gain insight into current performance, and guide future actions, by discerning patterns and relationships in data and using that understanding to guide decision making (Strome, 2013). Analytics in healthcare is principally aimed at improving the safety, efficiency, and effectiveness of healthcare delivery systems. Most importantly, analytics creates value in healthcare by providing powerful insights regarding a patient's experience. The combination of health information technology (HIT) and data analytics makes transformative improvements in healthcare possible. Healthcare organizations that do not devote sufficient attention to data analytics may only be able to speak of marginal success in their quality improvement journey. On the other end of the spectrum are organizations that are obsessively driven to measure and track anything and everything without the discipline of managing the psychosis that such tendencies produce. The key is to strike the right balance between process and outcomes, and between people and their work environment.

Technology can play a great role in the ability to capture the right information at the right time, in the right format, and to deliver it to the right stakeholders. One such technology is radio-frequency identification (RFID). The implementation of RFID technology in healthcare is on the rise. RFID has the potential to save healthcare organizations significant time and money by offering real-time traceability, identification, communication, and location data for people and resources. RFID technology utilizes radio waves for data collection and transfer (Rosenbaum, 2014). Historically, RFID technology has been used in supply chain management, primarily to track goods in warehouses (Bowen et al., 2011) because RFID can capture data automatically without human intervention. Compared to barcode scanning, RFID does not require line of sight for readers to capture information from tags.

Why Collect Data?

There are many reasons to collect data, including the following:

- To understand the gap between patient requirements and what an organization offers
- To gauge the impact of quality improvement activities on a process
- To answer research questions
- To provide information to support improvement efforts
- To monitor resource usage
- To determine the necessity for an improvement effort
- To track accomplishments
- To understand root causes
- To determine the viability of a solution or idea

Data Collection Methods

Before collecting data, it is important to answer the following questions:

- What do you hope to accomplish by collecting data?
- How will the data be collected?
- Who will collect the data and for how long?
- Where will the data be collected?
- What data collection instrument will be used?
- Is the data available?
- If the data is historical, in what format is it currently stored?
- How much disruption will data collection create?
- Will training be required for the people collecting or extracting the data?
- How much data is needed?
- How will the data be analyzed?
- Is the data adequately stratified?
- What is the cost of collecting the data?
- Is the cost of collecting data justified?

It is necessary to determine whether the data will have to be collected retrospectively or prospectively. When data is drawn from historical medical records, the process is called retrospective data collection. Conversely, data can be sampled prospectively by collecting it from current patients as they present for treatment on the day of the study visit. Collecting data retrospectively requires going into the past; that is, the data has already been collected and is available for use. Collecting data prospectively entails collecting data from this moment forward. It is common practice to collect data on prescribing encounters using both methods; however, patient care indicators often require the collection of prospective data. One of the key challenges in deciding between retrospective and prospective data is whether adequate sources of retrospective data exist. Possible sources of retrospective data can include chronological clinic visits, treatment records kept by individual providers, and drug prescription records kept at the health facility. Retrospective data sources must fulfill the following requirements: (1) a clearly defined method of selecting a random sample of patient encounters that occurred within a specified time period, (2) the exact names and definitions of all relevant variables, and (3) the proper sample size of encounters to examine.

Retrospective data is usually easier to collect than prospective data, and it is subject to fewer potential biases. It is often possible to define a retrospective study period of a year or longer with cases selected throughout this period. This reduces bias due to seasonal variations or interruptions in the event cycle. One of the challenges of retrospective data is that it is often incomplete, with individual or entire portions missing due to misplacement. Alternatively, the data was never captured. In addition, the validity of retrospective data is often difficult to ascertain.

Prospectively collected data are usually more likely to be complete. Prospectively collected data may suffer from biases because providers are aware that their behavior is being observed during the study period. The following are the various methods for collecting data:

■ Observation
■ Focus groups and interviews
■ Surveys
■ Documents and records
■ Experimentation

In what follows, each method of data collection will be described in greater detail.

Observation

Observation, particularly participant observation, has been used in a variety of disciplines as a tool for collecting data about people, processes, and cultures in qualitative research. Marshall and Rossman (Marshall and Rossman, 1989) define observation as "the systematic description of events, behaviors, and artifacts in the social setting chosen for study" (p.79). Observations enable the researcher to describe existing situations using the five senses, providing a "written photograph" of the situation under study (Erlandson et al., 1993).

Participant observation is the process that enables researchers to learn about the activities of the people under study in the natural setting through observing and participating in those activities. It provides the context for developing sampling guidelines and interview guides (DeWalt and DeWalt, 2002). Schensul, Schensul, and LeCompte (1991) define participant observation as "the process of learning through exposure to or involvement in the day-to-day or routine activities of participants in the researcher setting" (p.91). When feasible, direct observation allows the data collector to use all five senses in the data gathering process. The quality of the information gathered is usually very high. Moreover, certain facts can be learned only from direct observation. There are many things we learn only by watching patients in the waiting areas of hospitals, emergency rooms, and clinics. Surveys do not always address all the relevant issues. Field notes are the primary tool for capturing the data collected from participant observations. Notes taken to capture this data include records (such as videos) of what is observed, including informal conversations with participants and records of activities and events during which the researcher cannot question participants about their activities, and journal notes kept on a daily basis. DeWalt, DeWalt, and Wayland (1998) describe field notes as comprising both data and analysis, as the notes provide an accurate description of what is observed and are the product of the observation process. As they highlight, observations are not data unless they are recorded in field notes.

Focus Groups and Interviews

A focus group session is a facilitated group interview with individuals that have something in common. For example, a managed care company might want to bring together a group of disenrolled members to solicit their opinions regarding their reasons for disenrolling from the health plan. Focus groups require face-to-face interaction, as well as the opportunity to ask follow-up questions. Interviews and focus groups are the most common methods of data collection used in qualitative healthcare research. Interviews can be used to explore the perspectives, experiences, beliefs, and motivations of individual participants concerning a particular subject. Focus groups use group dynamics to generate qualitative data about a subject.

Conducting Focus Groups: Group Composition and Size

The composition of a focus group is vital to achieving great results. Group composition and group mix will always affect the data. Factors such as the mix of ages, gender, and the socioeconomic and professional statuses of the participants can be influential in the data collected. It is important for the researcher to give appropriate consideration to the impact of a group's mixture before commencing the focus group session. Group size is an important consideration in focus group research. It is preferable to slightly over-recruit for a focus group and potentially manage a slightly larger group than under-recruit and risk having to cancel the session or having an unsatisfactory discussion (Stewart and Shamdasani, 1990).

The optimum size for a focus group is six to eight participants, excluding researchers, but focus groups can work successfully with as few as three and as many as fourteen participants. Small groups risk limited discussions occurring, while large groups can be chaotic, hard to manage for the moderator, and frustrating for participants who feel they get insufficient opportunities to speak (Bloor et al., 2001).

Accordingly, the role of the moderator is vital to the process. The moderator should facilitate a group discussion, keeping it focused without leading it. He/she also should be able to ensure that the discussion is not being dominated by one member. The moderator should emphasize the importance of divergent viewpoints while ensuring that all participants have ample opportunity to contribute. Focus groups are usually recorded, often observed (by a researcher other than the moderator, whose role is to observe the interaction of the group to enhance analysis), and sometimes videotaped. At the start of a focus group, a moderator should acknowledge the presence of the audio-recording equipment, assure participants of their confidentiality, and give them the opportunity to withdraw if they are uncomfortable with being taped (Stewart and Shamdasani, 1990). The analysis of focus group data is different from other qualitative data because of its interactive nature, and this needs to be considered during analysis. The importance of the context of other speakers is essential to the understanding of individual contributions (Bloor et al., 2001). For example, in a group situation, participants will often challenge one another and try to justify their remarks in a way that perhaps they would not in a one-to-one interview. Therefore, the analysis of focus group data must account for the group dynamics that generated the remarks.

Interviews are a vital tool for research in healthcare. There are three basic types of research interviews: structured, semi-structured, and unstructured. Structured interviews are, essentially, verbally administered questionnaires with a list of predetermined questions. The questions are asked in a structured manner, with little or no variation and with no provision for follow-up questions. They are relatively quick and easy to administer. However, by their very nature, they only allow limited participant responses and are, therefore, not effective if elaboration is desired.

However, unstructured interviews do not reflect any preconceived mindset and are performed with little or no format. Such an interview may simply start with an opening question such as, "Can you tell me about your experience of going to the emergency room last month?" The direction of the interview depends on the direction of the initial response. Often lasting several hours, unstructured interviews tend to be very time-consuming and can be difficult to execute. The lack of predetermined interview questions encourages a free-form back and forth with undefined boundaries. Their use is, therefore, generally only considered when significant probing is desired or very little is known about the subject area.

Semi-structured interviews consist of several key questions that help to define the topic to be covered, but also allow the interviewer or interviewee to stray away to extract additional detail. This interview format is used most frequently in healthcare, because it provides participants with guidance on the boundaries of the discussion. When compared to structured interviews, this approach allows the elaboration of information that may be important to participants beyond what the researcher envisioned. As in any research, it is advisable first to pilot the interview questions on several respondents before data collection. This allows the research team to determine if the questions are clear, unambiguous, and properly aligned with the research questions and if changes to the interview questions are required.

Surveys

Surveys require designing an instrument and administering it to respondents. Using surveys makes it possible to collect data about existing information, processes, knowledge, perceptions, and the way things are or should be. Surveys can be administered via telephone, mailings, or face-to-face interviews. Low response rates can be a problem, particularly with mailed surveys. Other problems associated with mailed surveys are wrong addresses and the high cost of mailing. While using paper and pencil surveys is the traditional method of collecting data, technology continues to offer popular and often more efficient ways to collect data, especially quantitative data like the kind collected with a traditional survey tool. The types of technology often used to collect data traditionally captured via survey tools include online or web surveys, hand-held devices such as clickers and personal digital assistants (PDAs), text messages, and social networking sites such as Twitter and Facebook. The use of technology for surveys has advantages and disadvantages. The advantages include the following:

- Simpler and quicker way of collecting both quantitative and qualitative data
- Easy to access a large group of respondents in geographically diverse locations
- More cost effective than manually administering surveys

- Data can typically be exported, eliminating manual data entry
- Improves the accuracy of data entry (e.g. reduces omissions and duplicate entries)

There are also disadvantages, including the following:

- Limited to respondents with internet access
- Some may find online interfaces off-putting
- Does not guarantee the quality (reliability and validity) of actual survey design
- Potential lack of security

Responses to survey questions can be analyzed with quantitative methods by assigning numerical values to Likert-type scales. It is generally easier than qualitative techniques to analyze results. Surveys make it easy to compare and analyze pretests and post-tests.

Documents and Records

Documents and records consist of existing data in the form of databases, meeting minutes, reports, attendance logs, financial records, social media sources, electronic medical records systems, etc. They can be an inexpensive way to gather information but may be incomplete. Since accuracy is a function of manual data entry, such accuracy is often questionable.

Experiments

Experiments involve collecting information while allowing the control of one or more factors that influence the situation. If done correctly, they tend to be unbiased and statistically valid, and they are a methodical way to show cause and effect. Experiments' disadvantages include high costs and the need for technical expertise.

Stratifying Data

Stratification is the breakdown of the original data set into smaller but related subgroups. Stratification allows the data collector to have a better understanding of the context in which the problem or process exists. The ability to treat each subgroup separately makes data analysis more precise. For example, to study nurses' response times to call lights on a given nursing unit, it may be necessary to break the original data into shifts, as shown in Table 5.1.

In the example in Table 5.1, stratification is used because there is the suspicion of shift-to-shift and unit-to-unit variability, which the data confirms. Stratification allows a more precise analysis of this particular problem. Other stratification factors in healthcare include the following:

■ Day of the week
■ Walk-in vs. appointment patients
■ Salaried vs. non-salaried staff
■ Geographic locations
■ Time of day
■ Specialist vs. primary care physician
■ Medicare vs. Medicaid
■ Medicare, Medicaid, commercial, and individual HMO members

Data Variations

To understand the context of data, it is important to understand the sources of variations that could explain disparities in the data. Variations come from many sources and can be attributed to one or more of the following sources:

■ Human
■ Equipment
■ Material
■ Methods
■ Environment

Table 5.1 Average Response Time (in Minutes) to Call Lights

Nursing Unit	7:00 AM–3:00 PM	3:00 PM–11:00 PM	11:00 PM–7:00 AM
Unit 4 East	6.9 minutes	14.3 minutes	12.6 minutes
Unit 5 North	2.1 minutes	8.7 minutes	7.3 minutes
Unit 6 West	3.5 minutes	10.8 minutes	8.4 minutes

Humans are affected by many factors, including weather, traffic, emotional and personal problems, and level of resiliency. Technological distractions such as social media, text messages, tweets, etc. add a layer of complexity to the degree of variations attributable to humans. Equipment represents an important source of variations. The factors primarily responsible for variations due to equipment include the age, make, and model of the equipment, interface problems, maintenance (preventive vs. corrective), and complexity of the equipment. Variations due to material can be accounted for by examining the sources of raw materials and components. Multiple suppliers can mean multiple sources of variation. Even when an organization has a sole supplier, inspectors can be a source of variability. The lack of standardized methods continues to be a huge problem in healthcare. Over time, operators develop their own approaches to accomplishing their job duties. Consequently, it is very common to have five people performing the same function in five different ways. The environment plays a huge role in causing variations in a process. The leadership climate, temperature, noise level, teamwork or lack thereof, and culture can all contribute to the variations in an organization.

All processes have some form of inherent variation. Variations are simply unavoidable. For example, the proportion of medication or billing errors will vary every day. Accordingly, a conscious effort must be made to control and reduce variations. There are two types of variations: variations due to common cause and variations due to special cause. Variations due to common causes are variations due to causes that are inherent in a process. Employees should not be held responsible for the problems due to common cause variation; rather, these issues are within the purview of good management. Variations due to special causes fall outside the system. Special cause variations are avoidable, and they should be identified, studied, and eliminated. When variations are due to special causes, it implies the presence of certain meaningful factors that should be investigated.

Types of Data

Attribute or Discrete Data

Attribute or discrete data are countable data with a criterion of pass or fail, go or no go, good or bad, or yes or no.

The following are examples of this type of data:

- Number of misdiagnoses (a condition is either accurately diagnosed or misdiagnosed)
- Number of medication errors (a medication error either occurred or did not occur)
- Percentage of calls answered in over 50 seconds
- Number of patient-related accidents
- Percentage of provider claims processed within three weeks
- Number of phone rings before an answer
- Percentage of calls answered within three rings
- Number of negative entries on a survey instrument
- Number of patients arriving at an outpatient facility per hour
- Frequency of a diagnostic machine's failures
- Number of patients' complaints

Variable or Continuous Data

Variable or continuous data are measurable and reflect information such as how much, how big, or how long. The following are examples of this type of data:

- Response times to patients' call lights
- Patients' waiting time
- Average food temperature
- Ancillary cost for a given patient
- Average weight
- Average blood pressure reading
- Average height
- Distance walked by a patient
- Claims processing time in hours
- Time spent with a physician

Distinguishing Data Types

The data type can be determined based on the nature of the original data. For example, if data consists of the percentage of medication errors, the original data would have been the number of medication errors divided by the total amount of medication administered in that period. Because the original data is discrete, the percentage of medication errors is also discrete. If, however, the researcher is interested in the percentage of time that patients spend waiting, the original data is the time spent waiting (before receiving medical or nursing care) divided by the total time spent in the facility. Since time is always considered variable or continuous data, the percentage of waiting time would also be variable or continuous. It is necessary to distinguish between attribute and variable data because each requires different types of control charts. Attribute and variable control charts are discussed in Chapter 7.

Summary

Data provides the vital signs by which organizational performance can be measured. Without accurate data, it is impossible to keep up with the frantic pace of business. Indeed, data makes it possible to learn from the past, manage the present, as well as understand and predict the future. In addition, data provides an understanding of patients' needs and exceptions. Data also provides invaluable insight into the perceptions of patients and other customers of the healthcare process. When an organization strays from its mission, accurate data illuminates the effort to regain its success. To rely entirely on opinion and conjecture is not just dangerous; it is costly. There is no substitute for reliable, valid data.

Questions for Discussion

5.1. What are the costs associated with data collection? Give an example of a study in which it was necessary to consider such costs.
5.2. Describe a process one might follow to gather data about breast cancer screening for a managed care organization.
5.3. What methods of data collection would be appropriate for the following scenarios?
   – Name change for an HMO
   – Adverse drug reaction
   – Setting new visitation hours for guests
   – Cancellations of surgeries
   – High rate of cesarean births

    – Patient satisfaction

    – Meal choices in the cafeteria

5.4. What is the stratification of data? Give examples of how you might stratify data for the following:

    – Low birth weight in newborns

    – Patient falls

    – Medication errors

5.5. Give five examples each of attribute and variable data

References

Bloor, M., Frankland, J., Thomas, M. and Robson, K. 2001. *Focus Groups in Social Research*. London: Sage.

Bowen, M. E., Wingrave, C. A., Klanchar, A. and Craighead, J., 2011. "Tracking Technology: Lessons Learned in Two Healthcare Sites." *Technology and Health Care* 21: 191–197. DOI:10.3233/THC-130738

DeWalt, K. M. and DeWalt, B. R., 2002. *Participant Observation: A Guide for Fieldworkers*. Walnut Creek, CA: AltaMira Press.

Dewalt, K. M., Dewalt, B. R. and Wayland, C. B., 1998. Participant Observation. In: H. R. Bernard, editor. *Handbook of Methods in Cultural Anthropology*, 259–299. Walnut Creek, CA: AltaMira.

Erlandson, D. A., Harris, E. L., Skipper, B. L. and Allen, S. D., 1993. Doing naturalistic inquiry: a guide to methods. Newbury Park, CA: Sage.

Marshall, C. and Rossman, G. B., 1989. *Designing Qualitative Research*. Newbury Park, CA: Sage.

Rosenbaum, B. P., 2014. "Radio Frequency Identification (RFID) in Healthcare: Privacy and Security Concerns Limiting Adoption." *Journal of Medical Systems* 38(3). DOI:10.1007/s10916-014-0019-z

Schensul, S. L., Schensul, J. J. and LeCompte, M. D., 1999. *Essential Ethnographic Methods: Observations, Interviews, and Questionnaires* (Book 2 in Ethnographer's Toolkit). Walnut Creek, CA: AltaMira Press.

Stewart, D. W. and Shamdasani, P. M., 1990. *Focus Groups. Theory and Practice*. London: Sage.

Strome, T.L. 2013. *Healthcare Analytics for Quality and Performance Improvement*. Hoboken, New Jersey: John Wiley & Sons, Inc.

Chapter 6

Lean Management System

Lean management is a systematic approach to continuous improvement requiring those closest to the work to improve their work processes by achieving small, incremental changes that create value for the customer, improve efficiency and productivity, and reduce waste. The role of leadership in a lean organization is not to be the problem solver or the source of all answers. Instead, the primary focus of leadership is to create and facilitate an environment in which the workforce can feel empowered to solve problems. One of the goals of a lean organization is to have the entire organization actively engaged in problem solving, compared to traditional organizations in which 10%–20% of the workforce participates in problem solving.

Unfortunately, the lean philosophy has been bastardized by untrained practitioners and consultants. A popular misconception is that lean is suited only for manufacturing organizations. Not true! Lean applies to every business and every process. Businesses in all industries, including healthcare and governments, are using lean principles as the way to improve efficiency, productivity, reduce costs, and increase value.

The lean philosophy consists of several elements and guiding principles, including the ones listed below:

- The lean starting point is the creation of value from the customers' perspective. All inputs, activities, processes, and methods are aimed at value creation and waste elimination.
- Lean is built on a culture of continuous improvement, which is on display at every level of the organization and embraced by every team.
- Lean relies on the application of the scientific methods of process improvement and experimentation to create value for the customers.

■ Lean is founded on the value of respect for people—especially those who do the work and those who use the product or services. Lean assumes that those closest to the work are the most knowledgeable regarding improvement opportunities, and lean provides a platform for the customer's voice.

■ A lean culture has deep contempt for waste in all its forms. It is routine in a lean environment to distinguish between work that actually adds value to customers and work that does not. The elimination of waste makes it possible to free resources for value-adding activities that customers demand.

■ In a lean work environment, safety and quality are of the utmost importance and carry a sense of urgency.

■ Rather than blaming the employees and using fear to compel compliance, lean's focus is on the process that generates products or services. People do what the process allows them to do.

■ Lean is founded on a culture of teamwork, experimentation, collaborative problem solving, shared responsibility, and ownership that eliminate organizational walls or silos.

■ Lean creates a culture that promotes the joy of work. Lean is based on the belief that people do their best work when they derive joy from it.

■ In a lean environment, a seamless flow is perpetually desirable. The goal is an interruption-free process that flows from beginning to end. Lean achieves this smooth workflow by deploying technical tools and engaging both managers and employees.

One of the distinct characteristics of a lean organization is the emphasis on developing the problem-solving capabilities of the entire workforce. This is achieved by allocating specific categories of problems to each segment of the organization. The organization focuses on the performance of the entire value stream and the customer it serves. Lean management seeks to eliminate the waste of time, effort, or money by identifying each step in a business process and then revising or eliminating steps that do not create value.

The lean philosophy has its roots in manufacturing. The lean management approach is generally derived from the Toyota Production System, as developed by Taiichi Ohno, Shigeo Shingo, and others over a 40-year period. One of the most important features of the Toyota Production System is the way it links all production activity to real demand. Everything in the system happens only in the name of fulfilling dealers' actual orders. The system works thus because it is a "pull" system, unlike conventional "push" systems. Lean management has as its foundation the many lessons derived from the works of great quality pioneers, including Frederick Taylor, Henry Ford, Dr. Edwards Deming, Walter Shewhart, and Joseph Juran. The work of Fred Emery and Eric Trist, who founded the school of socio-technical systems, is integral to the nature of lean organizations.

However, it was not until the late 1980s that the term "lean" was promoted by a research team headed by Jim Womack at MIT's International Motor Vehicle Program to describe Toyota's business during that time. Today, despite indications that lean is prevalent in healthcare, many authors regard its implementation to be pragmatic, patchy, and fragmented (Burgess and Radnor, 2013). The application of lean management in healthcare can also be holistic, as in the transformation of an overall business strategy (Ulhassan et al., 2013). Although lean thinking originated from car making, research on its application and sustainability in healthcare is still limited (Mazzocato et al., 2012). Primary studies often lack appropriate concepts explicitly stated, research designs, appropriate analysis, and outcome measures (Mazzocato et al., 2012).

The ultimate vision is to deliver perfect value to the customer through a perfect value creation process that has zero waste. To accomplish this, lean thinking shifts the focus of management from optimizing the separate components of technologies, assets, resources, and functional areas/departments to optimizing the horizontal flow of products and services through entire value streams. See Figure 6.1.

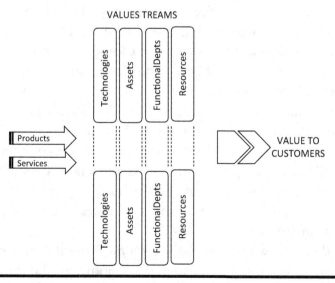

Figure 6.1   The lean value creation process.

Lean in healthcare is a management philosophy that pursues continuous improvement methodologies to create the most value for the patient. It targets the most value-eroding aspects of care delivery, such as wait times, long lines, delays, transportation, unsafe practices, and hospital-acquired infections. Lean in healthcare seeks to investigate the timeline from the moment a patient enters the system (either in person or via a phone call, an email, or otherwise) to the time when their needs have been met or their issues resolved. Lean aims to reduce that timeline by eliminating non-value-added activities or waste.

The Lean Process

The following steps are vital to the successful implementation of a lean culture:

1. *Understanding the Patient*: In Chapter 2, we discussed the need to define value in the context of the patient's experience, both clinical and non-clinical. A critical starting point for Lean is the process of thoroughly understanding what the patient values, given his/her condition and circumstances. The concept of value varies from patient to patient. The lean approach begins with a detailed understanding of what value the customer assigns to products and services, which determines what the customer will pay. Establishing value allows organizations to create a top-down target price. Subsequently, the cost to produce products and services is determined. The organization focuses on eliminating waste to deliver the value the customer expects at the highest profitability. Value is created by the producer, and in this case, by the healthcare delivery system and/or facility. From a patient's standpoint, this is why healthcare organizations exist. Value can only be defined by the ultimate customer—the patient. What a patient values can range from empathy, safety, or a resolution of the chief complaint to a physician's willingness to speak with the patient's family member. Once an organization understands what the patient values, it must seek to develop a mechanism for measuring it and creating services and processes that satisfy patients' needs.

2. *Identify all the Steps in the Value Stream for Patient Categories*: The value stream is the totality of the patients' journey (life cycle) throughout the duration of the visit, the conditions, interactions, etc. Processes

can be organized around value streams by re-examining the patient journey from start to end. For example, a patient's visit to a primary care physician's office might produce the steps depicted in Figure 6.2.

The entire flow, from the call to schedule an appointment to referrals and diagnostic tests, must be organized around the value stream. Every step must be scrutinized for the value it adds to the overall patient experience. Healthcare providers must make the value-creating steps occur in a tight sequence, so the patients' journey will flow smoothly toward the desired goal. Besides the traditional value streams, leaders must also consider the human resources value stream and think about how HR workers hire, reward, recognize, train, onboard, organize, and design systems for new and existing personnel.

3. *Maximize the Flow and Pull*: Lean adherents ensure the uninter-rupted and smooth flow of patients, information, supplies, doctors' notes, insurance verification, copays, etc. Lean seeks to eliminate the obstacles to flow by addressing wait times, delays, diagnostic machine malfunctions, inadequate capacity to handle patient volume, etc. The faster the process flow, the lower the costs associated with service delivery. All flow comes from the direct pull of the customer. In addi-tion, understanding flow is vital to the elimination of waste. If the value stream stops progressing or is hindered at any point, waste is the inevi-table byproduct. The lean principle of flow is about creating a value chain with no interruption in the service delivery process and a state where each activity is fully synchronized. The pull system responds to real demand, and if patients are spending excessive amounts of time waiting, then real demand is not being met. That means we must

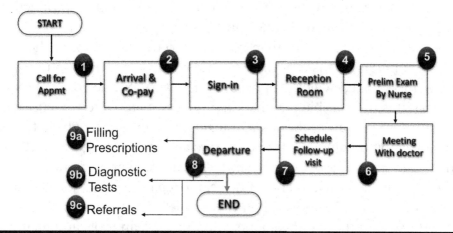

Figure 6.2   Patients' visit to the primary care physician.

conceptualize "pull" as the patient-pulling resources that are needed. Additionally, employees must work when patients need care, rather than when it is convenient or the capacity exists.

4. *Empower the Staff.* While doctors and nurses get the most attention, it is important for employers to engage all their employees. Asking employees their opinion can be extremely empowering. It shows that management values their input and cares how a decision might affect their daily work. Employees should be included in matters that affect them directly—for example, when implementing an electronic health record (EHR). The people on the frontlines and in the trenches (who contact patients every day, schedule appointments, and communicate with insurance companies about payments) will be most invested in seeing an EHR undertaking succeed. It makes sense, then, that these people should be consulted for input. Empowered nurses foster better health outcomes for patients (Laschinger, Gilbert, Smith and Leslie, 2010). Nurses who perceive themselves as empowered are more likely to use more effective work practices resulting in positive patient outcomes (Donahue, Piazza, Griffin, Dykes and Fitzpatrick, 2008). Leveraging employee empowerment is a force multiplier in generating thousands of process improvements. Without a climate of employee empowerment that is accepted and encouraged by management, production workers will seldom offer suggestions for process or quality improvement. One of the most important requirements of this step is the need to empower people for lean improvement every day. To accomplish this aim, one solution is to train the staff in root cause analysis and problem solving, standardized work, and visual management, as well as align each job to customer value creation. The lean concept of stopping production to fix a problem is called "jidoka" (in Japanese), which means "getting it right the first time" rather than passing it to the customer, or the next workstation. Jidoka is a prime example of the lean philosophy of "quality at the source," which emphasizes that every production worker (and supplier) is responsible for providing quality material to the customer.

The core of lean is about small teams of people throughout the entire organization coming together each day and trying to figure out how they can do their jobs better that day. It means that workers must gain the confidence to make critical decisions regarding their jobs or tasks, and simultaneously know when to seek help from experts. The only way to sustain the improvements afforded by lean tools and techniques is to fully embrace an environment of employee empowerment. One

distinct measure of success for employee empowerment is the percentage of the workforce that is engaged and participating in producing
countless improvements. Tremendous opportunities abound where
employees can showcase their problem-solving talents, including the
bedside, clinic, radiology suite, emergency room, laboratory, kitchen,
intensive care unit (ICU), operating room, business office, etc.

5. *Pursue Perfection*: Lean practitioners strive to achieve nothing short of
   perfection. The march toward the perfect process happens step-by-step
   as continuous improvements address the root causes of quality problems and production waste. The relentless pursuit of perfection drives
   users of the approach to dig deeper, measure more, and change more
   often than their competitors. As organizations understand how patients
   define value, accurately specify value, and identify the entire value
   stream, the value-creation steps for specific services flow continuously,
   letting patients pull value from the enterprise. Meanwhile, the staff naturally begins to accept the possibility of perfection in their future state.
   Lean improvement should be continued until every process adds value
   and every non-value-added process is eliminated. It is important to add
   that lean improvements come from aligned, empowered people making
   small changes daily.

Lean Tools and Their Applications

It is also key to note that no single lean tool will be effective alone or sustain a lean initiative. The lean methodology aims to eliminate waste and
increase efficiency by creating flow and allowing pull along a service value
stream, thereby creating value for the patient. Simply embracing one tool in
isolation will not achieve the objectives of lean thinking. Next, we will discuss some of these main tools of the lean approach.

Value Stream Mapping

First, let us define what we mean by a value stream. A value stream in
healthcare is a set of all the specific actions, steps, or activities a healthcare
organization uses to create or deliver a continuous flow of value to a patient.
The value stream is usually supported by the flow of information, supplies,
and materials. In addition, the flow of value is often triggered by certain

events, such as patient registration and triage in the emergency department. Value is achieved only when the patient receives the benefits of that intervention or encounter. It is the process steps that define the value stream.

Once the value stream has been identified, it is time to begin the task of mapping it. To create the value stream, one must literally walk the value stream of the facility, noting value-added time and non-valued-added time. This process leads to the creation of a visual map and exposes the ability to see areas for improvement. The purpose of a value stream map (VSM) is to identify activities that do not add value to the end product or service. By eliminating these activities, organizations will gain faster throughput and greater quality.

What Is Value Stream Mapping?

VSM is a lean methodology that consists of a flow chart used to illustrate, analyze, and improve the steps required to deliver a product or service. VSM is especially useful to find and eliminate waste. VSM reviews the flow of process steps and information from the start to the delivery of value to the customer. It uses a system of symbols to depict various work activities and information flows. Items are mapped as adding value or not adding value from the customer's perspective, with the goal of eliminating items that do not add value. Value stream maps have their roots in the Toyota lean production system. In this context, value can be conceptualized as anything the customer is willing to pay. Any process or activity that does not provide value is considered waste. Value stream mapping emphasizes "kaizen," or continuous improvement, in keeping with Toyota's kaizen philosophy. Because a value stream often crosses department boundaries, it is important to identify the individuals who must be involved in creating a map. Once the stakeholders have been identified, everyone should ideally gather in person to virtually or physically walk through each step in a process and document repeatable actions.

There is also the support value stream, which includes services like Human Resources and Information Technology. These are typically support functions: hence, the term support value stream. An organization can have several value streams depending on its size and the number of products and/or services it offers. The map itself is typically created as a one-page flow chart depicting the various steps involved in moving a patient through the system from start to finish. The low-tech yet effective method of developing the flow chart is to use a whiteboard with all the participants gathered in one place. Once the participants confirm the accuracy of the current state's VSM, stakeholders can use the shared visualization tool to identify potential sources of improvement and brainstorm ideas for eliminating waste. Typically, a mapping session concludes with the creation of a future state VSM. The VSM process is then continued iteratively. For an activity to meet the criteria for adding value, it must meet all three of the following:

■ The customer must be willing to pay for the activity.
■ The activity must directly transform the product or service in some way.
■ The activity must be done correctly the first time.

Lean thinking creates an environment that is obsessive about driving out waste, so all work adds value and meets the customer's needs. Identifying value-added and non-value-added steps in every process is a key element of the journey toward lean operations. For lean principles to take root, leaders must first commit to creating an organizational culture that is receptive to lean thinking. The commitment to lean must start at the very top of the organization and should involve all employees in the redesign processes to improve flow and reduce waste (Figure 6.3).

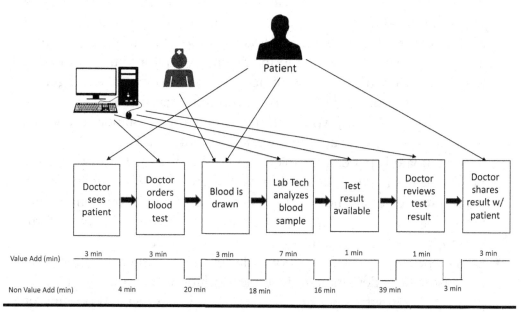

Figure 6.3   An example of a VSM for a segment of the patients' experience.

Defining Waste

Just creating a value stream map without using it would be a complete waste of time. Once the value stream map is accepted and verified by everyone involved, it is time to start looking for the "seven wastes" that could be eating up profits and destroying the customer experience. Waste is anything that adds no value. It represents what we aim to remove from processes. Lean manufacturing identifies seven forms of waste:

- *Transport*: The unnecessary (non-value-added) movement of parts, materials, or information between processes. It is not uncommon to find floor nurses going from floor to floor searching for the materials, supplies, and equipment needed to perform their duties.
- *Inventory*: Raw materials, work-in-progress (WIP), or finished goods that are not having value added to them. This includes holding inventory longer than required, discarding inventoried items because of obsolescence, and overstocked medications.
- *Motion*: The unnecessary movement of materials, people, equipment, and goods within a processing step. An example is a unit of a hospital facility in which the five nurses and staff travel a combined 14.3 miles each shift due to the location of a fax/copy machine.
- *Waiting*: People or parts, systems, or facilities idle, waiting for a work cycle to be completed. This includes wait time to be seen by a doctor, wait time for diagnostic services, wait time for a doctor's appointment, and wait time on the telephone. It is also important to include in this analysis staff's wait time due to inefficiencies built into the process. Staff have been known to spend significant amounts of time awaiting an answer from another department within the organization.
- *Over-processing*: Extra work performed beyond the standard required by the customer. One area this waste is manifested is the amount of (non-mandated) paperwork injected into the process because of an organization's inability to monitor its performance. Excess paperwork is used to create redundancy to insulate the organization from its inefficiency: for example, requiring the patient to submit the same information to different subsections of the same organization.
- *Overproduction*: Producing sooner, faster, or in greater quantities than the customer is demanding. Examples include information sent automatically, even when not required and the processing and printing of materials before they are needed by the next person in the process.

■ *Defects*: Any process results the customer would deem unacceptable, such as errors, mistakes, and rework. In healthcare, this would include mislabeled specimens, hospital-acquired infections, incomplete forms, medication errors, bed sores, surgical errors, and data entry errors.

Two other forms of non-value-added activities (according to Muda) are identified as follows:

■ *Type I Muda*: Non-value added, but necessary for the system to function. Minimize this type until it can be eliminated.
■ *Type II Muda*: Non-value added and unnecessary. Eliminate this first!

The value stream map represents the current state (status quo). The next question is, how should the future look (i.e., the future state)? The VSM team gets back to work by creating an ideal value stream map that eliminates, or at least reduces, all the wastes identified in the present state. It is unlikely that the VSM team could achieve the future state in one step. One approach to accomplishing this goal is to create a series of intermediate future state maps. The organization would aim to reach these milestones at specific dates and, ultimately, realize the goal identified in the ideal state map. Since nothing is ever perfect, the process starts all over with the goal of continuous improvement. Eliminating the seven wastes can be done through the implementation of lean and the various lean tools. However, the ultimate aim of implementation should not be to identify and remove waste. Instead, it should be how to use lean principles to identify value according to the customer and make those value-adding processes flow through the organization at the customer's pull.

The Process

1. Establish an interdisciplinary team closest to the process being studied. The aim is to improve the value-added process.
2. Make a high-level flow chart of the process. Include all the steps required to deliver a service or product. Focus on the current process of how work is done.
3. Identify and note customers' and suppliers' connections for each step in the diagram. The following questions should help:
   – What is the customer's need?
   – Who supplies what to whom?

    – How does each customer make a request?

    – How does each supplier respond?

    – How does a supplier do his/her other work?

4. Describe delivery and quality requirements: Determine key quality indicators.

5. Perform a value-stream waste "observational walk" through the process steps:

    – Follow the movement of a patient or product.

    – Note the information flow (i.e., paper, verbal, electronic).

    – Note the inventory.

    – Identify how work is "triggered" in the value stream.

    – Identify how each step knows what to do next (sequencing).

    – Calculate the process time, wait time, and first-time quality for process steps and the entire value-stream cycle (percentage complete, percentage accurate, number defect-free).

6. Create the future state. Use lean principles to design an improved flow and process based on the waste identified.

Figure 6.4 shows the flow of patients in an emergency room, with the associated process cycle efficiency.

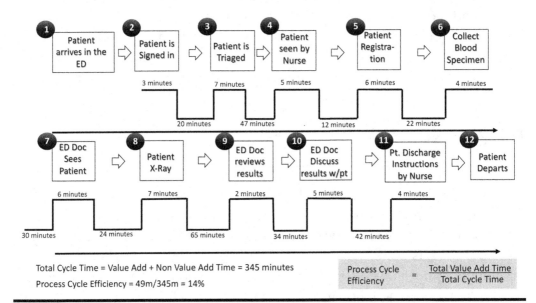

Total Cycle Time = Value Add + Non Value Add Time = 345 minutes

Process Cycle Efficiency = 49m/345m = 14%

$$\text{Process Cycle Efficiency} = \frac{\text{Total Value Add Time}}{\text{Total Cycle Time}}$$

Figure 6.4 Analyzing cycle time and process efficiency.

Poka-Yoke

"Poka-yoke" is a Japanese term that means "mistake-proofing" or "inadvertent error prevention." The key word in the second translation, often omitted, is "inadvertent." It is also referred to as "error-proofing." Some have described it as a system that allows employees to immediately catch any mistake so it can be corrected. Organizations pay a hefty price when mistakes reach the customer. The aim of poka-yoke is to design processes so mistakes are prevented or corrected immediately, thus eliminating defects at the source. Often, mistake proofing is accomplished by providing barriers that prevent people from taking the wrong action. Poka-yoke has been used in healthcare to prevent life-threatening mistakes. There are many examples in healthcare where mistake proofing through poka-yoke has been applied to medical devices. Human errors and faulty medical devices can threaten the safety of patients; poka-yoke techniques, used with employee training, can reduce the chances of these errors. Technology has become a powerful ally in the battle against mistakes and errors in healthcare.

The Agency for Healthcare Research and Quality has provided a catalog of poka-yoke examples in healthcare, as follows:

- *Infant Abduction Prevention*: With the aid of electronic sensor technology, an electronic device, or "tag," is clamped to the infant's umbilical cord. The tag ensures that the infant is not removed from the nursery. If the infant is removed without authorization, alarms sound, specified doors lock, and the elevators automatically return to the secured maternity floor. The elevator doors remain open.
- *Patient Identification and Safety*: Bar coding has been very effective in reducing certain types of mistakes in healthcare. Healthcare facilities have used bar coding to ensure a match between patients and their treatment, medicines, and supplies. Practitioners have emphasized the importance of radiologists matching the film they are reading to the right patient and how bar coding has been useful in that regard. Bar codes are attached to every order so the radiologist can electronically identify the patient and ensure the correct patient (information) has been entered into the digital dictation system. Bar coding has also been used to combat the problem of mislabeled specimens. Each specimen is labeled with a bar code specific to the patient and the test ordered. The instruments in the laboratory are programmed to identify the bar code

that ensures positive patient identification and to verify the correct test is performed. A word of caution! The use of bar codes does not automatically prevent errors. Staff should check that assigned bar codes match.

- *Computer-Aided Nutrition and Mixing*: Software profiles total parenteral nutrition (TPN). A patient's nutritional needs (i.e., protein, sugar, fat, vitamins, and electrolytes) are entered into the software application, which sends a message to an automixer that compounds the ingredients to create the base solution. The software issues a warning if certain concentrations of ingredients are exceeded based on values specified in the literature.

- *Drug Interactions*: The use of software to check for drug interactions has been quite effective in combating mistakes. The software alerts the user of an error. Shingo believes defect detection and rapid feedback following a mistake are nearly as effective as not making the mistake at all. Even after an initial mistake, staff can recover before substantial harm occurs. In this case, the pharmacist double-checks the prescriptions submitted by doctors. It is clear that there is no resultant harm if an error can be caught by the pharmacist before the patient receives the medicine, thereby avoiding, at the very least, significant difficulties for the pharmacist, doctor, and patient.

- *Computerized Physician Order Entry* (CPOE): Systems have been shown to reduce the incidence of serious medication errors. CPOE is computer software that physicians and other healthcare providers use to issue and record patient orders for diagnostic and treatment services such as medications, laboratory tests, and diagnostic tests. According to the experts, CPOE provides several mistake-proofing features:
  - Informs providers of common dosages and overdose warnings via drop-down menus
  - Eliminates the issue of illegible handwriting
  - Conducts drug interaction and allergy-checking routines
  - Employs sophisticated systems that function as a clinical decision support system (CDSS).

- *Hemoglobin Testing*: Precision hemoglobin testing is important because appropriate diagnosis and treatment are based on the results. Automatic hemoglobin testing devices that perform analyses in under one minute have replaced analyses that relied on visual judgment or time-consuming, complicated methods for their precision.

So, what are the requirements for implementing poka-yoke? One of the characteristics of a lean culture is a passion for error prevention.

Management must create an environment that encourages ideas and suggestions for improvement. Without an acceptance of experimentation and noble failures, it is difficult to cultivate a healthy contempt for mistakes. The era of digital transformation has opened the doors to creative instincts and new possibilities.

Kaizen

According to the Kaizen Institute, kaizen is the practice of continuous improvement in which everyone is involved. The word kaizen comes from two words: kai, which means "change," and zen which means "good." Its original Japanese meaning therefore is "Change for the better," which is continuous improvement. Kaizen was originally introduced to the West by Masaaki Imai, in his 1986 book *Kaizen: The Key to Japan's Competitive Success.* Today, kaizen is recognized worldwide as an important pillar of an organization's long-term competitive strategy. Kaizen's continuous improvement is based on the following guiding principles:

■ Good processes bring good results.
■ Go see for yourself to grasp the current situation.
■ Speak with data; manage by facts.
■ Take action to contain and correct the root causes of problems.
■ Work as a team.
■ Kaizen is everybody's business.

One of the most notable features of kaizen is that big results come from many small changes accumulated over time (Kaizen Institute, 1985). Imai describes kaizen as daily incremental improvements to a process. The kaizen methodology requires each employee to create as many as three to five ideas for improvement every month. The power of this methodology is not in the individual small improvement, but the combined force of hundreds of small improvements designed to continuously advance an organization.

These ideas and the many improvements that follow are expected in every part and process of the organization. They involve everyone from the housekeeping staff to the chief executive officer (CEO). Suggestion schemes are a simple and easy way to drive kaizen. Each area is measured based on the number of suggestions made and, of course, implemented. The performance of supervisors and managers are measured in terms of the number of ideas that their teams generate and subsequently implement. There is the belief that a supervisor or manager that cannot motivate his/her team to devise ways to improve the company or fails to support his/her team through implementation will not be helpful to the company in the long run. Equally important is the use of self-directed teams throughout the organization. Participants usually receive elaborate training in problem solving and analysis.

Even today, however, the concept of involving an entire workforce in the process of continuous improvement is very foreign to many American companies. Kaizen as a continuous improvement philosophy has been transformed into kaizen, the event. Consequently, now there are references to processes such as a Kaizen Event, Kaizen Blitz, and Kaizen Burst. These three processes will be described in what follows.

Kaizen Events

Kaizen events are short-duration improvement projects with a specific aim. Typically, they are week-long events led by a facilitator with the implementation team being predominantly members of the area in which the kaizen event is being conducted plus a few people from support areas and even management.

Although they are normally promoted as one-off events, kaizen events should be part of an overall program of continuous improvement to be successful and for gains to be sustained. Events in an environment where they are not supported or understood generally experience gains that are quickly eroded as people revert to their original ways of working. The following steps are vital to the successful implementation of a kaizen event:

1. Someone must lead and facilitate the event. While the area manager or team leader may be the leader, the preferred leader is experienced in lean techniques and philosophies who is adept at facilitating these types of events.
2. Identify team members and collect the relevant data regarding the current state of the process being improved. Voice of the customer data and all the associated process metrics should be collected about one month before the kaizen event.
3. The kaizen team leader will need to establish a team charter with the scope and objectives for the event at least two weeks beforehand.

Additionally, the team leader must notify the various departments and other stakeholders that will be affected by the work of the team.

4. Establish the deliverables of the kaizen event, including any financial implications. Use the charter to guide the development of a daily agenda for the process. This document will influence the planned resource requirements for each day. Be sure to include information about the management of down time and interruptions. Keep the project sponsor sufficiently briefed on the progress of the event.

Tripp et al. (Tripp et al., 2014) provide a description of each day in a typical five-day kaizen event, as follows:

Day 1—Current State Documentation

On Day 1, the focus of the team should be to lay the groundwork for the kaizen event by communicating the team charter, training participants, and physically viewing the process. In addition, a first draft of the detailed VSM should be created. Team members should be instructed on the objectives for the kaizen event and their individual responsibilities in the kaizen process. Site leadership should participate in the kickoff session to emphasize the importance of the event and grant authority to the team to make required changes. Training on the kaizen approach and philosophy should be limited to one hour or less; most of the learning experience will occur as the process evolves.

The bulk of Day 1 should be dedicated to observing the process, Voice of the Customer (VOC) synthesis, creating a VSM (or reviewing a recently created VSM), and identifying the elements of waste. These efforts should be informed by data and pertinent historical perspectives. Finance should provide a perspective on the cost benefits of the proposed change relative to the current state. The understanding gained on Day 1 will help set priorities for the activities of the second day. End the day by starting a storyboard with photos of the current process.

Day 2—Current State Evaluation

On Day 2, the team will quantify the impact of the waste in terms of process metrics, conduct time studies, identify and prioritize bottlenecks, update the VSM, and begin the root cause analysis of waste. Data analysis and display tools should be utilized with team-based tools such as brainstorming, affinity diagrams, fishbone diagrams, critical-to-quality trees, cause and effect matrices, process maps, spaghetti charts, and failure mode and effects analysis (FMEA). The work conducted on Day 2 is critical input for the third day: identifying solutions and prioritizing opportunities for improvement. At this point, the team should identify the additional resources necessary to complete the task list, report to management any potential roadblocks or barriers, and begin transferring knowledge to support culture change and reasons to embrace the new ways.

Day 3—Characterize the Future State; Plan Its Implementation

On Day 3, the team should be ready to develop and prioritize solutions aimed at eliminating critical waste, create flow scenarios with new standard work combinations, prioritize the proposed changes, plan the implementation, develop contingency plans, and begin implementing the solutions. A future state VSM or process map should be created to visually illustrate the impact of the proposed change. Proposed changes should also be reviewed with all stakeholders to save the time required for approvals and enrollment. The team should begin implementing changes on this day to alleviate the burden on the fourth day.

Day 4—Implement the Future State

The focus of Day 4 is on implementing changes with minimal disruption to the operation. The team may utilize the 5S techniques (sort, straighten, shine, standardize, sustain) during the implementation phase on Day 4 as equipment is rearranged, cleaned, and repaired. The use of visual aids is encouraged. Additionally, standard work documentation is revised, operators are trained, and the new process is piloted. It is critical that data is collected (including time studies) during the pilot to understand the impact of the process changes and provide feedback for multiple iterations of minor changes to optimize the process. Results are tallied and quantified, with their financial impact calculated. Resources and equipment must be coordinated to ensure the smooth execution of the changes and the pilot. Employees should be prepared to sequence the implementation of some changes over time with a project plan that tracks dates and accountabilities. All the meetings on this day should take place in the work area. The presence of management at the end of Day 4 will lend credence and support for the new processes. Going forward, the team should discuss ways to sustain changes and preserve gains.

Day 5—Operationalize the Future State and Debrief

Employees should live with the new process and prepare a report based on the results achieved on Day 5. Final documentation and approvals (legal, customer, safety, etc.) should be approved as necessary. A final, formal report of the event should not be required if the management team has been engaged during the rest of the kaizen event. Any final report should be a simple summary of the information already compiled on the kaizen storyboard. A post-mortem should be conducted with the kaizen team to deliberate on the lessons learned. Data collection plans and response plans should be in place to monitor performance and systematically respond to problems over the next several weeks. If layouts will need rearranged, electricians, moving equipment, and other support must be scheduled for the likely moving day/night. If flow will be created with defined areas and clear labeling, employees will need floor marking tape, paint, labeling machines, etc.

Employees must plan ahead to ensure everything is in place that likely will be needed for the specific project, from cleaning materials to cranes. Review the task list and kaizen metrics for completion every week for four weeks—or until all items are completed. The task list should assign responsibility to specific employees and list deliverable dates for each task.

No two kaizen events will be the same; the real skill in conducting them is deciding which tools to use, how rigorously to apply them, which individuals to involve in their administration, and what the desired outcomes are. The tools of kaizen are simple; their application requires diligent planning and considerable creativity from the team leader. Team leaders need to remain aware of the risks created by the short timeframe and physical demands of the events. The agendas described above represent a sample of tools that should be considered depending on the nature of the problem. Typically, the team should expect to complete about 80% of the task list during the event, with the remaining tasks to be completed within four weeks (Tripp et al., 2014). Kaizen is a powerful tool for positive change. With the proper planning, appropriate use of data, and effective tool application, these events deliver significant results to process improvement and a company's bottom line.

The 5S Method

The 5S method reduces waste in a work environment through better workplace organization, visual communication, and general cleanliness. The name *5S* comes from five Japanese words that all happen to begin with the letter "S": Seiri, Seiton, Seiso, Seiketsu, and Shitsuke. These five words, often translated in English as—Sort, Set in order, Shine, Standardize, and Sustain—represent a set of practices for improving workplace organization and productivity. These words will be explained in greater detail below.

- Seiri means "organization," or separating needed tools, parts, and instructions from unneeded materials and removing the unneeded ones.
- Seiton means "orderliness," which includes neatly arranging and identifying parts and tools for easy use. The goal is to have a place for everything and everything in its place, clean and ready for use.
- Seiso means "cleanliness," which entails conducting a cleanup campaign.
- Seiketsu means "standardization," which encompasses the daily conducting of seiri, seiton, and seiso daily to maintain a workplace in perfect condition and keep its gains. It calls for the development of common methods for consistency.
- Shitsuke means "discipline," or making a habit of following the proper procedures as set forth in the first four S items, while maintaining and improving on one's gains.

In recent times, the idea of a sixth "S" for "safety" has been mentioned.

The origin of 5S is linked to the history of lean production and the Toyota Production System. One key element of the Toyota system is to organize the workplace floor so needed items are convenient to locate, use, and easy to put away, thus eliminating or reducing the time for "search and select." The five-step method for accomplishing this became known as 5S. When companies around the world began turning to lean production in the 1990s, 5S became one of the most popular lean production tools, due in part to its simplicity. The 5S methodology has now been applied to the healthcare sector as a systematic method of organizing and standardizing the workplace for lean healthcare. In addition to being a workplace organization technique, 5S is a way to involve associates in the ownership of their workspace.

Figure 6.5 (previous page) illustrates the 5S system. Not an isolated event, but rather, 5S is part of the culture of a continuous improvement cycle. A proper step-by-step process must be followed to make 5S a practice and a success. Organizations maximize 5S when they deploy it within a PDSA framework (plan, do, study, act) or Deming Cycle (Figure 6.6).

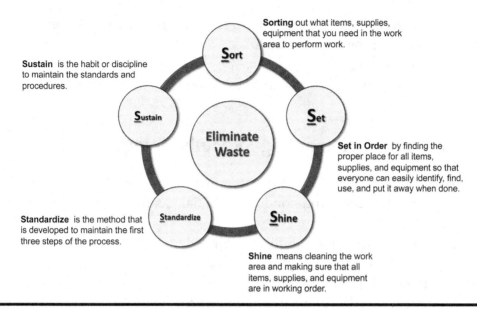

Figure 6.5   The five S cycle of continuous improvement.

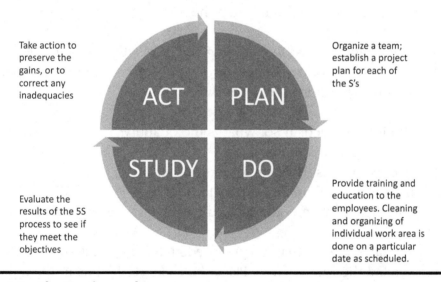

Figure 6.6   The Deming cycle.

Planning for 5S

Proper planning is vital to the successful implementation of 5S methodology. The planning steps include the following:

■ Assemble a 5S team.
■ Define the boundaries of the 5S work area.

■ Assign members of the work group to their respective 5S areas.
■ Install a 5S communication board.
■ Determine 5S targets, activities, scope, and schedules.
■ Review and finalize plans with the work group and site leaders.

The Steps for Implementing 5S Methodology

1. *First S—Sorting*: The objective of the first S is to separate the needed from the not needed and conduct an initial cleaning. The following steps are required:
   - Establish criteria for handling non-needed items
   - Take "before" photographs, as required
   - Identify not-needed items
   - Move not-needed items to a holding area
   - Conduct an initial cleaning
   - Use the red tag approach to tag the items

Begin the red tag process by providing red labels (tags) to every employee involved. Ask the employees to go through every item in the workplace and address the questions listed below.

   - Is the item needed? If so, what is the quantity?
   - If needed, what is the frequency of its use?
   - If needed, is this the ideal location for it?
   - Who has ultimate responsibility for the item?
   - What other items are adding to the clutter in the work area?

Apply red tags to items that are not needed. Store such items in a designated area called the red tag area. Place the suspected items in the red tag area for one week. Give staff time to re-evaluate the "needed items," just in case they change their minds. After one week, determine items that need to be returned for future use. Table 6.1 provides a guideline for item and equipment use and storage.

Individual departments should each have a holding area, which should be clearly visible and marked to ensure the visual control of items. Display pictures of items and place them on a bulletin board visible to all. Responsibility for the holding area should be assigned to certain

Table 6.1 Guideline for Item Use and Storage

Priority	Frequency of Use	Required Action
Low	Less than once/year to once/year	Throw away or store away from the workplace
Moderate	Once/month to once/week	Store together but offline
High	Once/day	Store within the work area
Super High	Hourly use	Store within arm's reach

employees at the beginning of sorting. The items in the holding area should be kept for three or four months. If the items are not needed, they can be disposed of. It is always necessary to discuss plans to dispose of items with anyone who has used them or are using the same or similar items. Items should be moved to a company-level holding area before final disposal. The facility manager or an authorized person should be involved in this process. Take "after" photographs wherever required.

2. *Second S—Set in Order*: This phase begins by ensuring that all unnecessary items are eliminated from the work area. Arrange workplace safety and efficiency by doing the following:
   - Identify key equipment and supplies.
   - Determine the location for each item based on the work flow.
   - Outline locations and zones.
   - Develop shadow boards; label items.
   - Document layout, equipment, and supplies.
   - Tools should be classified and stored by their frequency of use.
   - Take "before" photographs where necessary.
   - Utilize the five why methodology to decide where each item belongs.
   - Locate the needed items so they can be accessible in 30–60 seconds with ease.
   - Notify everyone about the new locations of the items.
   - Create a list of all items and their new locations; be sure to display the list for all to see.
   - Label each storage location or space to show what is there.

     – Use lines to outline the locations of equipment, supplies, common areas, safety zones, etc.

     – Take an "after" picture of the work area to document the process.

3. *Third S—Shine*: The aim of the third S is to clean for inspection. This process involves the following steps:
   - Take "before" photographs.
   - Perform daily cleaning before and after any work.
   - Define the responsibility for cleaning.
   - Identify every item that causes dirt or contamination.
   - Determine the cause of the dirt and contamination by using the five whys.
   - Keep a log of places and areas requiring improvement.
   - Take "after" photographs.

4. *Fourth S—Standardize*: This process requires the establishment of common methods for consistency. The following steps are vital to the success of the fourth S:
   - Take "before" photographs.
   - Check that the first three Ss are implemented correctly.
   - Establish the routines and standard practices for regularly and systematically repeating the first three Ss.
   - Create procedures and forms for regularly evaluating the status of the first three Ss.
   - Standardize cleaning schedules.
   - Create a maintenance system for housekeeping functions.
   - Take "after" photographs and post them for all to see.

5. *Fifth S—Sustaining*: The objective of the fifth S is holding and improving gains. In the healthcare setting, the true value of the 5S process is to sustain your customer/patient and joint commission ready approach at all times. Use simple but effective audit processes to accomplish this. Sustaining is the most important "S," and it requires the most discipline. The following action items are necessary for the success of this stage:
   - Assess the achievement of the 5S process.
   - Perform routine checks.
   - Analyze the results of routine checks.
   - Measure progress, and plan for continuous improvement.
   - Protect the system from bad habits or returning to its old ways.
   - Hardwire the changes into the organizational culture.

Benefits of 5S

The benefits of 5S include the following:

- A cleaner and safer workplace with reduced clutter
- Increased productivity due to an organized and efficient workplace
- An inspection-ready work environment that promotes compliance with regulatory standards
- Minimized overhead costs due to the recapturing and repurposing of valuable space
- Improved overall self-esteem due to an overall positive work environment

SMED

Lean Production defines single-minute exchange of dies (SMED) as a system for dramatically reducing the time it takes to complete equipment changeovers. SMED was developed by Shigeo Shingo, a Japanese industrial engineer who was extraordinarily successful in helping companies dramatically reduce their changeover times. His pioneering work led to documented reductions in changeover times averaging 94% (e.g., from 90 minutes to less than 5-minutes) across a wide range of companies. The SMED system seeks to convert as many of the changeover steps as possible to "external" (performed while the equipment is running) and to simplify and streamline the remaining steps. Each element of the changeover is analyzed to see if it can be eliminated, moved, simplified, or streamlined.

Changeover times that improve by a factor of 20 may be hard to imagine, but consider the simple example of a NASCAR tire change: An average driver can usually change a tire in 15–20 minutes with hand tools and a jack. A fully equipped NASCAR pit crew can change all four tires on their driver's car in less than 20 seconds! In races like these, speed is always of the essence. A few extra seconds in the pit can mean the difference between first and second place. Many techniques used by NASCAR pit crews are also used in SMED, for example, performing as many steps as possible before the pit stop begins, using a coordinated team to perform multiple steps in parallel, and creating a standardized and highly optimized process. In fact, the journey from a 15-minute tire changeover to a 15-second tire changeover can be considered a SMED journey (Lean Production, 2011).

In SMED, changeovers comprise steps called "elements." There are two types:

- Internal elements (must be completed while the equipment is stopped)
- External elements (can be completed while the equipment is running)

The SMED process focuses on making as many elements as possible "external," and simplifying and streamlining all elements. The following key steps are vital to the implementation of SMED (Lean Production):

1. Using hard data, understand where the opportunities are to apply SMED. In other words, where is the productive time lost? Establish a SMED team to analyze and review the opportunities.
2. Identify all the elements of the changeover. The most effective way of doing this is to videotape the entire changeover and then work from the videotape to create an ordered list of elements, each of which includes: a description (what work is performed) and cost in time (how long the element takes to complete). A typical changeover will result in 30–50 elements being documented. A fast method of capturing elements is to create a series of sticky notes that are stuck to a wall in the order in which they are performed during the changeover. Be sure to capture both "human" elements (where the operator is doing something) and "equipment" elements (where the equipment is doing something). As discussed later, the human elements are usually easiest to optimize. Only observe—let the changeover take its normal course. The deliverable from this step should be a complete list of changeover elements, each with a description and time "cost."
3. Identify and separate external elements. The changeover process that can be performed with little or no change while the equipment is running is identified and moved "external" to the changeover (i.e., performed before or after the changeover). It is not unusual for changeover times to be cut nearly in half with this step alone. For each element, the team should ask the following question: Can this element, as currently performed or with minimal change, be completed while the equipment is running? If the answer is yes, categorize the element as external and move it before or after the changeover, as appropriate. The deliverable from this step should be an updated list of changeover

elements, split into three parts: external elements (before the change-over), internal elements (during the changeover), and external elements (after the changeover).

4. Convert internal elements to external. In this step, the current change-over process is carefully examined, with the goal of converting as many internal elements to external as possible. For each internal element, the team should ask the following questions: How can these internal elements be made external? This will result in a list of elements that are candidates for further action. This list should be prioritized so the most promising candidates are acted on first. Fundamentally, this comes down to performing a cost/benefit analysis for each candidate element:
   – Cost as measured by the materials and labor needed to make the necessary changes.
   – Benefit as measured by the time that will be eliminated from the changeover.
   Once the list has been prioritized, work can begin on making the necessary changes.

5. Streamline the remaining elements. In this step, the remaining elements are reviewed with an eye toward streamlining and simplifying so they can be completed in less time. First priority should be given to internal elements to support the primary goal of shortening the changeover time. For each element, the team should ask the following questions: How can this element be completed in less time? How can we simplify this element? As in the previous step, a simple cost/benefit analysis should be used to prioritize actions.

Examples of SMED Healthcare Applications

One of the challenges for surgeons and other healthcare professionals is how to improve patient care handoffs. SMED is a lean tool that can improve changeovers in healthcare and beyond (Kashmer, 2014). As previously discussed, the essence of SMED is reducing changeover time by converting elements in the changeover process to elements that can happen before a machine is shut down for an actual changeover. Kashmer extended the analogy to a trauma and acute care surgery service, in which case the machine is the service rendered to patients or that time when the service is up and running and available. The "changeover" represents the morning handoff. The key to a successful handoff is to ensure that the required information (content and accuracy) for providing excellent clinical care is transmitted at the right time. Handoffs seldom go as planned. They often take too long, do not provide the kind of information needed by the team, sometimes are not aimed at the patients' needs, or mishandle the teaching points. Kashmer presents the following account of the steps followed in the implementation of SMED in trauma and acute care surgery:

1. Videotaping the sign-out or turnover. Patient confidentiality is preserved by destroying the video after reviewing it. This is part of a quality improvement study. Accordingly, expedited Institutional Review Board (IRB) standards usually apply, as do routine Health Insurance Portability and Accountability Act (HIPAA) protections.
2. The SMED team meets to discuss the desired elements (characteristics) of a good sign-out.
3. Next, caregivers review the tape (without the larger group) to gain a sense of its content and begin to apply SMED methodology.
4. Label elements of the sign-out as "essential to changeover" or as candidates to move externally. For example, factors can be determined like the number of times people waited for radiology films to load during sign-out or whether the films can be loaded and waiting beforehand, including the need to bring up labs.
5. Identify steps that make sign-out less effective, slow it down, or otherwise get in the way, so they can be made external relative to the sign-out process.
6. The options and possibilities include bringing up labs ahead of time or ensuring that radiologic films are ready and waiting. A teaching point of the day can be prepared from the night's events, typed, and printed for discussion. This makes it possible for the team to be focused on the single, relevant message for the day instead of 30 ad-hoc teaching points.
7. Next, review the video with the larger team and make sure to highlight with them the internal versus external parts of the process.
8. With the team, sign-out is redesigned, and the team determines what needs to be made an external process. The new process might take time to normalize. The first time the new process is tried, a trauma activation will be called just as the prep work is starting.
9. It is always helpful to build in a little redundancy or robustness into the process. For example: perhaps the in-house on-call person need not prepare a teaching point (when the group decides they want a daily

teaching point in the process). Perhaps someone not in-house and on-call can prepare the teaching point the night before and bring that to sign-out ready to discuss.

10. Last, run the pilot of the new turnover process for about a week. The kinks slowly work themselves out. After about a week, the team video-tapes the typical sign-out again. Compare the sign-out videos with the group in a follow-up meeting. The before and after confirms the value of the SMED process in improving the sign-out/turnover process for trauma and acute care surgery.

11. Last, destroy the tapes after the improvements have been recorded and noted by the team in terms of total time spent in sign-out, effectiveness of the sign-out, or any other endpoints selected.

Five Whys

The five whys technique involves a questioning protocol in which the question, "Why?" is asked five times to understand the cause of a problem. The technique is designed to drill down into the details of the cause of a problem beyond the symptoms to reach the cause. It is very common for process improvement teams to focus on the symptoms of a problem rather than its cause. The technique was originally developed by Sakichi Toyoda, a Japanese inventor, industrialist and the founder of Toyota Industries Co. He states, "By repeating 'why' five times, the nature of the problem as well as its solution becomes clear." Other sources have attributed the five whys technique to Taiichi Ohno, father of the Toyota production system. The following example illustrates how this process works:

A process improvement team was convened to address the problem of surgical cancellations. The team decided to ask "Why?" five times, as follows:

The first round of questioning asked:

1. Why are surgeries cancelled? There were several reasons offered in response to this question, including (a) The patient was eating; (b) Consent form issues; (c) The patient forgot, pre-op complications, etc. A round of multi-voting led the team to conclude that the most important reason is that the patient was eating.

2. The second round of questioning asked, "Why did the patient eat?" The team determined that the most important reason was because dietary services delivered a food tray to the patient's room.

3. The third "Why?" asked, "Why was a food tray delivered to the patient?" The most influential answer was, "Patient NPO Error." NPO is a medically approved abbreviation that means "nothing by mouth." The abbreviation is based on the Latin translation of *nil per os*, which also means "nothing by mouth."
4. Before scheduled surgery, it is recommended that the patient has nothing by mouth (no food or fluid) for a minimum of six hours and preferred eight to twelve hours before the surgery's start time.
5. The fourth round of questioning asked, "Why was there an NPO error?" The answer was a data entry error.
6. The fifth round of questioning asked, "Why was there a data entry error?" The answer was a lack of training of data entry personnel.

It may take less or more than five "Whys?" to reach the cause of a particular problem. What is clear is that, when you reach the actual cause, an actionable solution is easily identifiable.

Kanban

Kanban was developed in the 1940s by Taiichi Ohno, an industrial engineer at Toyota, as a system to improve and maintain a high level of production. With kanban, Toyota optimized its engineering process by modeling it after how supermarkets stock shelves. The approach was inspired by a Japanese management team's visit to a Piggly Wiggly supermarket in the United States, where Ohno observed that store shelves were stocked with just enough items to meet consumer demand and inventory would only be restocked when there was a visual signal—in this case, an empty space on the shelf. Only when an item was close to selling out did the clerks order more. Because inventory levels match consumption patterns, the supermarket gains significant efficiency in inventory management and optimizing for the customer.

In Japanese, the term "kanban" means "visual signal" or "card." Toyota line workers used a kanban (i.e., an actual card) to signal steps in their manufacturing process. The system's highly visual nature allowed teams to communicate more easily about what work needed to be done and when. It also standardized cues and refined processes, which helped to reduce waste and maximize value.

The essence of the kanban concept is that a supplier, warehouse, or manufacturer should only deliver components as and when they are needed, so there is no excess inventory. Within this system, workstations located along production lines only produce and deliver desired components when they receive a card and an empty container, indicating that more parts will be needed for production. In case of line interruptions, each workstation will only produce enough components to fill the container and then stop. In addition, kanban limits the amount of inventory in the process by acting as an authorization to produce more inventory. Since kanban is a chainlike process in which orders flow from one process to another, the production or delivery of components is pulled to the production line, unlike the traditional forecast-oriented method where parts are pushed to the line.

The Virginia Mason Institute has had significant success with applying the kanban system to the healthcare realm (Borbon, 2016). Most healthcare systems rely on the employee in charge of ordering supplies to operate on gut instinct, with no data. The result was that, for some supplies, availability was scarce, and many employees felt the need to hoard supplies so they could easily access the items they needed to care for their patients. For other supplies, the stockrooms were overflowing due to over-ordering, thus taking up space that could have been used for patient care. Borbon gives an account of Virginia Mason's success with the kanban system as follows:

> In the supply cabinets in orthopedics, for example, there's a two-bin system. Items are consistently stocked from the back, using the (First-In First-Out) FIFO approach. When the first bin runs out, the employee who uses the last item places the empty bin in a common area. Then, because Virginia Mason has developed a very effective replenishment process with its supply-chain vendors, the card on that bin is scanned the same day, activating a new order of supplies that will fill up that bin. While the team waits for the new supplies to arrive, there's already a full bin on the shelf—it's been there waiting behind the previous bin—and it's ready for the next employee who walks in. When the new supplies arrive, they're placed in the empty bin, and the bin filled with new supplies is stocked behind the current bin.

> With such a system, the supplies don't run out, and because supplies are stocked from the back, the supplies are not on the shelf long enough to expire. This not only makes the organization's system more efficient, but it also drastically reduces the inventory, saving costs. Even more, employees now have trust in a system that gives them what they need, when they need it.

The implementation of kanban in a healthcare setting requires the collaboration of everyone involved in the hospital's supply chain—frontline staff, purchasing department or materials management, and vendors/suppliers. Hospitals deal with thousands of supplies, and each supply requires a separate set of considerations. Similarly, hospitals deal with several vendors and suppliers, each with their unique lead times for supplies. The best way to get started is to implement it for non-critical items—the ones that do not pose a safety issue.

Employees should start in a small, controlled work area. To avoid running out of an item during the testing of more critical items, the use of a safety stock is recommended. Safety stock is the minimum amount of an item to keep on hand to accommodate variations in demand. There are six generally accepted rules for kanban:

1. Downstream processes may only withdraw items in the precise amounts specified on the kanban.
2. Upstream processes may only send items downstream in the precise amounts and sequences specified by the kanban.
3. No items are made or moved without a kanban.
4. A kanban must accompany each item at all times.
5. Defects and incorrect amounts are never sent to the next downstream process.
6. The number of kanbans should be monitored carefully to reduce inventories and to reveal problems and opportunities for improvement.

Steps for the Implementation of a Two-Bin Kanban System

1. Collect the usage data to decide the right levels of inventory needed for each supply item. Closely monitor the amount of inventory currently being used to know how much should be ordered when restocking. This process will take time, so an initial fluctuation in bin levels should be expected while inventory patterns and needs are being figured.
2. To help determine how many items should go into each bin, one must know how long it will take for a supplier to deliver the items. Then, that time should be built into determining how many items to put in each bin. For example, if five items are put in each bin and it takes ten days to go through each bin, the supplier needs to deliver new stock within six to eight days to avoid production delays.

3. Employees should decide what kind of signal will alert material managers that supplies need to be replenished.

4. One should decide on the right sizes for the bins, the right types of storage shelves, and the amount of shelving space required. Movable shelves are better than fixed or built-in storage shelves.

5. The most efficient option is to automate the process with RFID technology. Bar codes have also been used with great success. When RFID technology is used, the kanban system is equipped with an RFID digital restocking tag. Once the items in the primary bin are used, a nurse clicks the button on the restocking tag. While the nurses are waiting for supplies to be restocked, nurses pull items from the secondary bin.

6. A notification is automatically sent to the material managers with all the information relating to the items that need to be restocked (i.e., their quantity and location). Essentially, the RFID technology replaces steps in the counting process, saving valuable time while real-time information improves accuracy.

7. The two-bin system has the same items in each bin (bin A and bin B). The nursing staff retrieves items from bin A. When bin A is empty, the nurses move bin B forward, then retrieve the items from bin B. When the supply chain management staff comes around to count inventory, they only reorder items when bin A is empty by scanning the empty bin A and recording an inventory level of "0." The back-up bin (bin B) always ensures that the nurses will not run out of inventory. Ideally, by the time a nurse retrieves the last item from a second bin, the stock will be refilled. Before determining the amount of stock in any one bin, it is important to know how long it will take to get new inventory from the supplier (lead time). Stock that cannot be replenished by the time the second bin is empty will cause a lag in production.

8. Supplies are categorized into groups and are tagged with color-coded labels to quickly direct nursing and supply chain management staff to the items they are seeking.

9. Any unused items are returned to a bin labeled "returns" for reassignment by the material manager.

10. There is a list of all items and supplies with their specific locations so difficult-to-find items can be located easily.

11. A compatible inventory software system should be used.

12. All nursing staff should be trained on how to use the system

With the aid of barcodes, RFID tags, and software, monitoring inventory levels and patterns has been made much easier in recent years. There is a considerable number of kanban inventory software solutions that help auto- mate the process. A fully automated kanban inventory system can manage the complete supply chain. Such a system can signal and place a restocking order when the content of the first bin is emptied and can also monitor lead and replenishment times to ensure the right amount of stock is always avail- able on the nursing unit. Additionally, nursing managers can use the system to run reports on productivity to determine which items are used the most.

Benefits of Kanban in Hospitals and Clinics

1. Eliminates manual (handwritten) requisitions.
2. No more hoarding supplies.
3. No more running out of supplies.
4. The right supplies in the right place at the right time.
5. Reduced delay of supplies to patients.
6. Reduced use of expired (or obsolete) items via FIFO.
7. Reduced overstocking and obsolete inventory.
8. Eliminated cycle or daily counting.
9. Improved efficiency.
10. Better patient care.
11. Improved staff satisfaction.
12. Over time, the kanban system will show patterns such as which medi- cal products are used most often. This makes it possible to better man- age stock levels. Quantities can be easily refined and adjusted based on their usage patterns.

Standardized and Standard Work

Standard (or standardized) work is the most efficient method or procedure to safely carry out an activity to yield the best outcome and minimize waste. Since patients are not widgets and the labor involved in healthcare is sub- stantially emotional, it is important to state that standard work is not aimed at turning healthcare workers into robots. Standard work has become a key factor in reducing process waste, ensuring patient safety, and improving clinical outcomes. Standardized work is founded on the premise that people should analyze their work and have the latitude to determine how it would best meet the needs of stakeholders. With standard work, the employees doing the work are key players in developing the standard work process. That's why it is important to deploy the concept of standard work and other tools not in isolation, but in the context of a lean culture. This makes it imperative for healthcare employees to learn to analyze their processes, identify waste and other non-value-added activities, and prevent mistakes. Standard work becomes an opportunity to help employees do a better job. Rather than learning by mistakes, new healthcare employees can quickly learn to use the best practices of those who developed the standard work. If standard work is efficiently developed, it should allow virtually anyone to perform the work without variances in the desired output. Work can be described as standardized if the sequence of job elements has been efficiently organized and is repeatedly followed by the staff.

Each step in the process should be defined and must be performed repeatedly in the same manner. Any variations in the process will most likely increase cycle time and cause quality issues. Standardized work typically describes how a process should consistently be executed and documents current best practices. It also provides a baseline from which a better approach can be developed, allowing continuous improvement methods to leverage learning.

The Process

The process begins with the team obtaining the answers to the following questions:

- Who operates the process?
- Where is the process located?
- What specific steps are required to execute the process? Are the steps consistent with evidence-based practice? Are there sequence requirements for the steps?
- What are the special characteristics of the workspace (storage, work cells, tool storage, etc.)? Is the layout of the work area compatible with the goals of the process?
- How many people are required to operate the process?
- What are the prerequisite knowledge, licensure, and skills required to execute the process? Do the process operators possess the prerequisite knowledge, licensure, and skills?

■ What are the initial, intermediate, and final outputs of the process?
■ What steps can be taken to ensure the reliability of the process?
■ What are the quality checkpoints of the process?
■ What are the tools required to execute the process?
■ How long should the cycle time and "takt" time be? Does the process have a verifiable way to gather accurate performance data on the process?
■ What are the resource constraints of the process?
■ What are the technical and/or regulatory requirements or standards (internal or industry standards) affecting the way the process should operate? Are there manuals or operating procedures available for use? How frequently are they updated?
■ What is needed to start and finish the process? This includes how much raw material to have on hand and how often component levels must be replenished, as well as defining how often finished goods are retrieved from the work cell and how they are to be positioned for optimal flow.

Standardized work is a collection and implementation of the best practices known to date. Because improvements in quality, safety, and productivity will become apparent occasionally, standardized work should be updated via a work instruction document, training, and practice. Standardized work is created by the process's users, based on customer requirements provided by management, supervisors, and users. When applied correctly, Standardized work offers so many benefits to organizations.

Benefits of Standardized Work

1. Provides a basis for employee training
2. Establishes process stability
3. Reveals clear stop and start points for each process
4. Assists with audit and problem solving
5. Creates a baseline for kaizen
6. Enables effective employee involvement and poka-yoke
7. Maintains organizational knowledge

A lean organization understands customer value and designs its key processes to continuously increase it. Lean is not achieved by replicating what happened at Toyota; it is not a compilation of tools. For lean to take hold in an organization, the focus should be the management system, not just lean tools.

Questions for Discussion

6.1. Select three of the Lean tools and discuss how you would apply each of them to your organization.

6.2. Discuss the barriers to implement any of the Lean tools in your organization.

6.3. What aspect of the Lean culture would your organization find to be most challenging and why?

References

Borbon, M., 2016. "How Can a Kanban System Improve Health Care?" Virginia Mason Institute. https://www.virginiamasoninstitute.org/2016/01/how-can-a-kanban-system-improve-health-care/

Burgess, N. and Radnor, Z., 2013. "Evaluating Lean in Healthcare." *International Journal of Health Care Quality Assurance* 26(3): 220–235. doi:10.1108/09526861311311418.

Donahue, M. O., Piazza, I. M., Griffin, M. Q., Dykes, P. C. and Fitzpatrick, J. J., 2008. "The Relationship Between Nurses' Perceptions of Empowerment and Patient Satisfaction." *Applied Nursing Research* 21(1): 2–7.

Imai, M., 1986. *Kaizen (Ky'zen), the Key to Japan's Competitive Success.* Random House, New York, NY.

Kaizen Institute, 1985. https://in.kaizen.com/about-us/definition-of-kaizen.html

Kashmer, D., 2014. Single Minute Exchange of Die for Trauma & Acute Care Surgery. http://www.surgicalbusinessmodelinnovation.com/statistical-process-control/single-minute-exchange-of-die-for-trauma-acute-care-surgery/

Laschinger, H. K. S., Gilbert, S., Smith, L. and Leslie, K. (2010). "Towards a Comprehensive Theory of Nurse/Patient Empowerment: Applying Kanter's Empowerment Theory to Patient Care." *Journal of Nursing Management* 18(1): 4–13.

Lean Production, 2011–2017. SMED (Single-Minute Exchange of Dies), Vorne Industries. https://www.leanproduction.com/smed.html

Mazzocato, P., Holden, R. J., Brommels, M., Aronsson, H., Backman, U., Elg, M. and Thor, J., 2012. "How Does Lean Work in Emergency Care? A Case Study of a Lean-inspired Intervention at the Astrid Lindgren Children's Hospital, Stockholm, Sweden." *BMC Health Services Research* 12: 28. DOI:10.1186/1472-6963-12-28. DOI:10.1186/1472-6963-1112-1128. [PMC free article]

Tripp, R., Seider, C., Calderon, U. and Carnell, M., A Plan for a Five-day Kaizen, ISixSigma, 2014. https://www.isixsigma.com/methodology/kaizen/a-plan-for-a-five-day-kaizen/

Ulhassan, W., Sandahl, C., Westerlund, H., Henriksson, P., Bennermo, M., von Thiele, S. U. and Thor, J., 2013. "Antecedents and Characteristics

of Lean Thinking Implementation in a Swedish Hospital: A Case
Study." *Quality Management in Health Care* 22(1): 48–61. DOI:10.1097/
QMH.0b013e31827dec5a.

Additional Readings

Ahlstrom, J., 2018. Using the 5S Lean Tool for Health Care. Lean Is a Problem-
Solving Approach for Continuous Improvement—and the 5S Tool Is of Value
in Healthcare Settings. https://s3.amazonaws.com/rdcms-himss/files/product
ion/public/HIMSSorg/Content/files/MEPI/5S_ImpactArticle.pdf

Bialek, R., Duffy, G. L. and Moran, J. W., 2009. *The Public Health Quality
Improvement Handbook.* Milwaukee, WI: ASQ Quality Press: 168–170.

Graban, M., 2017. "#Lean: Clarifying Push, Pull, and Flow in a Hospital; the Patient
'Pulls.'" Lean Blog, https://www.leanblog.org/2014/02/flow-push-and-pull-in-
a-hospital/

Institute for Healthcare Improvement; IHI, 2005. Going Lean in Health Care. IHI
Innovation Series white paper. Cambridge, MA. www.IHI.org.

Mahalik, P., 2014. A Practical Approach to the Successful Practice of 5S. Six Sigma
Tools and Templates. iSix Sigma. https://www.isixsigma.com/tools-template
s/5s/practical-approach-successful-practice-5s/

Ohno, T., 1988. *Toyota Production System: Beyond Large-Scale Production.*
Portland, OR: Productivity Press.

Rouse, M., 2015. Kanban. http://whatis.techtarget.com/definition/kanban

Smartsheet, 2018. Understanding Kanban Inventory Management and Its Uses
Across Multiple Industries. https://www.smartsheet.com/understanding-kanb
an-inventory-management-and-its-uses-across-multiple-industries

Walters, C., 2012. What Is Standardized Work (And What Is It Not)? LEANBLITZ.
http://leanblitzconsulting.com/2012/09/what-is-standardized-work-and-what-i
s-it-not/

Womack, J. P. and Jones, D. T., 1996. *Lean Thinking: Banish Waste and Create
Wealth in Your Corporation.* New York: Simon & Schuster.

Womack, J. P., Jones, D. T. and Roos, D., 1990. *The Machine That Changed the
World: The Story of Lean Production—How Japan's Secret Weapon in the
Global Auto Wars Will Revolutionize Western Industry.* New York: Rawson
Associates.

Zarbo, R. J. and D'Angelo, R., 2006. "Transforming to a Quality Culture: The Henry
Ford Production System," *American Journal of Clinical Pathology* 126(suppl):
S21–S29.

Zarbo, R. J., Tuthill, J. M., D'Angelo, R. et al., 2009. "The Henry Ford Production
System: Reduction of Surgical Pathology in-Process Misidentification Defects
by Bar Code–Specified Work Process Standardization." *American Journal of
Clinical Pathology* 131: 468–477.

Chapter 7

Six Sigma

In Chapter 6, we discussed the lean concept and how it can be used to eliminate waste and create value for the customer. In this chapter, we present the concept of Six Sigma, which is aimed at reducing process variation and improving accuracy. Lean and Six Sigma (or as some call it, Lean Sigma) are often considered linked by people working on quality improvement projects. The goal of Six Sigma is to eliminate process variations, thereby achieving predictability.

Dr. W. Edwards Deming, the American statistician who is one of the people credited with Japan's revitalization, defines quality as "A predictable degree of uniformity and dependability at low cost and suited to the market." A lack of internal consistency confounds constancy of purpose and makes it impossible to create goods and services that would consistently meet or exceed customers' expectations. When present, variations rob an organization of the ability to deliver goods and services to customers predictably. A lack of predictability erodes the customers' trust in an organization's ability to deliver on its promises.

Process variations are deadly and should be handled with the urgency that their impact demands. Analyzing medical death rate data over an eight-year period, Johns Hopkins' patient safety experts (Makary and Daniel, 2016) have determined that more than 250,000 deaths per year are due to medical error in the United States. Their figure, published May 3, 2016 in *The BMJ*, surpasses the U.S. Centers for Disease Control and Prevention's (CDC's) third-leading cause of death—respiratory disease, which kills close to 150,000 people per year.

For the purposes of this chapter, the terms error and adverse event are defined as follows:

"An error is defined as the failure of a planned action to be completed as intended (i.e., error of execution) or the use of a wrong plan to achieve an aim (i.e., error of planning)" (Reason, 1990). An adverse event is an injury caused by medical management rather than the underlying condition of the patient. An adverse event attributable to error is a "preventable adverse event" (Brennan et al., 1991). Negligent adverse events represent a subset of preventable adverse events that satisfy legal criteria used in determining negligence, that is, whether the care provider failed to meet the standard of care reasonably expected of an average physician qualified to take care of the patient in question (Brennan et al., 1991). According to the Agency for Healthcare Research and Quality (AHRQ, 2017), one in seven Medicare patients in hospitals experience a medical error. However, medical errors can occur anywhere in the healthcare system: hospitals, clinics, surgery centers, doctors' offices, nursing homes, pharmacies, and patients' homes. Errors can involve medicine, surgery, diagnoses, equipment, or lab reports. They can happen during even the most routine tasks, such as when a hospital patient on a salt-free diet is given a high-salt meal (AHRQ, 2017).

The word "sigma," also known by its Greek letter σ, is a statistical measurement indicating the level of performance of a product or process. Higher sigma values indicate better performance, while lower values indicate a greater number of defects per unit. At 6σ—a rigorous and exacting approach to quality—defects are limited to just 3.4 per million opportunities. Organizations strive for this lofty goal by carefully applying Six Sigma methodology to every aspect of their product or process. This approach calls for a focus of time, energy, and resources to achieve a desired level of dependability, predictability, and uniformity to create real value for customers and profitability for the organization.

While Six Sigma has been steadily deployed in other industries, the approach is relatively new to the healthcare industry. Given the staggering and widely reported rate of medical errors, however, it is evident that the healthcare industry provides distinct and vital opportunities for the application of this methodology. The mounting evidence of Six Sigma's success in other industries suggests a tremendous opportunity for huge rewards for Six Sigma strategies and techniques in healthcare. If error reduction is a great concern to package delivery companies, it should be considered even more crucial to an industry that deals with life-and-death matters. Variation in healthcare is not just endemic; it is often avoidable.

The framework for Six Sigma application is: define, measure, analyze, improve, and control (DMAIC). An organization with the help of its highly trained Six Sigma experts uses the DMAIC model in a systematic order to develop, design, and redesign a process so there is, essentially, a one-in-a-million chance (or more specifically, a goal of 3.4 defects per million) that an error will occur. To attain their goal, the experts work to achieve 6σ, a measurement for standard deviation originating from statistics, to perfect their processes. This goal is congruent with the healthcare philosophy that, first, no harm should be done to patients. The statistical rigor required to achieve Six Sigma status can be daunting for small organizations. Even if a large organization is capable of collecting the amount of data necessary, with Six Sigma there is the potential for "analysis paralysis," where an exorbitant amount of time and resources are spent adhering to Six Sigma's rigid statistical targets and analyzing data instead of making quality improvements as soon as possible for patients.

Six Sigma is a heavily data-driven process designed to steer the improvement of work and eliminate defects—and that is why some organizations find achieving quality improvement goals with Six Sigma both difficult and time-consuming. These organizations often rely on professionals with advanced certifications in Six Sigma or Lean Six Sigma to help maintain the rigor of methodology, especially concerning statistical applications. The Six Sigma approach goes above and beyond other initiatives by insisting on facts rather than conjecture and ill-conceived implementation. At each step of the review process, the methodology demands the rigorous testing of assumptions. The figures in Table 7.1 illustrate several healthcare processes by sigma level. They also illustrate that, sometimes, being 99% effective is simply insufficient in healthcare delivery. Moreover, the figures show the value in striving for a Six Sigma level of excellence.

Table 7.1 Sigma Levels and Defects Per Million Opportunities

Sigma Level	Defects Per Million Opportunities (DPMO)	Percent Yield
3	66,800	93.32000
4	6,210	99.34900
5	230	99.97700
6	3.4	99.99966

Key Concepts of Six Sigma

The methodology of Six Sigma is driven by the following key concepts (Table 7.2).

A Six Sigma project team consists of members carefully selected for their skills and knowledge of the process under review. The roles of Six Sigma team members are described in Table 7.3.

Process variations weaken an organization's ability to deliver a predictable and uniform service to its customers. The inability to control variations has forced many healthcare organizations to accept defects as a permanent feature of their operations. Improvement strategies must address the challenges of defect detection and prevention in the processes used by healthcare organizations.

Examples of Defects

The following exemplify defect types found in healthcare processes:

- Cancellations of surgeries
- Adverse drug reactions
- Medication errors
- Errors in patient bills
- Poor visitor control
- Excessive waiting time in the emergency room
- Poor signage
- Inadequate parking
- Inadequate explanations to patients
- Delays in discharge
- Delays in room transfers
- Delays in admission
- Delays in answering call lights
- Rudeness of staff
- Failure to knock before entering patients' rooms
- Failure to update patient control board information
- Conflict between physicians and nurses in the presence of patients
- Failure to promptly deliver mail to physicians
- Delivering food trays to patients scheduled for surgery
- Delivering cold food to patients
- Poor telephone communication

- High telephone abandonment rate
- Accounts receivables over 60–90 days past due
- High rate of cesarean births
- Repeat visits for the same Diagnosis Related Groups (DRG)
- Infection rate during hospitalization
- Delays in turnaround times for X-rays
- Delays in turnaround times for lab results
- Surgical mortality rate
- Surgery performed on the wrong part of the body
- Incomplete medical records
- Missing charts
- Claims issues in managed care
- Mismatch between nurse and patient in home care
- Fragmentation, for example, too many nurses providing care to home-bound patients
- Nurses arriving late at patients' homes
- Patient falls
- Excessive use of physical restraints
- Incomplete registration forms
- Incomplete discharge summaries
- Patient complaints

Control Charts

One of the most powerful tools for monitoring and controlling process variation is a control chart, which is a statistical tool for managing process variability. A control chart is a run chart with a statistically determined center line (based on the mean), upper control limit (UCL), and lower control limit (LCL). Control charts are graphic aids for detecting variations in process output due to special causes. The limits are drawn at a calculated distance above and below the center line. There are two types of control charts—(a) Control charts for attribute data and (b) Control charts for variable data—both of which are discussed below.

Control Charts for Attribute Data

Attribute data is based on counts or the number of times we observe a particular event. Once the desired standards or guidelines have been defined,

Table 7.2   Key Concepts of Sigma Six

Key Concept	Explanation
Critical to quality (CTQ)	Attributes most important to the customer. Apply intensive analysis to processes, products, and services to determine whether the customers are receiving these CTQs.
Variation	The absence of predictability and dependability, ultimately experienced by the customer. Investigate what variations are occurring in the current processes and whether the processes are stable or predictable (i.e., is the same experience is provided to patients no matter the day of the week or time of day?). A defect is produced each time a process fails to deliver acceptable results. Determine what defects are being produced, how often, and how much they cost. A defect is anything that does not meet the customers' expectation or does not deliver acceptable results.
Focus areas	Choose focus areas based on company strategy, goals, and objectives.
Quantify the problem; identify possible causal relationships between the CTQs and input variables	Problem = $f(X_1, X_2, X_3, ...X_n)$, where X_i represents the variables affecting the problem. The problem could be one of the CTQs.
Stable process	A process that is predictable and only subjected to random or common causes of variation. Seek to bring a process into statistical control.
Process capability	What the process can deliver when it is stable.
Solutions to the problem	Use statistical rigor to analyze the process and devise sound solutions. Use data to validate the effectiveness and validity of the solutions. Refine the solutions if necessary using a PDSA process. Do a cost-benefit analysis to show the benefits of the solution, both tangible and intangible.
Design for Six Sigma	Designing a process to meet the needs of the customer, reduce variation, and improve accuracy. Design and implement process changes or adjustments to improve the performance of CTQs.
Implementation, monitor, and control	Regularly monitor the implementation and results of process improvement. Quantify and continually build upon improvements throughout the control phase. Hold the gains.

Table 7.3 Six Sigma Roles and Responsibilities

Roles	Responsibilities	Required Training
Champion	Each Six Sigma project team will have a champion whose responsibility is to facilitate a project, break down barriers, and ensure that resources are available and cross-functional issues are addressed. The champion is a middle- or senior-level executive.	Four to eight hours' training is sufficient for creating a basic understanding of Six Sigma concepts and a champion's role.
Black Belt	A black belt leads strategic and high-impact process improvement projects and helps to coach green belts. Black belts serve as a team leader for a Six Sigma project. In some organizations, black belts work full-time on Six Sigma projects.	About 160–200 hours of classroom training in statistical tools, process improvement methods, and team building skills. Usually, the training culminates in a written exam and a Six Sigma project demonstrating mastery of Six Sigma tools and methods as well as significant cost savings.
Master Black Belt	A master black belt is considered an expert who has managed several Six Sigma projects. He/she is responsible for coaching, mentoring, supporting, and training black belts.	The primary training for a master black belt comes from the supervision of several black belts in their Six Sigma endeavors. Additionally, some places require 40–80 hours of classroom training in project management and advanced statistical tools.
Green Belt	Green belts participate on project teams or lead process improvement projects within their own areas.	Green belt training typically requires 40 hours of training on the basics of Six Sigma.
Project Team Member	Team members are typically process stakeholders with some basic knowledge of Six Sigma concepts. They apply their knowledge to help the team achieve its goals.	A few hours of introductory materials on Six Sigma.
Process Owner	The professional that is accountable for the process being improved.	A few hours of introductory materials on Six Sigma.

it becomes necessary to count the number of non-confirming items, the fraction of non-conforming items, or the number of defects or inadequacies. For example, if the acceptable number of cesarean births is 12 percent, a cesarean birth rate exceeding that number is considered non-confirming. As another example, registration forms can be classified as either complete or incomplete. The number of discrepancies within each registration form is yet another example.

Attribute Data Chart Categories

There are two categories of attribute control charts:

1. Attribute Charts for Non-Conforming Items. The types of charts in this category, both explained below, are as follows:
   - p-charts
   - np-charts
2. Attribute Charts for Non-Conformities. Also explained below, the types of charts in this category are as follows:
   - c-charts
   - u-charts

Attribute Charts for Non-Conforming Items

Attribute charts for non-conforming items are based on a binomial distribution and the assumption that, for every trial, there are only two possible outcomes, such as acceptable/unacceptable, conforming/non-conforming, and so on. A "p-chart" is used to plot the fraction of non-conforming items for each subgroup or sample. An "np-chart" is used to plot the number of non-conforming items per subgroup or sample.

Attribute Charts for Non-Conformities

Attribute charts for non-conformities are based on the Poisson distribution. Any random phenomenon that occurs on a per-unit basis (or a per-unit area, per-unit volume, per-unit time, or the like) is often well-approximated by the Poisson distribution. The charts are used to count the number of non-conformities per inspection unit or non-conformities in a given area of opportunity.

A "c-chart" is used to plot the number of non-conformities per inspection unit where the area of opportunity is constant. A constant area of opportunity is one in which each subgroup used in constructing the control chart provides the same area or number of places in which the characteristic of interest may occur. For example, a constant area of opportunity would be a patient registration form. Each form has the same number of entry lines and information. The number of discrepancies observed in each form may be information of interest to hospitals. The types of discrepancies may include incomplete addresses, inaccurate birthdate information, incomplete or omitted telephone numbers, omission of other demographic information, and the like. However, from one form to another, the opportunity exists to observe the same set of discrepancies.

A "u-chart" is used where the area of opportunity is not constant. For example, the weekly number of respondents to a customer satisfaction survey may vary. A u-chart can be used to study the number of negative, positive, neutral, or no responses.

P-Chart Example

Assume an inspection of hospital patient accounting records is performed to gather information about billing errors. Table 7.4 shows the data from that inspection. Note that, on day 19, there is a high rate of billing errors.

Procedure for Constructing a P-Chart

Follow the steps below to construct a p-chart using the data from Table 7.4.

Step 1: Plot the fraction of billing errors against time. Select an appropriate scale for both axes. The Y axis is the fraction of billing errors, and the X axis is the day or subgroup. Use a dot to indicate each pair of data (see Figure 7.1).

Step 2: Consecutively connect the points with straight lines. After completing this step, the result is a run chart.

Step 3: Calculate the control limits using the equations given below. The center line for a p-chart is also the average of the samples taken:

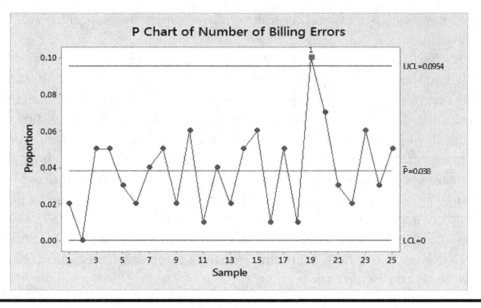

Figure 7.1 A p-chart showing fraction of billing errors.

$$\bar{P} = \frac{\text{Total number of billing errors in all subgroups}}{\text{Total number of units examined in all subgroups}}$$

$$\bar{P} = 95 \div 2500 = 0.038$$

$$\text{Center line} = \bar{P} = \frac{\sum P_i}{m}$$

$$\text{UCL} = \bar{P} + 3\sqrt{\frac{\bar{P}(1-\bar{P})}{n}}$$

$$\text{LCL} = \bar{P} - 3\sqrt{\frac{\bar{P}(1-\bar{P})}{n}}$$

The UCL is set at the value of $\bar{P}$ plus three times the standard error, while the LCL is set at the value of $\bar{P}$ minus three times the standard error.

Table 7.4   Hospital Billing Error Information

Day (Subgroup)	Number of Records Inspected	Number of Billing Errors	Proportion Billing Errors
1	100	2	0.02
2	100	0	0.00
3	100	5	0.05
4	100	5	0.05
5	100	3	0.03
6	100	2	0.02
7	100	4	0.04
8	100	5	0.05
9	100	2	0.02
10	100	6	0.06
11	100	1	0.01
12	100	4	0.04
13	100	2	0.02
14	100	5	0.05
15	100	6	0.06
16	100	1	0.01
17	100	5	0.05
18	100	1	0.01
19	100	10	0.10
20	100	7	0.07
21	100	3	0.03
22	100	2	0.02
23	100	6	0.06
24	100	3	0.03
25	100	5	0.05

A minimum of 24 subgroups are recommended to construct a control chart. Using the equations given above, the value for the UCL is 0.095, and the LCL is a negative number, which is approximated to 0 since we cannot have a negative value for a fraction of a non-conforming item.

UCL	Center Line	LCL
0.095	0.038	0.000

Results

Figure 7.1 reveals that the process lacks control. On day 19, the mean fraction value is above the UCL. Three important steps must be taken when this situation occurs. First, investigate the incident on day 19 to determine if it truly occurred due to a special cause. If so, determine what steps should be taken to prevent a recurrence and, finally, implement the necessary steps to ensure that this never happens again. The investigation of the process for day 19 might reveal that a new hire was put in charge of billing, replacing an employee who had performed that function for many years. To address the problem and eliminate this special cause of variation, management could decide that any new billing employee must undergo three weeks of training instead of the usual two days before being assigned any task. Thus, the process changes to eliminate a special cause of variation. After the process changes and the special cause of variation has been removed, the subgroup statistics for day 19 must be removed from the data and the chart, and that information is skipped on the graph. Removing this point also changes the process average and standard error. Therefore, the center line and control limits must be recalculated. Table 7.5 shows the remaining data after removing the data for day (subgroup) 19. The new center line and the control limits are shown in Figure 7.2.

An NP-Chart Example

An np-chart serves the same purpose as a p-chart, except that an np-chart is based on the number of items that are defective or non-conforming, rather than the fraction of non-conforming items. It is sometimes easier to grasp the number, not the fraction, of non-conforming items.

Table 7.5 Information from Table 7.1 After Removing Data for Day 19

Day (Subgroup)	Number of Records Inspected	Number of Billing Errors	Proportion Billing Errors
1	100	2	0.02
2	100	0	0.00
3	100	5	0.05
4	100	5	0.05
5	100	3	0.03
6	100	2	0.02
7	100	4	0.04
8	100	5	0.05
9	100	2	0.02
10	100	6	0.06
11	100	1	0.01
12	100	4	0.04
13	100	2	0.02
14	100	5	0.05
15	100	6	0.06
16	100	1	0.01
17	100	5	0.05
18	100	1	0.01
19	–	–	–
20	100	7	0.07
21	100	3	0.03
22	100	2	0.02
23	100	6	0.06
24	100	3	0.03
25	100	5	0.05

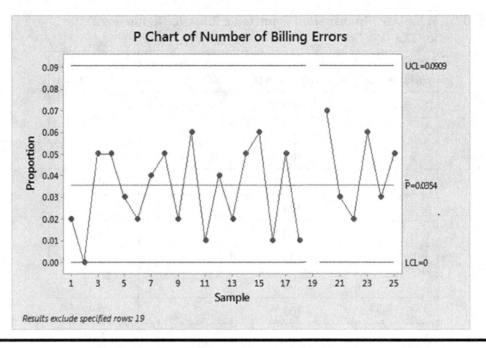

Figure 7.2 A p-chart for fraction billing errors (revised).

Because the two types of charts are interchangeable, the np-chart uses the same steps as the p-chart. To construct an np-chart for the information in Table 7.1, the following equations are required:

$$\text{Center line} = n\bar{p} = n\frac{\sum P_i}{m}$$

$$\text{UCL} = n\bar{P} + 3\sqrt{n\bar{P}\left(1 - \bar{P}\right)}$$

$$\text{LCL} = n\bar{P} - 3\sqrt{n\bar{P}\left(1 - \bar{P}\right)}$$

UCL	Center Line	LCL
9.54	3.80	0.00

Figure 7.3 is an example of an np-chart using the data from Table 7.1.

Results

An examination of the np-chart in Figure 7.3 reveals the absence of a stable process. Again, on day 19, something unusual happened. As with the p-chart, this special cause of variation must be investigated, the data removed, and the process brought under statistical control.

Variable Sample Size

In the p-chart example in Table 7.1, we assumed that the number of records (subgroup size) was constant at 100. It is also possible to have a variable subgroup size. We illustrate this with the following example:

Results

The control chart displayed in Figure 7.4 reveals a stable process or the absence of any special (assignable) causes, as all the points fall within the UCL and LCL.

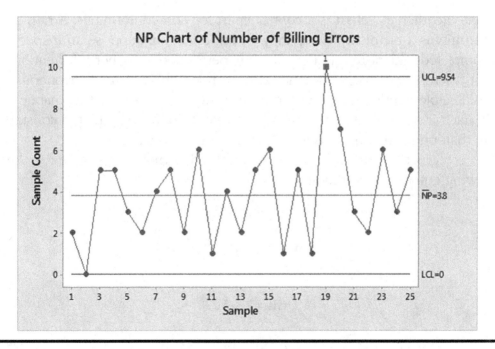

Figure 7.3   An np-chart for number of billing errors.

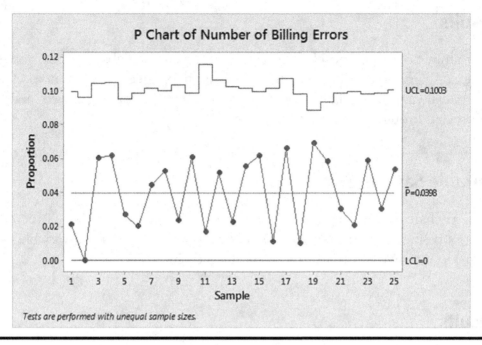

Figure 7.4   P control chart with variable subgroup size.

A C-Chart Example

As stated earlier, a c-chart is a control chart for non-conformities. A non-conformity is a blemish, discrepancy, or imperfection. Suppose an inspection of completed patient registration forms is performed to gather information about discrepancies. A discrepancy can include a missing field, erroneous data, illegible handwriting, etc. Table 7.6 shows the data from that inspection. Each inspected form represents an area of opportunity that is constant. Note that, on form 9, there is a high rate of discrepancies.

To construct the appropriate c-chart for the information in Table 7.6, the following equations are required:

$$\text{Center line} = \bar{c} = \frac{\sum c_i}{m}$$

$$\text{UCL} = \bar{c} + 3\sqrt{\bar{c}}$$

$$\text{LCL} = \bar{c} - 3\sqrt{\bar{c}}$$

Table 7.6   Number of Discrepancies Found on 25 Patient Registration Forms

Form Number	Number of Discrepancies
1	2
2	5
3	0
4	3
5	1
6	4
7	2
8	1
9	9
10	3
11	5
12	2
13	0
14	4
15	1
16	3
17	5
18	2
19	2
20	6
21	1
22	4
23	3
24	5
25	2

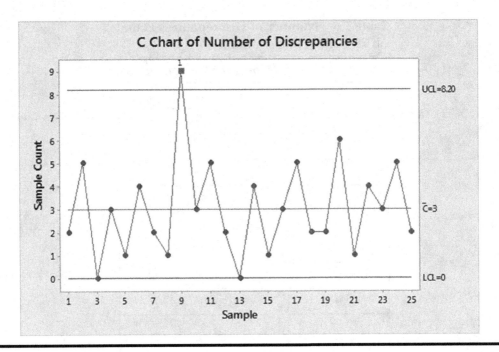

Figure 7.5   A c-chart for discrepancies in patient registration forms.

UCL	Center Line	LCL
8.196152	3	0

Figure 7.5 is an example of a c-chart using the data from Table 7.3.

Results

Figure 7.5 reveals an unstable process. Form 9 had an unusually high rate of discrepancies. Further investigation would reveal that form 9 was completed by a non-registration clerk, a situation that is rarely allowed. Thus, a policy would be instituted to prohibit the recurrence of such events. Figure 7.6 shows the resulting process after the data for form 9 is removed and new control limits for the c-chart are calculated.

A U-Chart Example

Suppose a nursing floor wishes to study the number of patient falls using a control chart. The patient census on the floor is a variable area of

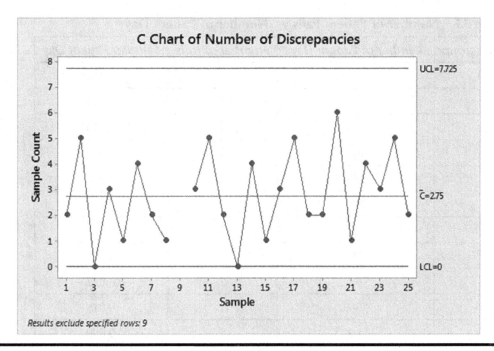

Figure 7.6   A c-chart for discrepancies in patient registration forms (revised).

opportunity; so are the patient days. Table 7.7 shows the data from that review.

To construct the appropriate u-chart for the information in Table 7.7, the following equations are required:

$$\text{Center line} = \bar{u} = \frac{\sum u_i}{\sum a_i}$$

Where:

$$\bar{a} = \frac{\sum a_i}{m}$$

$$\text{UCL} = \bar{u} + 3\sqrt{\frac{\bar{u}}{\bar{a}}}$$

$$\text{LCL} = \bar{u} - 3\sqrt{\frac{\bar{u}}{\bar{a}}}$$

UCL	Center Line	LCL
Variable	0.0387	0

Table 7.7   Number of Patient Falls vs. Number of Patient Days

Subgroup	Number of Patient Days	Number of Falls	Falls Per Patient Day
1	68	3	0.044
2	77	1	0.013
3	83	4	0.048
4	56	0	0.000
5	103	8	0.078
6	100	7	0.070
7	87	4	0.046
8	59	1	0.017
9	62	2	0.032
10	66	1	0.015
11	60	0	0.000
12	75	3	0.040
13	86	5	0.058
14	91	6	0.066
15	54	1	0.019
16	58	1	0.017
17	60	2	0.033
18	61	1	0.016
19	84	5	0.060
20	88	5	0.057
21	74	3	0.041
22	72	2	0.028
23	70	2	0.029
24	82	3	0.037
25	57	1	0.018

Results

Figure 7.7 reveals a stable or predictable process. All points fall between the control limits.

Bringing the Process Under Control

After removing the points outside of the control limits and recalculating the new and narrower limits, it is still possible to find other points falling outside the new limits. Such points should also be investigated for special causes. Several iterations may be needed to stabilize the process and bring it under control.

Evidence of an Unstable Process

A process exhibits a lack of statistical control if a subgroup statistic falls outside either control limit. However, it is possible for a process to exhibit a lack of control even when all subgroup statistics are within the control

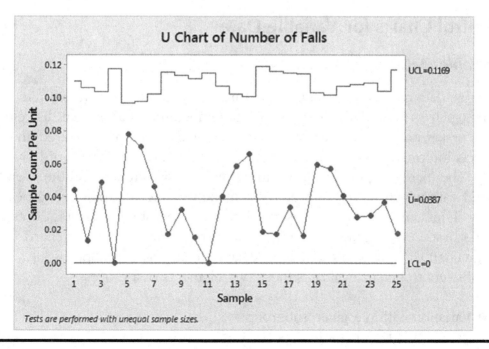

Figure 7.7   A u-chart for number of patient falls.

limits. A stable process can be expected to exhibit random patterns of variation, with most data points spread around the center line and an approximately equal number of points distributed above and below the center line. A few data points would tend to lie close to either control limit. Only in rare cases would a point be outside the control limits.

Apply these conditions to decide when to investigate processes that may be outside the control limits:

■ Any point is outside either control limit.
■ Two of three consecutive points are near the control limits.
■ There are runs of seven or more points above or below the center line.
■ There are trends showing seven or more points moving up or down.

The Meaning of a Stable Process

A stable process does not imply a perfect or good process. It simply means no special causes of variation exist and only common causes of variation are present. Reducing the number of variations due to common causes further improves the predictability of the process.

Control Charts for Variable Data

Variable Data

Variable data represent quantities measured on a continuous and infinite scale (such as time, distance, pressure, or temperature) rather than discrete units or yes/no options. Variable or continuous data can be measured and reflects information about processes such as how much, how big, or how long. The increasing interest in waiting times, services times, and the overall speed with which service is performed make variable control charts especially significant. Variable data is also known as measurement data. Control charts based on variable data include an average bar chart (X-bar chart), range chart (R-chart), and standard deviation chart (S-chart). Specifically, a variable control chart evaluates these two elements of a process:

■ Variation within a given subgroup
■ Variation between subgroups

There are several examples of healthcare applications of variable control charts, including the following:

- Waiting time in the emergency room
- Waiting time for an appointment
- Amount of time taken to answer call button
- Amount of weight lost or gained by patients in a diet program
- Blood pressure measurement for patients under observation
- Average number of accounts receivable days
- Turnaround time for lab tests and results
- Turnaround time for X-rays
- Underwriting time for new managed care patients
- Number of days to obtain authorization for salaries for prospective job candidates
- Amount of time spent by a physician with new patients
- Amount of time spent by a physician with patients on a follow-up visit
- Amount of time taken to fill a prescription
- Amount of time taken to prepare for surgery
- Amount of time taken to perform routine ambulatory surgery
- Amount of time to prepare a meal
- Amount of time to deliver food trays to patients
- Average food temperature
- Patient registration time
- Amount of time housekeeping takes to clean a room
- Amount of time between a doctor's order to discharge a patient and when patient leaves the hospital
- Amount of time patients wait for clean rooms to become available
- Amount of time it takes to resolve doctors' claims inquiries
- Amount of blood lost by patients during surgery
- Length of patients' stays in the hospital
- Amount of time it takes a home health agency to find staff for a case

A variable control chart provides an opportunity to track process performance in terms of the mean and the range. Neither the mean nor the range alone sufficiently describes the process performance.

Presented here are descriptions of two control charts for variable data:

- R-chart, which monitors variations within a subgroup. This type of chart shows the spread or dispersion of the individual samples within the subgroup. The calculation of spread is necessary to determine the degree of consistency in the service being delivered.
- X-bar chart, which monitors variations between subgroups. This type of chart provides an understanding of where the process is centered.

Judging Process Stability

The data in Table 7.8 illustrates the importance of a process's range and mean. The data was collected for three subgroups, where each subgroup represents five randomly selected patients. The subgroup mean (or average) is a measure of central tendency, and it is used to chart the process's location. The range (calculated as the difference between the highest and the lowest item in a given subgroup) is a measure of spread, and it is used to measure process variability. Based on subgroup averages or mean ($\bar{X}$), even though more subgroup data is needed, the process seems predictable or stable. However, examining the values for the range suggests huge differences among all three subgroup statistics (Table 7.9).

Example of an $\bar{X}$ – R-Chart

Table 7.10 below shows the waiting time (in days) for managed care patients to obtain an appointment to see a specialist physician. Time is defined as the time between when the patients call and the date of their appointment to see the doctor. Table 7.10 shows the data collected for 25 subgroups.

Procedure for Constructing an R-Chart

Step 1: Select an appropriate scale for the R-chart values. For example, the Y axis is the waiting time, and the X axis is the subgroup (see Figure 7.7).

Step 2: Plot the range of values for each of the 25 subgroups. Each point represents the range of values for each subgroup. Note that the range of values is calculated as:

$$X_{max} - X_{min}$$

Table 7.8 Data for a p-Chart with Variable Subgroup Size

Day (Subgroup)	Number of Records Inspected	Number of Billing Errors	Proportion Billing Errors
1	96	2	0.02
2	108	0	0.00
3	83	5	0.06
4	81	5	0.06
5	112	3	0.03
6	100	2	0.02
7	90	4	0.04
8	95	5	0.05
9	85	2	0.02
10	99	6	0.06
11	60	1	0.02
12	78	4	0.05
13	88	2	0.02
14	90	5	0.06
15	97	6	0.06
16	91	1	0.01
17	76	5	0.07
18	101	1	0.01
19	145	10	0.07
20	120	7	0.06
21	100	3	0.03
22	97	2	0.02
23	102	6	0.06
24	99	3	0.03
25	94	5	0.05

Table 7.9   Data on Waiting Time (in Minutes) to See a Doctor

Subgroup	X_1	X_2	X_3	X_4	X_5	$\bar{X}$	Range (R)
Subgroup 1	35	45	24	63	52	43.8	39.0
Subgroup 2	44	46	39	48	42	43.8	9.0
Subgroup 3	43.8	43.8	43.8	43.8	43.8	43.8	0.0

Step 3: Connect the points for each range value. The result is a run chart for the range.

Step 4: Calculate the values for the center line, LCL, and UCL based on the equations given below. The values for A_2, D_3, and D_4 are constants and are found in Table 7.11 (insert Stat Table).

Equations for $\bar{x}$ Control Chart

$$\text{Center line}\left(\bar{x}\right) = \bar{\bar{x}} = \frac{\sum \bar{x}}{k} = \frac{404.6}{25} = 16.184$$

$$\text{UCL}\left(\bar{x}\right) = \bar{\bar{x}} + A_2\bar{R} = 16.183 + 0.577\left(9.2\right) = 21.492$$

$$\text{LCL}\left(\bar{x}\right) = \bar{\bar{x}} - A_2\bar{R} = 16.183 - 0.577\left(9.2\right) = 10.876$$

Equations for R-Control Chart

$$\text{Center line}\left(R\right) = \bar{R} = \frac{230}{25} = 9.2$$

$$\text{UCL}\left(R\right) = D_4\bar{R} = 2.114\left(9.2\right) = 19.45$$

$$\text{LCL}\left(R\right) = D_3\bar{R} = 0\left(9.2\right) = 0$$

Note: A_2, D_4, and D_3 are constants found in Table 7.11.

Step 5: Determine if there is evidence of an unstable process. If there is, do not analyze or construct an X-bar chart until or unless the R-chart shows evidence of a stable process. Once the R-chart is stabilized (by any number of interventions; for example, eliminating an out-of-control

Table 7.10 Average Waiting Time (in Days) for Appointments for HMO Commercial Patients

Subgroup	X_1	X_2	X_3	X_4	X_5	$\bar{X}$	Range (R)
1	10	15	17	8	20	14	12
2	15	9	21	14	16	15	12
3	12	12	15	9	24	14.4	15
4	16	18	14	22	19	17.8	8
5	6	11	15	18	14	12.8	12
6	18	19	21	10	15	16.6	11
7	22	20	10	19	9	16	13
8	16	15	9	13	17	14	8
9	14	16	21	19	14	16.8	7
10	12	21	11	15	16	15	10
11	13	15	18	11	19	15.2	8
12	19	18	15	10	20	16.4	10
13	23	12	13	16	18	16.4	11
14	15	16	15	17	20	16.4	6
15	18	12	15	17	19	16.2	7
16	14	21	20	16	15	17.2	7
17	16	23	14	21	11	17	12
18	13	16	19	19	20	17.4	7
19	17	17	21	14	15	16.8	7
20	16	21	19	12	20	17.6	9
21	18	18	18	25	20	19.8	7
22	15	11	16	12	14	13.6	5
23	19	14	14	19	21	17.4	7
24	14	23	21	19	10	17.4	13
25	16	18	20	13	19	17.2	7

point), it is appropriate to construct and analyze an X-bar chart. If the X-bar chart shows evidence of an unstable process, the entire process is unstable. Hence, for process stability, both the R- and X-bar charts must show evidence of a stable process. Note that Figure 7.8 shows a stable process.

Step 6: If the R-chart shows evidence of a stable (in control) process and if the corresponding X-bar chart reveals an unstable process, take the appropriate action to stabilize the X-bar chart. If the appropriate action implies removing one or more subgroup statistics that fall outside the control limits, it may be necessary to reconstruct the R-chart without including the specific subgroup statistics eliminated in the X-bar chart.

Results

Figure 7.8 shows a stable process regarding the range (variations between subgroups). An X-bar chart should be drawn next to verify this information. If the R-chart had shown an unstable process, it would be appropriate to take action to prevent the recurrence of the special cause of the variation. After stabilizing the process, an X-bar chart should be constructed.

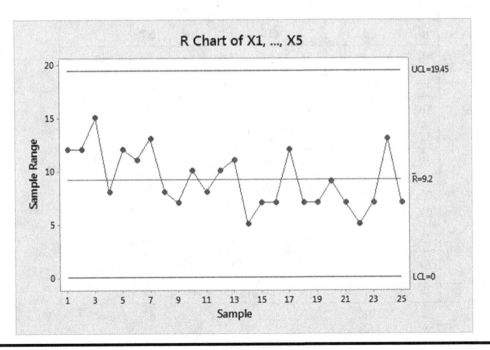

Figure 7.8   An R-chart showing waiting time for a specialist appointment (in days).

Procedure for Constructing an X-Bar Chart

Step 1: If the R-chart shows a stable process, plot the X-bar chart by adding three horizontal lines representing the center line, LCL, and UCL (see Figure 7.8).

Step 2: If the X-bar chart reveals one or more points outside the control limits, the process is unstable. If all the points fall within the limits, the process is stable.

Results

As Figure 7.9 reveals, the process is also stable regarding the mean. All the subgroup statistics or points fall between the control limits. In addition, none of the rules for process stability have been violated.

An $\bar{X}-S$-Chart

The $\bar{X}-S$-chart is very similar to the $\bar{X}-R$-chart in many ways, the major difference being the subgroup standard deviation is plotted when using the

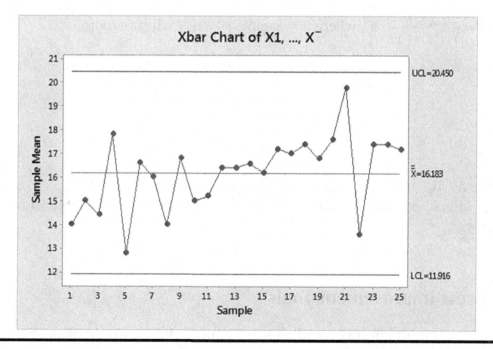

Figure 7.9   An X-bar chart showing waiting times for an appointment (in days).

$\bar{X}-S$-chart, while the subgroup range is plotted when using the $\bar{X}-R$-chart. One advantage of using the standard deviation instead of the range is that the standard deviation considers all the data within a subgroup, not just the maximum and the minimum. The constants used to calculate the control limits and to estimate the process standard deviation are different for the $\bar{X}-S$-chart than for the $\bar{X}-R$-chart. The $\bar{X}-S$-chart is used when the subgroup size is 10 or more, because the standard deviation gives a better estimate of the variation in large subgroups than the range does.

Equations for $\bar{x}$ Control Chart

$$\text{Center line}(\bar{x}) = \bar{\bar{x}} = \frac{\sum \bar{x}_i}{k}; \text{ where k is the number of samples in each}$$

subgroup (k≥10)

$$\text{UCL}(\bar{x}) = \bar{\bar{x}} + A_3\bar{S}$$

$$\text{LCL}(\bar{x}) = \bar{\bar{x}} - A_3\bar{S}$$

Equations for S Control Chart

$$S = \sqrt{\frac{\sum(x_i - \bar{x})^2}{n-1}}; \text{ where n = sample size of each subgroup}$$

$$\text{Center line}(S) = \bar{S}$$

$$\text{UCL}(S) = B_4\bar{S}$$

$$\text{LCL}(S) = B_3\bar{S}$$

Note: A_3, B_4, and B_3 are constants found in Table 7.11.

A sample problem format for an $\bar{X}-S$-chart is presented in Table 7.12 below:

Process Improvement Tools

One of the most effective problem-solving methodologies is the Plan-Do-Study-Act (PDSA) cycle. It is a simple yet powerful process for driving

Table 7.11   Control Chart Constants and Formulae

	Control Chart Factors							
	X-Bar and R-Charts					X-Bar and S-Charts		
Subgroup Size	X-bar Chart Limits	Hartley's Constant	Factors for Control Limits			c4 Constant	Factors for Control Limits	
n	A2	d2	D3	D4	A3	c4	B3	B4
2	1.880	1.128	0.000	3.267	2.659	0.7979	0.000	3.267
3	1.023	1.693	0.000	2.575	1.954	0.8862	0.000	2.568
4	0.729	2.059	0.000	2.282	1.628	0.9213	0.000	2.266
5	0.577	2.326	0.000	2.114	1.427	0.9400	0.000	2.089
6	0.483	2.534	0.000	2.004	1.287	0.9515	0.030	1.970
7	0.419	2.704	0.076	1.924	1.182	0.9594	0.118	1.882
8	0.373	2.847	0.136	1.864	1.099	0.9650	0.185	1.815
9	0.337	2.970	0.184	1.816	1.032	0.9693	0.239	1.761
10	0.308	3.078	0.223	1.777	0.975	0.9727	0.284	1.716
11	0.285	3.173	0.256	1.744	0.927	0.9754	0.321	1.679
12	0.266	3.258	0.283	1.717	0.886	0.9776	0.354	1.646
13	0.249	3.336	0.307	1.693	0.850	0.9794	0.382	1.618
14	0.235	3.407	0.328	1.672	0.817	0.9810	0.406	1.594
15	0.223	3.472	0.347	1.653	0.789	0.9823	0.428	1.572
16	0.212	3.532	0.363	1.637	0.763	0.9835	0.448	1.552
17	0.203	3.588	0.378	1.622	0.739	0.9845	0.466	1.534
18	0.194	3.640	0.391	1.609	0.718	0.9854	0.482	1.518
19	0.187	3.689	0.404	1.596	0.698	0.9862	0.497	1.503
20	0.180	3.735	0.415	1.585	0.680	0.9869	0.510	1.490
21	0.173	3.778	0.425	1.575	0.663	0.9876	0.523	1.477
22	0.167	3.819	0.435	1.565	0.647	0.9882	0.534	1.466
23	0.162	3.858	0.443	1.557	0.633	0.9887	0.545	1.455
24	0.157	3.895	0.452	1.548	0.619	0.9892	0.555	1.445
25	0.153	3.931	0.459	1.541	0.606	0.9896	0.565	1.435

Table 7.12 **Problem format for an $\bar{X}-S$-chart**

Subgroup	X_1	X_2	X_3	X_4	X_5	X_6	X_7	X_8	X_9	X_{10}	$\bar{X}$	S
1												
2												
3												
4												
5												

quality improvement efforts. Once a process improvement team has been formed and the measures developed to determine whether a change leads to an improvement, the next step is to implement the change on a trial basis in the real work setting. The PDSA cycle provides a framework for implementing a change—by planning it, testing it, observing the results, and acting on what is learned.

The steps in the PDSA cycle are:

Step 1: Plan—Plan the test or observation, including a plan for collecting data.
Step 2: Do—Try the test on a small scale.
Step 3: Study—Set aside time to analyze the data and study the results.
Step 4: Act—Refine the change, based on what was learned from the test.

Process improvement is both an art and a science. No two problems are similar. There are fundamental steps every team should consider when trying to improve a process. Certain problem-solving tools make it easier for a team to quickly gain insight into a problem. Sometimes, teams struggle with the question of when to use a given problem-solving tool. Figure 7.10a,b serves as a guide for the team problem-solving process.

Tools for Managing Ideas

Brainstorming and multi-voting are tools for managing the ideas created during the team problem-solving process. Both are discussed in greater detail in the following pages.

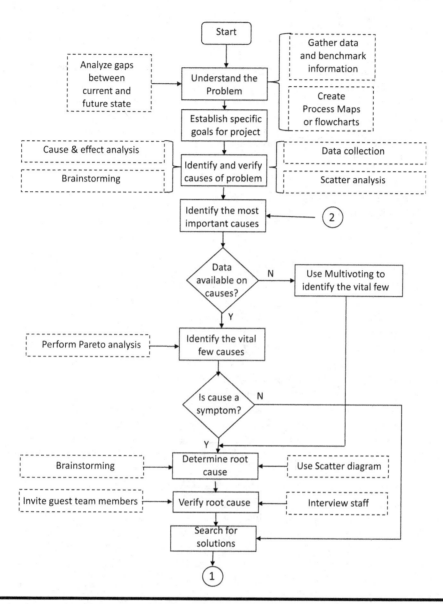

Figure 7.10a   Team problem-solving process.

Brainstorming

Brainstorming is a technique developed in the 1930s by the Father of Brainstorming, Alex F. Osborn. According to Osborn, "It is easier to tone down a wild idea than to think up a new one." Brainstorming is used to generate a large quantity of ideas within a short time. Brainstorming ignites the creativity of team members and is used to do the following:

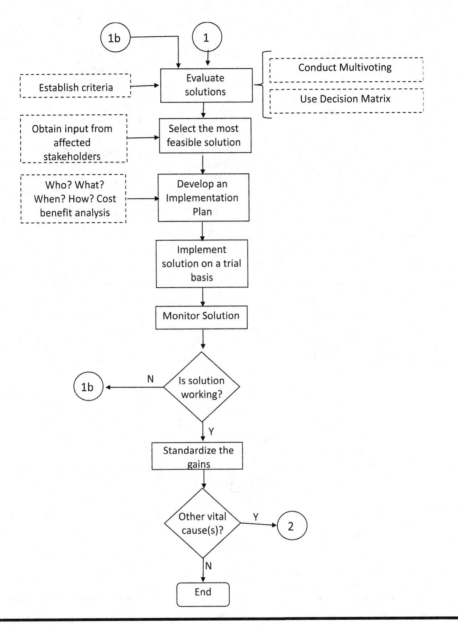

Figure 7.10b   Team problem-solving process.

- Generate ideas on any subject or area
- Identify problems deserving a team focus
- Identify possible causes of a problem
- Identify the causes of a problem's symptom
- Identify possible solutions to a problem
- Identify obstacles to implementing a solution

Initially, the emphasis is on the quantity of ideas, not their quality. All the ideas are evaluated in later phases of the brainstorming process. Representation from all process owners is mandatory in a brainstorming session. It may be necessary to invite non-team members to participate in the brainstorming session as guests if they possess relevant knowledge about the process being studied or if information generated through brainstorming would be rendered invalid or inadequate without them. The three phases of a brainstorming session are the creativity phase, the clarification phase, and the assessment phase.

The Creativity Phase

A team member is selected as the recorder. The recorder's responsibility is to write down the ideas generated by the team. Ideas are recorded so they are visible to all team members. Ideas are usually displayed in large handwriting on flip charts, which are then placed against the walls for clear visibility. The recorder is also expected to engage in the brainstorming session. The team leader first states the purpose of the session. All participants must understand the topic before the brainstorming session begins. Next, the rules of the brainstorming session are presented and may include the following:

- Each member takes a turn, in sequence, to supply one idea at a time.
- The creativity phase continues until all ideas are exhausted.
- Criticism, judgment, or discussion of any ideas is not permitted.
- It is acceptable to say, "pass" if a participant has no new idea to offer during a round.
- Participants are expected to build on others' ideas.
- It is acceptable for participants to say whatever comes to mind, even if it seems silly or outrageous.
- A brisk pace must be maintained throughout this phase.

The Clarification Phase

During this phase of the brainstorming session, team members review the compiled list of ideas to ensure everyone understands them. Once clarification is obtained, the recorder makes the appropriate modifications on the flip chart to reflect the new information. There is no discussion or criticism of ideas in this phase.

The Assessment Phase

During this phase, the team reviews the list to eliminate duplications, redundancies, and issues that are not germane to the topic. Teams may use a technique called multi-voting to reduce the number of ideas for consideration.

Multi-Voting

Multi-voting takes place after brainstorming and is used to reduce a list of ideas or issues to the most important ones. Team members vote for between 20% and 25% of the ideas on the list; 20% is more commonly used. Before multi-voting, the team agrees on the criteria with which it will select the most important ideas from the list. Depending on the topic, the most common criteria used are the following:

- Impact on patient care
- Impact on member disenrollment or retention
- Impact on patient satisfaction
- Impact on the bottom line
- Ease of implementation
- An issue the team can control
- Increased competitiveness for the organization
- Greatest frequency of occurrence

It is recommended to use as few criteria as possible because each idea selected must meet all the criteria established by the team. Following the vote count, the ideas receiving the largest number of votes are noted. It may then become necessary to vote again for 20% of the items from the previous round of voting. As an example, say a team started with a list of 30 ideas from their brainstorming session. During the first round of voting, each member voted for the six most important ideas out of the 30 ($30 \times .20 = 6$). After counting the votes (mostly done by asking how many people voted for number 1, number 2, and so on), the six ideas receiving the most votes are recorded. The second round of voting is conducted to select 20% of the top ideas, and the criteria remain the same. At the end of the second round of voting, the most important ideas emerge.

Tools for Gathering and Analyzing Data

Discussed below are some of the tools for gathering and analyzing data during the problem-solving process.

- Flow charts
- Pareto analyses
- Cause and effect diagrams
- Scatter diagrams

Each of these tools will be discussed in turn in the following sections.

Flow Charts

A flow chart is a graphical depiction of how a process currently works, not how the process should work. It is an important tool of choice for Process Improvement (PI) teams. Flow charts are useful for many reasons.

- They document how a process really works.
- They provide a way to see and understand where and how every team member fits into the total picture.
- They reveal bottlenecks in a process.
- They are useful for training employees.
- They can be used as diagnostic tools for process problems.

Most processes can be sufficiently described using the following symbols:

- Ovals represent a process's beginning and end.
- Rectangles stand for process activities.
- Diamonds symbolize decision points.
- Arrows indicate the direction of flow.
- Small circles denote continuation.

Process for Creating Flow Charts

The following steps are essential for creating a flow chart:

- Define the process to chart. The team sets boundaries for the process by indicating starting and ending points. Using an ER's intake process as an example, the team would set the process's boundaries to begin when a patient arrives in the ER and to end when the patient is registered (see Figure 7.11).

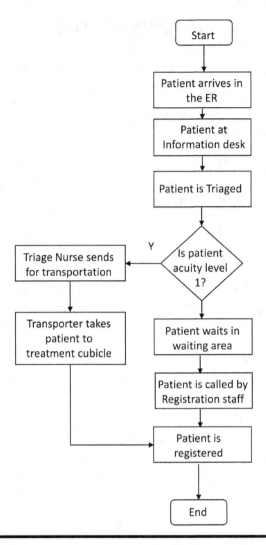

Figure 7.11 Flow chart of an emergency room's intake process.

- Define the type of information expected from the flow chart: the who, what, where, when, why, and how of the process.
- Identify a list of key individuals whose input is critical for providing a complete description of the process.
- Select volunteers from the team to conduct interviews of these individuals.
- Generate a draft of the flow chart for review.
- Verify all the facts about the process from key process owners.
- Make final modifications and create the final flow chart.

Pareto Analysis

In 1897, Vilfreo Pareto, an Italian economist, presented a formula showing the unevenness of income distribution. In 1907, M.C. Lorenz, an American economist, diagrammatically expressed a similar theory. Both Pareto and Lorenz noted that, by far, the largest share of income or wealth was in the hands of a few people. J. M. Juran, an economist and management consultant applied this concept to quality problems to classify them into the vital few and the trivial many, and he named this procedure the Pareto analysis. Pareto analysis is a way of organizing and presenting data to show the vital few causes of a problem in contrast to the trivial many. This analysis is based on data presented in a diagram. The 80-20 rule exemplifies this point—80% of problems are instigated by 20% of the causes. Pareto analysis works best for zero-based types of data such as the number of complaints or mistakes. The ideal situation is to reduce a problem to zero.

An Example

This example illustrates steps 1 through 5 of the process for creating a Pareto diagram. A local hospital formed a PI team to study the incidents of cancellations in surgeries and how to reduce the number of cancellations. Since there is sufficient documentation regarding the causes of cancellations, the team used a tally sheet to collect data retrospectively from the department of surgery records (see Table 7.13). The hospital had 80 cases of surgery cancellations during the period under study. The team then arranged the data in descending order, and calculated the probabilities and cumulative probabilities. Table 7.13 shows the causes of cancellations, their frequency of occurrence, probabilities, and cumulative probabilities.

Table 7.13 Causes of Surgery Cancellations (Arranged in Descending Order)

Causes	Frequency	Probability	Cumulative Probability
Patient ate	33	0.41	0.41
Adverse test result	24	0.30	0.71
Failure to sign consent form	10	0.13	0.84
Surgeon no-show	5	0.06	0.90
Other	8	0.10	1.00

At this point, the team constructs a Pareto diagram from the data in Table 7.13 (see Figure 7.12). The team concludes that "Patient ate" and "Adverse test result" together account for 71% of the cases of surgery cancellations. The team can now devote its attention to the one or two causes that constitute the vital few. It is not cost efficient to address every cause of a problem. A PI team must evaluate how the remaining issues (the trivial many) on the Pareto diagram compare with other opportunities for improvement in the hospital in terms of priority. It is quite common to make the "Other" category the last item on a Pareto chart even if it is not the lowest in frequency.

Cause and Effect Diagrams (Ishikawa or Fishbone Diagrams)

A cause and effect diagram displays and explores sources of variation in a process. It depicts a relationship between cause and effect, and is used primarily to display symptoms and their causes. In 1953, Professor Kaoru Ishikawa of the University of Tokyo applied the concept of cause and effect to a quality problem. The Ishikawa diagram (or fishbone diagram because it resembles a fish's skeleton) is a chart comprising lines and words that represent a meaningful relationship between an effect and its causes. Brainstorming is one technique used to provide the data for this diagram.

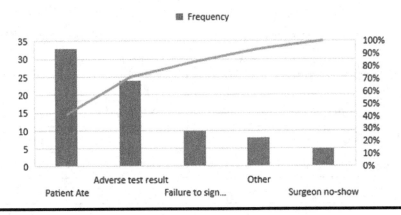

Figure 7.12 **Pareto chart showing reasons for surgery cancellations.**

Process for Creating a Cause and Effect Diagram

Construct a cause and effect diagram by doing the following:

■ Draw a box on the extreme right-hand side of a page, and write the problem (the effect) clearly inside the box (see Figure 7.13).
■ Draw a horizontal line (the backbone) running from left to right with an arrowhead touching the box and stating the effect.
■ Draw a horizontal box for each major category. Place the boxes above and below the backbone line. Label the boxes as distinct and major categories (primary causes). In general, the following major categories are used:

Another round of brainstorming might reveal that inadequate food temperature is one of the most common complaints from patients (hence the cloud around it in the diagram). The team should conduct another round of brainstorming to determine the causes of inadequate food temperature and develop another cause and effect diagram for it.

Scatter Diagrams

A scatter diagram is a technique for studying the relationship between two variables. It verifies the relationship between a dependent variable, such as

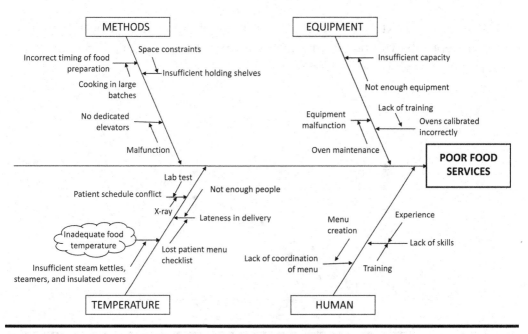

Figure 7.13   Cause and effect diagram for poor food services.

absenteeism, and an independent variable, such as length of employment. A scatter diagram reveals existing patterns in data and shows the strength of the relationship between both variables. Although the technique is often used for discrete (countable) data, its correct application is when two variables are continuous (measurable) data (see Figure 7.14).

The following are examples of where scatter diagrams can be used:

■ To study the relationship between number of patient falls and the census on the hospital unit.
■ To study the relationship between food temperature (upon delivery to the patient) and speed of delivery in minutes (the amount of time between the food being removed from the oven and the patient receiving it).
■ To examine the relationship between the patient's waiting time after pushing the call button and the time of day.
■ Hospital readmission rates and how full the hospital was at the time of discharge. The point is that, if extra beds are available, patients can stay an extra night as a precautionary measure. If beds are in high demand, some hospitals might send patients home earlier than if there were extra beds.
■ To investigate the relationship between hours spent training new nurses and the number of mistakes made on patient charts.

An Example

The data on the next page (Table 7.14) represents information on the number of patient falls vs. the staffing levels in man hours. Figure 7.15 shows the scatter plot using Minitab software.

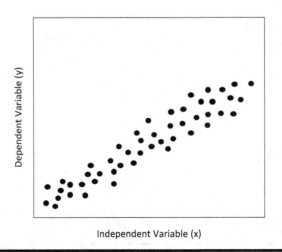

Independent Variable (x)

Figure 7.14 Scatter diagram showing a positive correlation.

Table 7.14   Data for Patient Falls vs. Staffing Levels (man hours)

Week	Number of Patient Falls	Staffing Level (man hours)
1	23	402
2	34	368
3	12	488
4	45	323
5	55	305
6	19	430
7	16	476
8	6	520
9	31	377
10	3	560
11	24	401
12	49	315
13	67	298
14	14	490
15	29	383
16	37	356
17	51	318
18	18	436
19	25	399
20	5	563

Coefficient of Correlation (R)

The correlation coefficient (r) measures the strength of the relationship between two variables. The value of correlation lies between minus one and plus one ($-1 \leq r \leq +1$), where -1 means a perfect negative correlation and $+1$ means a perfect positive correlation. Searching for causes can sometimes lead a PI team to investigate the relationships between two variables. If the strength of the relationship is strong, it justifies the need to probe further for a causal relationship. Causation only exists if it occurs every time.

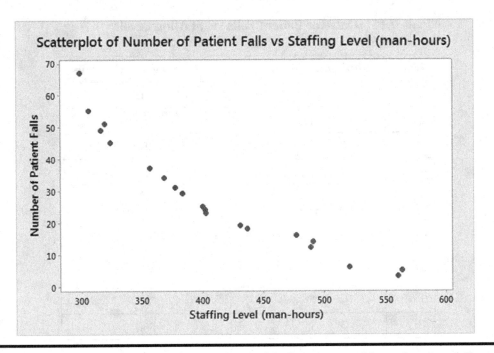

Figure 7.15 Scatter plot showing the relationship between number of patient falls and staffing levels in man hours.

Correlation, however, has a significantly lower standard that establishes a relationship to a condition. Two variables with a high correlation do not necessarily prove causation. By knowing the strength of the relationship, a PI team can determine whether to solve a problem by focusing solely on that cause. Even though Minitab provides an effortless way to do these calculations, we provide the formulae below as a reference.

$$r = \frac{n\sum(xy) - \sum x \sum y}{\sqrt{\left[n\sum(x^2) - \left(\sum x\right)^2\right]\left[n\sum(y^2) - \left(\sum y\right)^2\right]}}$$

Where:
  n = sample size
  y = dependent variable (e.g., number of patient falls)
  x = independent variable (e.g., staffing levels in man hours)
  r = coefficient of correlation

Using Minitab, the coefficient of correlation r for the example in Table 7.14 is −0.948, which is a very strong negative correlation.

Discussion Questions and Problems

7.1. Give at least one example of attribute data in each of the following areas of a hospital:
  - Dietary services
  - Business office
  - Pharmacy
  - Radiology
  - Nursing
  - Housekeeping
  - Facilities maintenance
  - Human resources

7.2. The following data represents the number of misdiagnoses for a particular DRG based on a subgroup size of 50 patients:

Subgroup	Subgroup Size	Number Misdiagnosed
1	50	2
2	50	4
3	50	1
4	50	6
5	50	2
6	50	3
7	50	5
8	50	0
9	50	5
10	50	2
11	50	4
12	50	10
13	50	5
14	50	2
15	50	6
16	50	1
17	50	5

18	50	3
19	50	7
20	50	2
21	50	0
22	50	4
23	50	1
24	50	5

  – What type of control chart is needed for this problem?
  – Calculate the center line, UCL, and LCL.
  – Is there evidence of an unstable process? If so, what actions would you take to stabilize the process?

7.3. The dietary department of a hospital has recently implemented a short survey instrument for its cafeteria. The survey consists of only four questions. Each question has a five-point rating system. A rating of 1 or 2 is considered negative, while a 4 or 5 is considered positive. The table on the next page shows the number of negative responses in each of the 24 subgroups. Each subgroup contains 25 surveys.

Subgroup	Subgroup Size	Number of Negative Response
1	25	4
2	25	4
3	25	10
4	25	6
5	25	9
6	25	6
7	25	5
8	25	8
9	25	5
10	25	8
11	25	4
12	25	10

13	25	20
14	25	8
15	25	10
16	25	8
17	25	5
18	25	11
19	25	6
20	25	4
21	25	4
22	25	12
23	25	1
24	25	5

- What type of control chart is needed for this problem?
- Calculate the center line, UCL, and LCL.
- Is there evidence of an unstable process? If so, what actions would you take to stabilize the process?

7.4. The table on the next page represents the turnaround time (in hours) for lab results at the local hospital. Statistics for 25 subgroups were gathered, with each subgroup consisting of the turnaround times for four lab test results selected at random.

Subgroup	X_1	X_2	X_3	X_4
1	20	15	17	22
2	15	19	21	14
3	17	12	15	23
4	16	18	14	22
5	20	17	15	18
6	18	19	21	10
7	22	20	18	19
8	16	15	24	16
9	14	16	21	19

10	19	21	17	15
11	13	15	18	19
12	19	18	15	15
13	23	12	13	16
14	15	16	15	17
15	18	16	15	17
16	23	21	20	16
17	16	23	17	21
18	14	16	19	19
19	17	17	21	14
20	16	21	19	18
21	18	18	18	25
22	15	17	16	22
23	19	14	14	19
24	14	23	21	19
25	16	18	20	13

- Calculate the values for the average (x) and the range (R).
- Determine the values for the center line.
- Calculate the UCL and the LCL
- Is there any evidence of an unstable process? If so, what action would you take to correct it?

7.5. Provide three examples of variable data in each of the following hospital-based departments:
- Dietary services
- Housekeeping
- Pharmacy
- Facilities maintenance
- Telephone switchboard
- Nursing services

7.6. Give three examples of variable data in each of the following service-based departments of a managed care organization:
- Member services
- Underwriting claims processing

- Physician credentialing
- Care coordination
7.7. Give three examples of variable data in each of the following home health-care agency functions:
  - Patient intake
  - Accounts receivable
  - Coordination of care

References

AHRQ, 2017. 20 Tips to Help Prevent Medical Errors: Patient Fact Sheet. Content last reviewed May 2017. Agency for Healthcare Research and Quality, Rockville, MD. http://www.ahrq.gov/patients-consumers/care-planning/errors/20tips/index.html

Brennan, T. A., Leape, L. L., Laird, N. M., Hebert, L., Localio, A. R., Lawthers, A. G., Newhouse, J. P., Weiler, P. C. and Hiatt, H. H., 1991, February 7. "Incidence of Adverse Events and Negligence in Hospitalized Patients. Results of the Harvard Medical Practice Study." *The New England Journal of Medicine* 324(6): 370–376.

Makary, M.A. and Daniel, M., 2016 "Medical Error – the Third Leading Cause of Death in the US. *BMJ* doi: https://doi.org/10.1136/bmj.i2139.

Reason, J. T., 1990. *Human Error.* Cambridge, MA: Cambridge University Press.

Additional Readings

AHRQ Health Care Innovation Exchange, 2008. https://innovations.ahrq.gov/qualitytools/plan-do-study-act-pdsa-cycle

General Electric (GE). What Is Six Sigma? https://www.ge.com/en/company/companyinfo/quality/whatis.htm

Omachonu, V., 1999. *Healthcare Performance Improvement.* Norcross, GA: Engineering and Management Press, Institute of Industrial Engineers, IIE.

Pexton, C., 2018. Measuring Six Sigma Results in the Healthcare Industry. In Six Sigma. https://www.isixsigma.com/industries/healthcare/measuring-six-sigma-results-healthcare-industry/#comment-165753

Chapter 8

Creating Value Through Digital Transformation

Digital transformation is a recurring theme among healthcare executives and industry leaders. No sector of the economy is insulated from the effects of digital transformation and the wave of transformative change occurring at every level. It is important to know that digital transformation is not just about introducing computers in a hospital, creating apps, enabling patients to make appointments online, giving healthcare staff the option of using their own smartphones or tablets, or opening a Facebook or Twitter account for the hospital. While these technological options may be part of the digital transformation journey, the merit of digital transformation cannot be reduced to the use of a specific technology.

Digital transformation assesses factors beyond the walls of healthcare organizations, including the patients' experience before, during, and after interacting with the healthcare system. It goes to the very core of what an organization does, including why and how it does it. The journey begins with the simple realization that this is not a fad or technology to be installed, but what could be the engine that drives an organization's existence. The most logical starting point is to put the patient at the center of the transformation.

To compete today, healthcare organizations must retool the skillset of their workforce to be digitally agile and fluent. These qualities cannot be achieved when healthcare organizations lack skilled teams, new data, and technology integration; have slow or inflexible processes; and use outdated or obsolete technology. As the healthcare industry becomes more value-based, there is mounting pressure on hospitals and health systems to change the way they do business by improving quality of care, efficiency, and the patients' experience. Hence, digital technology is helping many hospitals navigate healthcare's changing landscape.

The Meaning of Digital

Digital refers to a broad range of technologies and applications that enable more efficient automation, better decision making, stronger connectivity with customers and other external stakeholders, and more advanced data-driven innovations. Digital technologies include electronic systems, devices, tools, and resources that generate, store, or process data. These include mobile devices, cloud computing, social media, multimedia, productivity technology, and interoperable systems. These technologies are deployed as intelligent processes that create a cycle of continuous improvement and feedback, as well as develop sophisticated models that allow people and software to make real-time adjustments and decisions. Digital technologies enhance our ability to identify opportunities for adaptation, analyze cost benefits, and then adapt quicker and more efficiently. Digital capabilities make it possible for intelligent processes to swiftly identify opportunities for improvement and for other digital technologies such as artificial intelligence (AI) and robotics to execute these changes quickly.

Most healthcare executives believe that quality healthcare can be achieved by leveraging information technology (IT) services and a digital platform. What remains unclear is where to invest, what technologies deliver the greatest benefits for patients and healthcare providers, and the corresponding return on investment. The key players in the healthcare ecosystem are beginning to recognize the value of digitization and digital transformation. They are visualizing digital transformation in the context of enhancing patient-centeredness, improving productivity and the employee experience, and finding new ways of delivering care. Newer digital technologies such as mobile apps, social media, smartphones, big data, predictive analytics, and the cloud, among others, touch the patients directly and in that process create value while increasing revenue. In the aggregate, digital healthcare and healthcare information technology consist of four key areas (i-SCOOP, 2016):

1. Electronic medical records (EMR)/electronic health records (EHR)—digital versions of patients' medical history (patient chart); tied to a specific practice

2. Telehealth—information and health (data/communications) via electronic communication (also email)
3. Mobile health (or mHealth)—via mobile devices (including wearables, smartphone, laptop)
4. Wireless health—wireless technology for medicine (diagnosis, treatment, remote monitoring)

Digital transformation is not just about technology. It is about the challenges facing healthcare across the entire ecosystem, including innovation, building a viable and sustainable future for healthcare, and leveraging technology and the abundant, yet unstructured data and information. This is especially important because of the challenges of dealing with security, privacy, and compliance as they relate to personal data. Organizations slow to digitize their offerings and operations (i.e., to adopt a digital-native operating model) over the next three years will find themselves competing for only a minority—and a progressively shrinking minority—of their market segments' opportunities (IDC FutureScape, 2017). According to FutureScape, by 2020, 60% of all enterprises will have effected an organization-wide digital transformation platform strategy and will be in the process of implementing that strategy as the new IT core for competing in the digital economy. This prediction is about a new enterprise IT foundation for digital transformation: a new way of designing, sourcing, integrating, and running IT that accelerates digital innovation at the scale and pace required to compete in the digital transformation economy. The increasing role of AI is inescapable to healthcare executives. By 2019, 40% of digital transformation initiatives will use AI services; by 2021, 75% of commercial enterprise apps will use AI; over 90% of consumers will interact with customer support bots; and over 50% of new industrial robots will leverage AI (IDC FutureScape, 2017).

Digital Health Applications

Mobile applications offer people the ability to monitor, manage, and improve their health, reach their wellness goals, and interact with their healthcare provider. In 2017, there were 325,000 mobile health apps in use via the App store. Since 2016, 78,000 new apps have been added to major app stores (Research2Guidance, 2017). The majority of the applications utilize advanced technology and are quite easy to use.

Digital health apps can improve value-based care through appointment reminders, the monitoring of patients with chronic conditions, and other functions that can improve the overall health of a patient population. There are several types of digital health tools in use today. The IQVIA Institute for Human Data Science lists 11 categories of digital health tools in their report "The Growing Value of Digital Health" (IQVIA Institute for Human Data Science, 2017):

- Consumer mobile apps
- Consumer wearables
- Connected biometric sensors
- Smartphone cameras
- Clinical trial patient information collection tools
- In-home connected virtual assistants
- Telemedicine and virtual physician visits
- Personal health records
- Web-based interactive programs
- Text messaging or email
- Health system disease management apps

In the IQVIA definition, digital health is mHealth.

Healthcare organizations seeking digital transformation must transform processes, business models, and the customer experience by creating the appropriate digital connections among systems, people, locations, and things. Large or small, all hospitals, clinics, urgent care centers, nursing homes, and emergency rooms can use digital technology to achieve their aims. Most healthcare professionals (physicians, nurses, technicians, medical assistants, nurse practitioners, etc.) serve only one small slice of their patients' overall ecosystem, thus limiting their opportunity to meet their customers' end-to-end needs. An inside-out focus on delivering healthcare services ignores the fact that patients' desires are at the heart of their personal value ecosystems.

Medical professionals who can pivot their approach to a fundamentally outside-in patient-outcome mindset create new opportunities for growth. To do this, healthcare organizations must re-envision themselves not as a set of products and services, but as part of a personal value ecosystem. This notion challenges the nature of a healthcare organization's relationships with its patients and partners. It also enables healthcare organizations to increase the value that they provide by digitally enhancing existing services. As a start, a healthcare company must first focus on how digital assets enhance the outcomes that its patients most value.

Organizations must create new sources of value through digital partnerships. By focusing on the patient's desired outcome, healthcare organizations can uncover opportunities to achieve those outcomes in new ways by partnering with other providers already in the patient's personal value ecosystem. The use of data and analytics to help patients achieve their desired outcomes is vital to any culture of digital transformation. Healthcare businesses that collect data from thousands or even millions of patient encounters have access to a potential treasure trove of insights. The real opportunity lies in mining the data that is already collected and combining it with external data, which together opens new digital business possibilities. Hospitals and other leading healthcare organizations are using predictive analytics for identifying and stratifying patient risks for chronic and acute conditions, including hepatitis C, sepsis, suicide risks, mental health, medication adherence, and diabetes, among others. When hospitals can combine data from patients (including wearables, fitness monitors, mobile health applications, and weight scales) with data from hospital EHRs and other available records, hospitals can fully take advantage of predictive analytics to help manage the health of the patient as well as the population. Digital businesses understand that, to win in the age of the patient, they must become a patient-centered organization. Success means investing in constantly evolving patient experiences and understanding that technology has become fundamental to how patients perceive value. Digital and AI technologies can help enable on-demand interaction and seamless processes aimed at improving the patient experience. Robotic process automation (RPA) and AI can allow caregivers to spend more time providing care and less time documenting it.

Impact on Employees

One of the benefits of digital transformation is employee satisfaction. When employees are equipped with innovative technologies that can improve their productivity while enhancing the process of care delivery, it is a win-win for all stakeholders. Employees across all age groups, especially Millennials, want to work for organizations that show a strong commitment to the pursuit of digital maturity. Healthcare leaders must consider this factor to attract and retain the best talent. According to a survey of more than 4,800 business executives by the *MIT Sloan Management Review* and Deloitte, across age groups from 22 to 60, the vast majority of respondents want to work for digitally enabled organizations (Kane et al., 2015).

Employees will be on the lookout for the best digital opportunities, and businesses must continually up their digital game to retain and attract them (Kane et al., 2015).

Role of Leadership

A successful business strategy for a digital transformation, therefore, requires a comprehensive digitization talent strategy with the right leadership competencies. There are striking distinctions between digital and non-digital leaders. The distinctions include the ability to create and articulate a clear digital strategy combined with a culture and leadership poised to drive the transformation. The healthcare industry is replete with examples of companies focusing on technologies without investing in organizational capabilities that ensure their impact.

Although leaders do not need an IT degree to lead a digital culture, they must understand what is possible and what lies at the intersection of patient needs and technology. They should also be prepared to lead the way in making the case for how technology can transform their organization. According to Kane et al., 2015, the digital agenda is led from the top. Their survey revealed that digitally maturing organizations are nearly twice as likely as less digitally mature entities to have a single person or group leading the effort (Kane et al., 2015). In addition, employees in digitally maturing organizations are highly confident in their leaders' digital fluency. However, Kane et al. noted that digital fluency does not demand mastery of these technologies. Instead, it requires the ability to articulate the value of digital technologies to the organization's future.

Generally, digital strategies go beyond the technologies themselves. They include improvements in process innovation, decision making and, ultimately, transforming how the business achieves its aims. Many healthcare organizations will be forced to postpone the journey toward digital transformation because their organizational culture would make such an undertaking daunting. Essential ingredients in the quest for digital transformation such as increased collaboration and risk taking constitute major constraints in the pursuit of digital transformation. Healthcare leaders must also understand what aspects of the current culture could spur greater digital transformation growth. Healthcare organizational cultures must be prepared to embrace analytics and the use of data in decision making and processes.

Important First Steps in Implementing a Digital Strategy

1. *Senior Leadership Education*: The leader's role in the early stages of the journey is to become educated on the subject of digital transformation and its importance. There are several offerings of executive seminars, webinars, and educational sessions by reputable organizations regarding digital transformation. Senior management should be digitally fluent, which means it must be able to articulate the value of digital technologies to the organization's future.

2. *Develop a Strategic Vision*: Armed with this new knowledge and the organization's reality, the leader should develop a strategic vision for digital transformation. This vision should center on the impact of digital transformation on the patient experience, employee experience, other healthcare partners, and organizational efficiency.

3. *Make the Case for Digital Transformation*: The leader should "take the show on the road" to make his/her case and sell the concept to the staff and the governing board. It is imperative that senior management understands the significance of a digital future and should drive support for its implementation at all organizational levels.

4. *Define the Current and Future Culture and Its Gaps*: Using a series of focus group sessions, a staff survey/s, senior leadership insights, and industry best practices, the leader should identify the current and future state of digital transformation for the organization. The gaps should be mapped between the current and future states and a plan developed for mitigating these gaps. This process should be done cross-functionally across several layers of the organization. In addition, the leader should be sure to involve Millennials and newer employees in the process.

5. *Develop a Priority Action List*: Establish a list of priority areas, metrics, and an action plan, or road map, for implementation. The roadmap should include the required leadership competencies for digital transformation and the steps to achieve them.

6. *Connect Interdependent Technologies for Improved Communication*: Digital implementation is complex and involves several moving parts. Connecting disparate applications, devices, locations, and

technologies—all highly interdependent—and making certain they talk to each other are all essential to a successful digital implementation journey. Digital technologies are always evolving; thus, adaptability and scalability are critical.

7. *Reliance on Solid Data*: The need for reliable data cannot be overemphasized. To achieve the goals of data scalability, interoperability, productivity, and adaptability, the entire process should be based on a solid framework of capturing, storing, securing, and analyzing data.

8. *Fine Tune the Talent Pool*: The investment in digital technologies should be matched with a significant investment in cultivating the talent pool that will use the technologies. Senior leadership should provide employees ample opportunities to develop and master the corresponding digital skills.

Questions for Discussion

8.1. Name three companies within or outside the healthcare industry that represent best practice when it comes to digital transformation. How has digital technology transformed these organizations?

8.2. What are some of the barriers to digital transformation in the healthcare industry? How can the industry overcome them?

8.3. Which of the digital technologies pose the most challenge or risk to patients, and why? What steps can the industry take to mitigate the risks?

8.4. What are some of the lessons learned from other industries that could help the healthcare industry regarding digital transformation? Why are these lessons significant?

8.5. Give an example of the applications of digital technologies in the areas of treatment, diagnosis, communication, patient education, prevention, safety, and medication adherence.

References

IDC FutureScape, 2017. Worldwide IT Industry 2018 Predictions. IDC #US43171317.
IQVIA Institute for Human Data Science, 2017. The Growing Value of Digital Health. https://www.iqvia.com/institute/reports/the-growing-value-of-digital-health

i-SCOOP, 2016. Healthcare in Digital Transformation: Digital and Connected Healthcare. https://www.i-scoop.eu/digital-transformation/healthcare-industry /#Healthcare_and_digital_transformation_challenges_and_considerations

Kane, G. C., Palmer, D., Phillips, A. N., Kiron, D., and Buckley, N., 2015. Deloitte Insights. Strategy, Not Technology, Drives Digital Transformation. MITSloan Management Review. https://www2.deloitte.com/insights/us/en/topics/digital -transformation/digital-transformation-strategy-digitally-mature.html

Research2Guidance, 2017. 325,000 Mobile Health Apps Available in 2017—Android Now the Leading mHealth Platform. https://research2guidance.com/32500 0-mobile-health-apps-available-in-2017/

Chapter 9

Telemedicine: The Quest for Quality and Value

What Is Telemedicine?

Telemedicine is the use of telecommunications technology such as phones and computers to provide clinical services to patients who lack access to care. Healthcare professionals can diagnose, treat, and monitor patients by using teleconferencing, phone calls, emails, mobile apps, image sharing, and even video chat without the need for long journeys or in-person hospital consultations. Telemedicine is rapidly transforming how healthcare is delivered throughout the world. There were just over one million telehealth consults in 2016, with an addressable market estimated of more than 400 million potential telehealth consults (Guttman, 2017). For older Americans, Guttman notes, a review of medical records found that 38 percent of doctor visits, including 27 percent of emergency room (ER) visits could have been replaced with telemedicine. A report from information and analytics firm IHS Markit (reported by Japsen, 2015) says video consultations will jump to nearly 27 million in the U.S. market, driven by the primary care market, where insurance coverage is rapidly widening. IHS Markit projects there will be a cumulative annual growth of nearly 25 percent a year over the next five years to 5.4 million video consultations between primary care providers and their patients by 2020 (reported by Japsen, 2015).

There are many advantages to the use of telemedicine, including the following:

- A significant reduction in the time to see a doctor or to obtain an expert diagnosis

- Access to care twenty-four hours a day, seven days a week.
- Dramatic reduction in the time, cost, and risk associated with transporting frail or very ill patients to the point of treatment.
- Reduces the need for expensive and unnecessary emergency room visits.
- New technologies make it possible to remotely monitor the health conditions of patients, thus leading to early intervention.
- Mitigates the problem caused by shortages of specialist physicians.
- Increased patient engagement as patients are becoming more tech-savvy and even more aware of their health because of the rise of telemedicine and the wide variety of healthcare apps available today. Telemedicine increases patient engagement by helping them maintain checkup appointments and care schedules. Virtual consultations also make it easier for patients to reach out to their physicians, report early warning signs or any health concerns, and follow through on their appointments.
- Telemedicine services can also help businesses, employers, and employees save time and money by reducing absences from work and billable expenses incurred from hospital visits.

Although the use of telemedicine technology comes with significant risks, its benefits, taken individually or collectively, make a forceful case for a healthcare patient value proposition. Patients and physicians are expected to have appropriate hardware and software security in place to ensure the safe transmission of protected health information (PHI) and personally identifiable information (PII) such as Social Security Numbers (SSNs) and detailed medical records. Accordingly, the federal government has set conditions for participating in telemedicine. The conditions outline what facilities must do to be allowed to provide and receive telemedicine services, especially concerning the credentials of participating physicians, their privileges, and the licenses of these doctors and other caregivers. Only Health Insurance Portability and Accountability Act (HIPAA) compliant, encrypted, and secure telemedicine software solutions and messaging apps can be used in transmitting sensitive patient data or electronic protected health information (ePHI) between patients and healthcare providers. Email, SMS, and mobile apps such as Skype, Facebook Messenger, and Google Hangouts were not designed for telemedicine and are not approved for use in communicating private health information and records. When it comes to telemedicine, different states have different licensing rules.

Many studies have examined the impact of telemedicine on healthcare quality. However, very few studies have addressed the quality of telemedicine applications. LeRouge et al. proposed a model for the attributes of quality telemedicine video conferencing (LeRouge et al., 2002). The model contains four quality attribute groups: technical, usability, the physical environment, and the human element.

The challenges of accessing health services in isolated populations where human resources and infrastructure are constrained by vast geographical landmasses create tremendous opportunities for healthcare providers, patients, and families. Telemedicine programs provide specialty health services to remote populations using telecommunications technology. This innovative approach to medical care delivery has been expanding for several years and currently covers various specialty areas such as cardiology, dermatology, rehabilitation, radiology, surgery, home health, and pediatrics. Terms such as telesurgery, telecardiology, telerehabilitation, teledermatology, teledentistry, telehomehealth, teleassessment, telepathology, telemonitoring, etc. have flooded the literature in the last 15 years.

Telemedicine describes a variety of interactions via telephone lines. Telemedicine may be as simple and commonplace as a conversation between a patient and a health professional in the same town or as sophisticated as surgery directed via satellite and video technology from one continent to another.

More than 30 years ago, a physician named Avedis Donabedian proposed a model for assessing healthcare quality based on structures, processes, and outcomes. He defined structure as the environment in which healthcare is provided, process as the method by which healthcare is provided, and outcome as the consequence of the healthcare provided.

Two decades later, the healthcare field adopted continuous quality improvement strategies, which use teams to improve processes. According to Donabedian's model, processes are constrained by the structures in which they operate.

According to Donabedian (1988), before assessment can begin we must decide how quality is to be defined, and that depends on whether one assesses only the performance of practitioners or in addition the contributions of patients and the healthcare system. It also depends on how broadly health and responsibility for health are defined and whether individual or social preferences define the optimum. Donabedian added that we also need detailed information about the causal linkages among the structural attributes of the settings in which care occurs, the processes of care, and the outcomes of care. Even though so much work has been done regarding quality assessment in healthcare, quality assessment remains in its infancy as it relates to telemedicine.

Telemedicine presents the opportunity to use information and communication technology to overcome some of the limitations imposed by scarce resources. For example, the lack of physicians with specialty stroke training represents a significant challenge to the future of stroke research (Switzer et al., 2009). This deficit limits both quality stroke care and clinical research initiatives. According to Switzer et al., the use of telemedicine for stroke (telestroke) has been an attempt to overcome this shortage and extend stroke expertise to locations lacking coverage. However, initial telestroke systems required a point-to-point connection for transmission and only provided videoconferencing, which limited their generalizability and usefulness (Switzer et al., 2009). Singh et al. (2009) note that telestroke based on the remote evaluation of an acute ischemic stroke model can also be utilized so that selected stroke patients can be given an intravenous tissue plasminogen activator in the emergency department (ED) of a regional hospital with the supervision of a stroke neurologist.

The growing influence of telemedicine across the globe has created the need to examine the issues of quality of care. An increasing number of people can send data from their home to their doctor using the Internet. Moreover, the widespread availability of broadband opens up the possibility of real-time videoconferencing with clinicians. It is already possible for patients at home to monitor simple variables, such as heart rate and blood pressure, and send their results using communication technologies to their doctors, who can promptly review the information to diagnose problems. As healthcare approaches a point of convergence among diagnostic, treatment, health education, and communication technologies, more patients can now transmit more complex healthcare data periodically to their doctors, who can identify problems early and thus modify disease management to prevent the exacerbation of patients' medical conditions. According to Malik, this will allow improved patient care in a wide range of healthcare situations, from acute medical conditions to chronic disease (Malik, 2009).

Aoki et al. reviewed 104 articles published from 1966 to 2000 to investigate telemedicine evaluation studies respecting methods and outcomes (Aoki et al., 2003). A total of 112 evaluations were reported in these 104 articles. Two types of evaluations were assessed: clinical and nonclinical. Within the clinical evaluations, three dealt with clinical effectiveness; twenty-six with patient satisfaction; forty-nine with diagnostic accuracy;

and nine with cost. In the non-clinical evaluations, 15 articles discussed technical issues relating to digital images, such as bandwidth, resolution, and color, and 10 articles assessed management issues concerning efficiency of care, such as avoiding unnecessary patient transfers or saving time. Of the 112 evaluations, 72 were descriptive in nature. The main methods used in the remaining 40 articles used quantitative methods. Nineteen articles employed statistical techniques, such as a receiver operating characteristics curve (three evaluations) and kappa values (seven evaluations). Only one article utilized a qualitative approach to describe a telemedicine system.

Currently, there are several good reports on diagnostic accuracy, satisfaction, and technological evaluation. However, clinical effectiveness and cost-effectiveness are important parameters, and they have received limited attention. Since telemedicine evaluations tend to explore various outcomes, it may be appropriate to evaluate them from a multidisciplinary perspective and to utilize various methodologies (Aoki et al., 2003).

According to Durrani and Khoja, the number of published articles on telehealth in Asia increased during the study review period (Durrani and Khoja, 2009). The largest number of studies were conducted in Japan (37 percent). Most telehealth applications were based on the store-and-forward modality (43 percent), with 35 percent using videoconferencing and 15 percent using a hybrid approach. Most of the studies were descriptive (75 percent), and only eight included a control group against which telehealth was compared. The most common means of telecommunication was Integrated Services Digital Network (ISDN) lines, which were employed in 32 percent of the studies. Some 40 percent of the studies mentioned improved quality of healthcare; about 20 percent mentioned improved access to healthcare. Although most studies mentioned cost, only 13 assessed resource utilization and cost (Durrani and Khoja, 2009).

Boaz et al. (2009) note that patient satisfaction can be enhanced through telemedicine. They added that, though post-treatment metabolic differences were not observed between treatment groups, the telemedicine group reported significantly greater post-treatment experiences regarding improved quality of life and sense of control over the disease.

Quality, access, and efficiency are the general key issues for the success of eHealth and telemedicine implementation (Vitacca et al., 2009). The real technology is the human resources available to organizations. For eHealth and telemedicine to grow, it will be necessary to investigate their long-term efficacy, cost-effectiveness, possible improvement to quality of life, and impact on the public health burden (Vitacca et al., 2009). Since the implications for outcomes and costs are high, it is imperative to address the quality issues affecting telemedicine as the technology evolves. Telehealth, a cost-effective way to promote improved health management, is suitable for most patients. Only minor adjustments in management will be needed to accommodate individual preferences to increase patient satisfaction (LaFramboise et al., 2009).

Donabedian's (1988) classic paradigm for assessing quality of care is based on a three-component approach—structure, process, and outcomes. Donabedian's model proposes that each component has a direct influence on the next. Structure refers to the attributes of the settings in which providers deliver healthcare, including material resources (e.g. EHRs), human resources (e.g. staff expertise), and organizational structure (e.g. hospitals vs. clinics). For example, a cardiologist may use a disease registry to track whether a patient with cardiovascular disease is receiving drugs for lowering cholesterol. Process of care denotes what is actually done to the patient in the giving and receiving of care. Building on the example above, the provider could review whether an eligible patient has been placed on an angiotensin-converting enzyme inhibitor to help prevent future heart attacks. Health outcomes are the direct result of a patient's health status because of his/her contact with the healthcare system. In the above example, the patient's receiving the preventive medications mentioned could decrease the chance of dying from a heart attack. For the purpose of this paper, we focus on two of the three components of Donabedian's model—structure and process. Many previous studies have addressed the subject of outcomes quite comprehensively.

Structure-Related Measures of Quality

Healthcare's structure reflects the setting or system in which care is delivered. Many structural measures describe hospital-level attributes, such as the physical plant and resources or staff coordination and organization (e.g. RN–bed ratios or a designation as a Level I trauma center). Other structural measures reflect attributes associated with the relative expertise of individual physicians (e.g. board certification, subspecialty training, or procedure volume).

Process of Care Measures

Processes of care are the clinical interventions and services provided to patients. Although they are only occasionally applied as performance measures for surgery (e.g. the appropriate use of perioperative antibiotics), process measures are the predominant quality indicators for both inpatient and outpatient medical care. Switzer et al. (2009) envision Telestroke 2.0, an integrative web-based telestroke system combining high-quality audiovideo transmission, the ability for consults and teleradiology to be conducted from any desktop or laptop computer with web access, decision and technical support, the creation of billable physician documentation, and electronic medical record connectivity (Switzer et al., 2009). In addition, a multimedia messaging service can transmit important scan images to experienced staff to facilitate accurate and prompt diagnosis and commence optimal treatments.

The Institute of Medicine (IOM) Model

Another model for evaluating quality issues in telemedicine is based on the Institute of Medicine's (IOM's) six aims of quality healthcare. The report *Crossing the Quality Chasm: A New Health System for the 21st Century* calls for national action to address serious and well-documented quality shortcomings in the U.S. healthcare system (IOM, 2001). The report proposes a restructuring of the healthcare delivery system so Americans will consistently receive the quality of care they deserve. To this end, the report recommends the adoption of six quality aims for improvement, defined as follows:

- *Safe*: Avoiding injuries to patients from the care intended to help them
- *Effective*: Providing services based on scientific knowledge to all who could benefit and refraining from providing services to those not likely to benefit (avoiding underuse and overuse, respectively)
- *Patient-Centered*: Providing care that is respectful of and responsive to individual patient preferences, needs, and values and ensuring that patient values guide all clinical decisions
- *Timely*: Reducing wait times and sometimes harmful delays for both those who receive and those who give care
- *Efficient*: Avoiding waste, including waste of equipment, supplies, ideas, and energy
- *Equitable*: Providing care that does not vary in quality because of personal characteristics such as gender, ethnicity, geographic location, and socioeconomic status

Despite the attractiveness of tele-intensive care unit (ICU) and its increasing adoption, few trials have evaluated its effect on outcomes. Therefore, it is not yet clear in what situations, if any, the potential benefits might be realized. Early studies, each performed at a single center and comparing care before and after the implementation of a tele-ICU system, documented decreases in length of stay (LOS), mortality, and cost, first in an academic-affiliated community hospital and subsequently in a tertiary-care hospital (Rosenfeld et al., 2000; Breslow et al., 2004).

In this chapter, we propose a merger between Donabedian's model (structure and process), and the IOM model to identify 12 dimensions for evaluating quality in telemedicine (Table 9.1). In Table 9.2, we explain the intersections between the two models (Figure 9.1).

Dimensions of Quality Measurement in Telemedicine

Using the combination of the models from the IOM and Donabedian, we arrive at a confluence of powerful ideas that make it possible to evaluate quality in telemedicine. This combination presents 12 dimensions for evaluating quality, as shown in Tables 9.1 and 9.2, above. The following is a brief description of the dimensions and the corresponding research questions:

Safety and Structure: Safety addresses how to avoid injuries to patients from the care intended to help them. Structure refers to the attributes of the settings in which providers deliver healthcare, including material resources (e.g. EHRs), human resources (e.g. staff expertise), and organizational structure (e.g. hospitals vs. clinics). The healthcare structure reflects the setting or system in which care is delivered. The research question is: Does the structure of the telemedicine application help

Table 9.1   Twelve Dimensions of Quality Telemedicine

Institute of Medicine Model	Donabedian's Partial Model	
	Structure	Process
Safety	1	2
Effectiveness	3	4
Patient-Centered	5	6
Timely	7	8
Efficient	9	10
Equitable	11	12

Table 9.2   Explanation of Intersections between Donabedian's Model and IOM Model

Institute of Medicine Model	Donabedian's Process/Structure	
	Structure	*Process*
Safety	How is safety affected by the structure of TM?	How is safety affected by the TM process?
Effectiveness	How does the structure of TM affect effectiveness?	How effective is the process used in delivering TM?
Patient-Centered	What is the impact of the structure of TM on patient-centeredness?	Is the TM process as patient-centered as it needs to be?
Timely	How does the structure of TM affect timeliness?	How does the process affect the timeliness of TM?
Efficient	How does the structure of TM affect efficiency?	How does the process affect the efficiency of TM?
Equitable	Does the structure of TM make it possible to deliver services in an equitable manner?	What is the impact of the process on the equitable delivery of care?

avoid or prevent injuries to the patients from the care intended to help them? According to the Telemedicine Research Center (TRC), a nonprofit public research organization based in Portland, Oregon, two types of technology are used in most telemedicine applications. The first type stores and sends digital images taken with a digital camera from one location to another. The most common application of this kind of telemedicine is teleradiology—sending X-rays, computerized tomography (CT) scans, or MRIs from one facility to another. The other type of technology described by the TRC is two-way interactive television

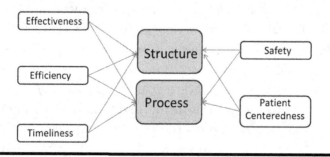

Figure 9.1   Framework of intersections between models.

(IATV), which uses video-teleconferencing equipment to create a meeting between a patient and primary care physician in one location and a physician specialist elsewhere when a face-to-face consultation is not feasible because of time or distance. Peripheral equipment even enables the consulting physician specialist to perform a virtual physical examination and hear the patient's heart sounds through a stethoscope.

The availability of desktop videoconferencing has expanded this form of telemedicine from a novelty found exclusively in urban, university teaching hospitals to a valuable tool for patients and physicians in rural areas who were previously underserved and unable to access specialists readily. The same technology may be used to send slides or images from the pathology laboratory to another physician or laboratory for a second opinion.

Another example of the use of digital image transfer is the rural primary care physician who, miles from the nearest dermatologist can send a photograph of a patient's rash or lesion and receive an immediate, long-distance consultation from the dermatologist. There are significant safety challenges posed by locations in rural areas, especially regarding technology, power supply, and qualified personnel.

One application of telemedicine that uses only the standard telephone line in a patient's home is transtelephonic pacemaker monitoring. Cardiac technicians at the other end of the telephone can check the implanted cardiac pacemaker's functions, including the status of its battery. Transtelephonic pacemaker monitoring can identify early signs of possible pacemaker failure and detect potential pacemaker system abnormalities, thereby reducing the number of emergency replacements. It can also send an electrocardiogram (ECG) rhythm strip to a patient's cardiologist. Additionally, some of the communities that would benefit most from telemedicine do not have the telecommunications equipment necessary to deliver the bandwidth for telemedicine (http://www.libraryi ndex.com/pages/1866/Change-Challenges-Innovation-in-Health-Care-D elivery-INFORMATION-COMMUNICATION-TECHNOLOGY.html, 2009).

Safety and Process: *Safety* addresses how to avoid injuries to patients from the care intended to help them. *Processes of care* are the clinical interventions and services provided to patients. *Process of care* denotes what is actually done to the patient in the giving and receiving of care. The risk factors vary depending on the particular application of telemedicine. Teleradiology, for example, involves sending X-rays, CT scans, or MRIs from one facility to another. The same technology may be used to send slides or images from the pathology laboratory to another physician or laboratory for a second opinion. There is no independent way to verify the qualifications of the individuals interpreting the images or ascertain the quality of the images. Varghese and Phillips (372009) studied how advanced practice nurses (APNs) cared for their telehealth patients. According to Varghese, they did so by (1) being with them, (2) personifying the images, and (3) possessing certain attributes. The major constructs that emerged from the data together formed a model of how APNs conveyed caring in telehealth.

As the menu of telehealth services (telesurgery, telecardiology, telerehabilitation, teledermatology, teledentistry, telehomehealth, teleassessment, telepathology, etc.) grows, it is imperative to evaluate the point of convergence between safety and process. According to Lee et al. (2010), parents reported positive perceptions about telemedical retinopathy of prematurity (ROP) diagnoses, but expressed a preference for face-to-face care. Thus, telemedicine has the potential to alter the nature of the patient-physician relationship. The resulting research question is: What are the safety issues involved in the widely divergent scope of applications in the field of telemedicine? Are the risk factors significantly different from process to process for each application? Does the absence of a face-to-face interaction predispose certain patients to safety concerns? Does the departure from traditional physician-patient communication create possible safety issues?

Sandberg et al. (2009) conducted a study to better understand the experiences of providers and the factors they perceive contribute to the success of telehealth interventions and their own satisfaction. Face-to-face or telephone interviews were conducted with 10 diabetes educators (nurses and dietitians) who served as providers of a telemedicine case management intervention for older adults who have diabetes. Qualitative analyses revealed that providers were very satisfied with their experience and felt their efforts with patients were generally successful. Providers also identified several unique benefits to telehealth interventions. These included opportunities for more frequent contact with patients, greater relaxation and information due to the ability to interact with the patients in their own homes, increased ability to reach the underserved, more timely and accurate medical monitoring, and improved data management. The primary disadvantages of telehealth they identified were technology problems and a concern about the lack of physical contact with patients.

Effectiveness and Structure: Effectiveness is determined in the context of providing services based on scientific knowledge to all who could benefit and refraining from providing services to those not likely to benefit (avoiding underuse and overuse, respectively). Structure refers to the attributes of the settings in which providers deliver healthcare, including material resources (e.g. EHRs), human resources (e.g. staff expertise), and organizational structure (e.g. hospitals vs. clinics). Healthcare structure reflects the setting or system in which care is delivered. Two important questions arise, as follows: i) Does the structure of a telemedicine application support the quest for effectiveness? and ii) Is effectiveness compatible with the structure of a telemedicine program?

Despite the promise of telemedicine, several obstacles prevent Americans from realizing all its potential benefits. As of July 2004, many states in the United States did not permit physicians who are not licensed in their states to practice telemedicine, and the Centers for Medicare and Medicaid Services will reimburse for interactive teleconference services but not digital image transfer. Although insurance coverage is rapidly widening, some private insurers are reluctant to pay for telemedicine, and some physicians fear additional liability (i.e., medical malpractice suits or other litigation) arising from telemedicine.

Warshaw et al. (2009) investigated the diagnostic and management effectiveness of teledermatology. They noted that, in general, the diagnostic accuracy of teledermatology was inferior, whereas the management of teledermatology was equivalent to a clinic's dermatology. However, for the important subgroup of malignant pigmented lesions, both the diagnostic and management accuracy of teledermatology was generally inferior to a clinic's dermatology and up to seven of thirty-six index melanomas would have been mismanaged via teledermatology. They advised that teledermatology and teledermatoscopy should be used with caution for patients with suspected malignant pigmented lesions.

A study conducted by the Mayo Clinic, Rochester, Minnesota, and the University of California, San Diego, California, shows the benefit of telemedicine in stroke diagnosis. Six rural hospitals were connected to specialists at two primary stroke centers using a video feed from a mobile robotic telemedicine camera system positioned near the patients' beds. Subsequently, 276 patients with stroke symptoms at their respective emergency departments were randomly assigned to telephone consultations versus two-way telemedicine consultations. Using telemedicine, the correct diagnosis was made 96 percent of the time versus 83 percent by telephone. The percentage of patients eligible for thrombolysis was raised from 5 percent to 29 percent. In other words, the study confirmed that telemedicine is a viable evaluation tool for acute stroke. The results of the study were presented at the 2010 International Stroke Conference in San Antonio, Texas, in February 2018. These results support the hypothesis that, compared with telephone consultations, the telemedicine evaluation of stroke patients results in more accurate diagnoses, better emergency decision making, fewer complications, and encouraging long-term outcomes.

Stroke Team Remote Evaluation using a Digital Observation Camera (STRokE DOC) connects stroke specialists at a hub site to a remote spoke site using an internet connection. Current data reveals that only 55 percent of Americans have access to primary stroke centers within 60 minutes. Roughly 135 million people in the United States do not have access to a primary stroke facility within an hour of their home.

Effectiveness and Process

The better we manage the technical, organizational, medical, legal, and economic challenges of telemedicine, the better we can minimize the limitations of telemedical home monitoring (Jurgens et al., 2009).

There has been growth in home healthcare technology in rural areas. However, a significant limitation has been the need for costly, repetitive training for patients to efficiently use their home telemedicine unit (HTU). A study by Lai et al. (2009) describes the evaluation of an architecture for remotely training patients in a telemedicine environment. This work examines the viability of a remote training architecture called Remote Patient Education in a Telemedicine Environment (REPETE). REPETE was implemented and evaluated in the context of the Informatics for Diabetes and Education Telemedicine (IDEATel) project, a large-scale telemedicine project focusing on Medicare beneficiaries with diabetes in New York state. Patients not only reported that the training was beneficial, but also showed significant improvements in their ability to effectively perform tasks on their home telemedicine unit. REPETE was determined to be an effective remote training tool for older adults in the telemedicine environment.

According to Sevean et al. (2009), patients and families' experiences of their telehealth visits centered on three key themes: lessening the burden (costs of travel, accommodations, lost wages, lost time, and physical limitations), maximizing supports (access to family, friends, familiar home environment, nurses, and other care providers), and tailoring specific eHealth systems to enhance patient and family needs. Their study indicates that video telehealth is an effective mechanism for delivering nursing and other health services to rural and remote communities and can ameliorate the quality of healthcare. Hence, the integration of telehealth practices can enhance the coordination, organization, and implementation of healthcare services.

In a study on the effectiveness of physician-patient communication, Agha et al. (2009) state that the quality of physician-patient communication is a critical factor influencing treatment outcomes and patient satisfaction with their care. To date, there is little research to document the effect of telemedicine on physician-patient communication. In the study by Agha et al., they measured and described verbal and nonverbal communication during clinical telemedicine consultations and compared telemedicine with in-person consultations concerning the quality of physician-patient communication. The study's findings indicate differences between telemedicine and in-person consultations in terms of physician-patient communication style. The researchers suggest that, when comparing telemedicine and in-person consultations in terms of physician-patient communication, telemedicine visits are more physician-centered, with the physician controlling the dialogue and the patient taking a relatively passive role. They called for further research to determine whether these differences are significant and whether they have relevance respecting health outcomes and patient satisfaction with care. While the debate continues over the effectiveness and outcomes of telemedicine, there are researchers on both sides of the debate.

Patient-Centeredness and Structure

The intersection between patient-centeredness and structure is both vital and challenging. An adequate structure is necessary to support an effective telemedicine environment. One aspect of structure that raises concerns for telecommunications professionals is data security. In the United States and Germany, there have been significant advancements in these areas. Heydenreich et al. (2009) note that data security must be considered seriously in the context of telemedical home monitoring because of the transmission and communication of patients' personal data. The contract governing medical treatment allows an ophthalmologist to process all data relevant to treatment. In Germany, the legal framework for this purpose is provided by the Data Protection Act, various German hospital acts, and codes of medical professional conduct. In principle, these rules apply to telemedical home monitoring and to common physician-patient relationships. The patient must be informed extensively in an understandable manner and must give his/her written consent. However, the advanced options of new IT technologies demand the development of technical and organizational concepts that guarantee compliance with legal and regulatory affairs, ensure data security, and prevent data abuse.

Another aspect of structure is the hardware and software components of telemedicine. Malone et al. (1998) conclude that remote sonographic viewing of fetal anatomy was adequate using both 256 and 384 kbps systems, although a motion artifact was significantly more likely to occur using the slower system. This problem may affect the ability of the lower-bandwidth system to allow the optimal detection of fetal anomalies.

Patient-Centeredness and Process

Store-and-forward telemedicine is an emerging technology by which medical data is captured for subsequent interpretation by a remote expert. This has the potential to improve the accessibility, quality, and cost of ROP management. In their article, Richter et al. (2009) summarize the current evaluation data on applications of telemedicine for ROP, particularly involving the diagnostic accuracy and reliability of remote image interpretation by experts. One of the challenges faced by patients regarding telemedicine is their access to consultants. Nijland et al. (2009) note that, as healthcare continues to evolve toward a more patient-centered approach, patient expectations and demands will be a major force in driving the adoption of e-consultations.

Timeliness and Structure

Mitchell et al. (2009) reported on their work with the telemedicine project at Yorkhill Hospital, Glasgow, which was set up in 2004 to aid with the rapid diagnosis of children at a distant location. The Child and Adolescent Mental Health Services (CAMHS) uses this service for clinical work, service development, and research. Twenty-four CAMHS professionals with experience of the telemedicine facility were asked to complete questionnaires outlining their opinions on the strengths and weaknesses of the facility; 19 responded. The results showed a wide variety of professionals use the facility and that clinical work makes up the majority of the use. The respondents noted that the most significant benefit of the system was in terms of what it offers to rural populations in Scotland. Saving time and improving communication were also highlighted as important. Technology failures and problems with sound quality were highlighted as drawbacks. Seventy-nine percent of the subjects stated that they preferred telemedicine to telephone conferencing. The results show the telemedicine facility is perceived as a positive addition to CAMHS in Scotland. Therefore, its use should be encouraged in other areas of medicine and surgery.

Timeliness and Process

Regarding timeliness and process, Barrett et al. (2009) note that, in the rural midwest region of Western Australia (WA), wound care is a major burden on the healthcare system. Optimal wound care was found to be impeded by issues that included the involvement of multiple healthcare providers, incomplete and inconsistent documentation, and limited access to expert review. Barrett et al. (2009) examined the systemic barriers encountered in implementing a telehealth program in rural WA and provided recommendations for future telehealth initiatives.

The study investigated the use of a shared electronic wound imaging and reporting system in combination with an expert remote wound consultation service for managing patients with chronic wounds in midwestern WA. The trial sites included rural hospital outpatient clinics, a private domiciliary nursing service, residential aged-care facilities, general practices, and a podiatry clinic. The implementation conformed to accepted best practices in introducing telehealth initiatives. Major obstacles were workforce issues and significant delays in installing the software at some sites. Only 47 percent of the healthcare providers trained to use the software at the beginning of the trial were still employed when the trial ended. Prolonged periods of vacant positions at one remote clinic and an aged-care facility made it impossible for the remaining providers to allocate time for using the wound care software.

Efficiency and Structure

Rocha et al. (2009) note that, in the last few years, telepathology has benefited from progress in the technology of image digitalization and transmission through the world wide web. The applications of telepathology and virtual imaging are more current in research and morphology teaching. In surgical pathology daily practice, this technology still has limits and is more often used for case consultation. Many of the limitations of virtual imaging for the surgical pathologist reside in the capacity to store images, which thus far has hindered the more widespread use of this technology.

While it is undeniable that telemedicine has contributed to improving the prevention, diagnosis, and treatment of disease, as well as access to healthcare, it must be emphasized that the enthusiasm and the infatuation it evokes hide a sad reality. Indeed, it is not enough that things are technically possible and medically desirable to be simple. Telemedicine faces, like most other radical technological innovations, cultural, structural, economic, organizational, and legal obstacles that undermine its full deployment (Yaya and Raffelini, 2009).

Efficiency and Process

The confluence of efficiency and process holds a great deal of promise for telemedicine. The efficient deployment of telemedicine requires an effective management of a process. Organizations that adopt telemedicine strategies must be willing to incorporate some form of learning and education for the process to be successful. Mishra et al. (2009) report that India, with its diverse landmass and huge population, is an ideal setting for telemedicine. There, telemedicine activities began in 1999. Since then, the Indian Space Research Organization has been deploying a satellite communication (SATCOM) based telemedicine network across the country. Various government agencies—the Department of Information Technology and the Ministry of Health & Family Welfare, state governments, and premier medical and technical institutions of India—have undertaken initiatives with the aim of providing quality health-care facilities to the rural and remote parts of the country. The Government of India has planned and implemented various national-level projects and even extended telemedicine services to South Asian and African countries.

Efforts are taking place in medical e-learning to establish digital medical libraries. Some institutions that are actively involved in telemedicine activities have started curriculum and non-curriculum telemedicine training programs. To support telemedicine activities within India, the Department of Information Technology has defined standards for telemedicine systems, and the Ministry of Health & Family Welfare has constituted the National Telemedicine Task Force. There are various government and private telemedicine solution providers and a few societies and associations actively engaged to create awareness about telemedicine within the country. With its large medical and IT manpower and expertise in these areas, India holds great promise and has emerged as a leader in the field of telemedicine.

The telecommunications revolution has offered medical professionals the possibility to transmit information of any sort while zeroing in on transmission time latency and annihilating spatial distances. Robotically mediated telesurgery has made it possible for surgeons to operate standing at a considerable distance from the operating table and without even touching or directly seeing the surgical field. Medical education and medical consulting have acquired new, wider ranges of applicability thanks to the introduction of teleproctoring, telementoring, and teleconsulting (Karamanoukian et al., 2003).

According to Charters (2009), interoperability issues are critical for home telehealth applications, EHRs, EMRs, and personal health records. Issues of interoperability affect clinical decision making and clinician information synthesis. The ability to exchange data collected in the home with an EMR has been positively related to improvements in process outcomes for chronic illness. However, to realize this benefit, risks must be minimized. The evaluation of interoperability challenges and their potential solutions support data-driven risk management decisions.

Equitability and Structure

The central question here is whether the structure can support the equitability of care. According to Yoo and Dudley (2009), one of the most common applications is in the ICU, where ICU telemedicine (tele-ICU) can increase access to intensivist physicians. In this care model, intensivist physicians and nurses in a central monitoring facility can visually monitor patients across multiple ICUs in many hospitals using bedside cameras while electronically tracking relevant clinical information, such as vital signs or laboratory data. The remote care team can communicate orally with bedside caregivers to provide real-time, around-the-clock patient care. Research has shown that dedicated on-site intensivist staffing is associated with reductions in hospital and ICU LOS and mortality. The real challenge of this model lies in the requirements of the structure that would support it.

Equitability and Process

Equitability is significantly affected by access to care. While the field of telemedicine specifically targets access to care, it is important to understand the link between access to care and equitability. George et al. (2009) explore perceptions about telemedicine among underserved urban African American and Latino populations. Telemedicine has been advanced as a vehicle to increase access to specialty care among the urban underserved, yet little is known about its acceptability among these populations. George et al. (2009) found that concerns about telemedicine varied between the two racial/ethnic groups. These findings have implications for important issues such as the adoption of telemedicine, patient satisfaction, and doctor-patient interactions. It will be critical to consider perceptions of this healthcare innovation in the development of strategies to market and implement telemedicine among underserved urban African American and Latino populations.

One of the greatest challenges facing people in underserved neighborhoods is the access to consultants. Nijland et al. (2009) address the role of e-consultation in this regard. The patients' motivations to use e-consultation strongly depended on demands being satisfied, such as getting a quick response. When analyzing socio-demographic and health-related characteristics, it turned out that certain patient groups—the elderly, the less educated, chronic medication users, and frequent general practitioner visitors—were more motivated than other patient groups to use e-consultation services, but also were more demanding. Less-educated patients, for example, more strongly demanded instructions regarding e-consultation use than highly educated patients.

Sicker patients with greater care needs are being discharged to their homes to assume responsibility for their own care with fewer nurses available to aid them. This situation brings with it a host of human factors and ergonomic (HFE) concerns, both for the home care nurse and the home dwelling patient, that can affect quality of care and patient safety (Or et al., 2009). Many of these concerns relate to critical home care tasks concerning information access, communication, and patient self-monitoring, equitability, and self-management.

Implications for Outcomes

Outcome measures reflect the result of care, from a clinical or patient perspective. Although mortality is by far the most commonly used measure, other outcomes that could be used as quality indicators include complications of care, hospital admission or readmission, visits to the emergency room, and a variety of patient-centered and staff-based measures of satisfaction, health status, or utility. Outcomes can also be defined in the context of patients' and staff experiences.

Ramaekers et al. (2009) conducted a study on telemonitoring aimed at assessing its short-term impact on patients' disease-specific knowledge, adherence, and depression. The improved adherence rates within the three-month study period underscored the potential of telemonitoring to enhance self-management among heart failure patients and its potential impact on other outcomes. Longer-term results will enable solid conclusions to be reached concerning the relationship between telemonitoring and patients' adherence.

Figure 9.2 shows the interaction between the variables that drive structure and process and telemedicine quality. In this framework, telemedicine quality manifests in two ways—patient satisfaction and provider satisfaction—with vital implications for clinical outcomes.

Any attempt to understand quality in telemedicine must account for the following key variables:

- Access to care by patients
- Access to service providers
- Patient safety
- Diagnostic accuracy
- Clinical effectiveness (communication among care providers, documentation and records, outcomes, reliability of interpreted data at remote locations, etc.)
- Confidentiality of health records
- Patient satisfaction, patient perception, and acceptability
- Provider satisfaction
- Structure—(technology, facility, transmission, efficiency of care delivery, costs, etc.)

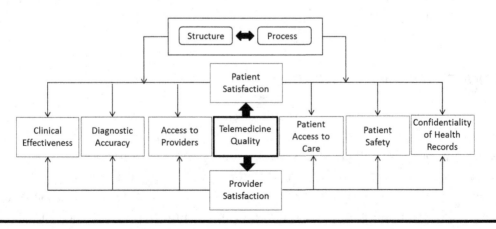

Figure 9.2 Quality variables in telemedicine.

While the benefits of telemedicine and its many derivatives are laudable, it is important to recognize the challenges that lie ahead for practitioners, healthcare administrators, providers, and patients. Many of the discussions regarding telemedicine have failed to consider quality. Perhaps the most significant benefit of telemedicine is its ability to expand access to care. However, access to care does not occur in a vacuum. The fusion of technology and medicine creates its own set of risk factors. Our ability to understand, measure, and improve such risk factors is vital to the long-term sustainability of telemedicine.

Questions for Discussions

9.1. What are some of the barriers to the implementation of telemedicine at your organization? What can be done to overcome them?
9.2. How does an organization deal with the challenges of resistance to change regarding the adoption of telemedicine?
9.3. Describe how telemedicine can serve as a value proposition for healthcare organizations.

References

Agha, Z., Roter, D. L. and Schapira, R. M. 2009. "An Evaluation of Patient-Physician Communication Style During Telemedicine Consultations." *Journal of Medical Internet Research* 30; 11(3): e36.

Aoki, N., Dunn, K., Johnson-Throop, K. A. and Turley, J. P., 2003, December. "Outcomes and Methods in Telemedicine Evaluation." *Telemedicine Journal and e-Health* 9(4): 393–401.

Barrett M., Larson A., Carville K., Ellis I., 2009. "Challenges Faced in Implementation of a Telehealth Enabled Chronic Wound Care System. *Rural Remote Health* 9(3): 1154.

Boaz, M., Hellman, K. and Wainstein, J., 2009. "An Automated Telemedicine System Improves Patient-Reported Well-Being." *Diabetes Technology & Therapeutics* 11(3): 181–186.

Breslow, M. J., Rosenfeld, B.A., Doerfler, M. et al., 2004. "Effect of a Multiple-Site Intensive Care Unit Telemedicine Program on Clinical and Economic Outcomes: An Alternative Paradigm for Intensivist Staffing. *Critical Care Medicine* 32(1): 31–38.

Charters, K., 2009. "Home Telehealth Electronic Health Information Lessons Learned." *Studies in Health Technology and Informatics* 146: 719.

Donabedian, A., 1988. "The Quality of Care: How Can It Be Assessed?" *JAMA* 260(12): 1743–1748.

Durrani, H. and Khoja, S., 2009. A Systematic Review of the Use of Telehealth in Asian Countries. *Journal of Telemedicine and Telecare* 15(4): 175–81.

George, S. M., Hamilton, A. and Baker, R., 2009. "Pre-experience Perceptions about Telemedicine among African Americans and Latinos in South Central Los Angeles." *Telemedicine Journal and e-Health* 15(6): 525–30.

Guttman, D., 2017. How Telemedicine Is Transforming the Healthcare Industry. https://www.fshealth.com/blog/how-telemedicine-is-transforming-the-healthcare-industry

Heydenreich, F., Jürgens, C. and Tost, F., 2009. Data Security and the Handling of Patient Data in Home Monitoring Systems. *Ophthalmologe* 106(9): 800–4.

IOM (Institute of Medicine), 2001. *Crossing the Quality Chasm: A New Health System for the 21st Century.* Washington, DC: National Academy Press.

IOM (Institute of Medicine), 2003. *Priority Areas for National Action: Transforming Health Care Quality.* Adams, K. and Corrigan, J. M., eds. Washington, DC: The National Academies Press.

Japsen, B., 2015. *Doctors' Virtual Consults with Patients to Double by 2020.* https://www.forbes.com/sites/brucejapsen/2015/08/09/as-telehealth-booms-doctor-video-consults-to-double-by-2020/#461c2e364f9b

Karamanoukian, H. L., Pande, R. U., Patel, Y., Freeman, A. M., Aoukar, P. S. and D'Ancona, G., 2003, December. "Teleoperations Systems." *Journal of Pediatric Endosurgery & Innovative Techniques* 7(4): 421–425.

LaFramboise, L. M., Woster, J., Yager, A. and Yates, B. C., 2009. "A Technological Life Buoy: Patient Perceptions of the Health Buddy." *Journal of Cardiovascular Nursing* 24(3): 216–224.

Lai, A. M., Kaufman, D. R., Starren, J. and Shea, S., 2009. "Evaluation of a Remote Training Approach for Teaching Seniors to Use a Telehealth System." *International Journal of Medical informatics* 78(11): 732–744.

Lee, J. Y., Du, Y. E., Coki, O., Flynn, J. T., Starren, J and Chiang, M. F., 2010. "Parental Perceptions Toward Digital Imaging and Telemedicine for Retinopathy of Prematurity Management." *Graefes Archieves for Clinical and Experimental Ophthalmology* 248(1):141–147. Epub

LeRouge, C., Garfield, M. J. and Hevner, A. R., 2002. Quality Attributes in Telemedicine Video Conferencing, Proceedings of the 35th Hawaii International Conference on System Sciences.

Malik, N. N., 2009. "Integration of Diagnostic and Communication Technologies." *Journal of Telemedicine and Telecare* 15(7): 323–326.

Malone, F. D., Athanassiou, A., Nores, J. and D'Alton, M. E., 1998. "Effect of ISDN Bandwidth on Image Quality for Telemedicine Transmission of Obstetric Ultrasonography." *Telemedicine Journal* 4(2): 161–165.

Mishra, S. K., Kapoor, L. and Singh, I. P., 2009. "Telemedicine in India: Current Scenario and the Future." *Telemedicine Journal and e-Health* 15(6): 568–575.

Mitchell, S. A., MacLaren, A. T., Morton, M. and Carachi, R., 2009. "Professional Opinions of the Use of Telemedicine in Child & Adolescent Psychiatry." *Scottish Medical Journal* 54(3): 13–16.

Nijland, N., van Gemert-Pijnen, J. E., Boer, H., Steehouder, M. F, Seydel, E. R., 2009. "Increasing the Ise of e-consultation in Primary Care: Results of an Online Survey among Non-users of e-consultation." *International Journal of Medical informatics* 78(10): 688–703.

Or, C. K., Valdez, R. S., Casper, G. R., Carayon, P., Burke, L. J., Brennan P. F. and Karsh, B. T., 2009. "Human Factors and Ergonomics in Home Care: Current Concerns and Future Considerations for Health Information Technology." *Work* 33(2): 201–209.

Ramaekers, B. L., Janssen-Boyne, J. J., Gorgels, A. P. and Vrijhoef, H. J., 2009. Adherence among Telemonitored Patients with Heart Failure to Pharmacological and Nonpharmacological Recommendations." *Telemedicine Journal and e-Health* 15(6): 517–524.

Richter, G. M., Williams, S. L., Starren, J., Flynn, J. T. and Chiang, M. F., 2009. "Telemedicine for Retinopathy of Prematurity Diagnosis: Evaluation and Challenges." *Survey of Ophthalmology* 54(6): 671–685.

Rocha R., Vassallo J., Soares F., Miller K., Gobbi H. 2009. "Digital Slides: Present Status of a Tool for Consultation, Teaching, and Quality Control in Pathology. *Pathology – Research and Practice* 205(11): 735–741.

Rosenfeld, B. A., Dorman, T. and Breslow, M. J. et al., 2000. Intensive Care Unit Telemedicine: Alternate Paradigm for Providing Continuous Intensivist Care. *Critical Care Medicine* 28(12): 3925–3931.

Sandberg, J., Trief, P. M., Izquierdo, R., Goland, R., Morin, P. C., Palmas, W., Larson, C. D., Strait, J. G., Shea, S. and Weinstock, R. S., 2009. "A Qualitative Study of the Experiences and Satisfaction of Direct Telemedicine Providers in Diabetes Case Management." *Telemedicine Journal and e-Health* 15(8): 742–7450.

Sevean, P., Dampier, S., Spadoni, M., Strickland, S. and Pilatzke, S., 2009. "Patients and Families' Experiences with Video Telehealth in Rural/Remote Communities in Northern Canada." *Journal of Clinical Nursing* 18(18): 2573–2579.

Singh, R., Ng, W. H., Lee, K. E., Wang, E., Ng, I. and Lee, W. L., 2009. "Telemedicine in Emergency Neurological Service Provision in Singapore: Using Technology to Overcome Limitations." *Telemedicine Journal and e-Health* 15(6): 560–565.

Switzer, J. A., Levine, S. R. and Hess, D. C., 2009. Telestroke 10 Years Later—"Telestroke 2.0." *Cerebrovascular Diseases* 28:323–330. DOI:10.1159/000229550

Varghese, S. B. and Phillips, C. A., 2009. "Caring in Telehealth." *Telemedicine Journal e-Health* 15(10): 1005–1009.

Vitacca, M., Mazzù, M. and Scalvini, S., 2009. "Socio-technical and Organizational Challenges to Wider eHealth Implementation." *Chronic Respiratory Disease* 6(2): 91–97.

Warshaw, E. M. et al., 2009. "Accuracy of Teledermatology for Pigmented Neoplasms." *Journal of the American Academy of Dermatalogy* 61(5): 753–765.

Yaya, S. and Raffelini, C., 2009. "Technological Transformations and Evolution of the Medical Practice: Current Status, Issues and Perspectives for the Development of Telemedicine," *Review of Med Brux*, 30(2): 83–91.

Yoo, E. J. and Dudley, R. A., 2009. "Evaluating Telemedicine in the ICU." *JAMA* 302(24): 2705–2706.

Index

A

AAOS, *see* American Academy of Orthopaedic Surgeons (AAOS)
ACP, *see* American College of Physicians (ACP)
Acute care appointment, 6
Advance practice nurses (APNs), 19
Adverse events, 140
Affordable Care Act, 9
Aging population in United States, 3–4
AI, *see* Artificial intelligence (AI)
AMA, *see* American Medical Association (AMA)
American Academy of Orthopaedic Surgeons (AAOS), 36
American College of Physicians (ACP), 5
American Medical Association (AMA), 5
American Nursing Association (ANA), 19
AMI, *see* Any mental illness (AMI)
ANA, *see* American Nursing Association (ANA)
Analytics, defined, 87
Any mental illness (AMI), 11
APNs, *see* Advance practice nurses (APNs)
Artificial intelligence (AI), 13–14, 16
Assessment phase, 174
ATD, *see* Attention to detail (ATD)
Attention to detail (ATD), 39
  core value principles of, 83–85
  culture of, 80–81
    distraction, 81–83
  power of, 79–80
  principle, 44
Attentiveness, 76–79
Attribute data, 96–97
  chart
    categories, 146
    for non-conforming items, 146
    for non-conformities, 146–147
  control charts for, 143–146
Availability of information, 39–40

B

Baby Boomers, 3
Behavioral healthcare, 10–12
Beryl Institute, defines, 51–52
Black belt, 145
Brainstorming
  assessment phase, 174
  clarification phase, 173
  creativity phase, 173
Burnout prevention, 65–66

C

CAMHS, *see* Child and Adolescent Mental Health Services (CAMHS)
Care coordination, 37–39
  principle, 46
C-chart example, 154–156
CDC, *see* Centers for Disease Control and Prevention (CDC)
CDSS, *see* Clinical decision support system (CDSS)
Centers for Disease Control and Prevention (CDC), 8

Centers for Medicare & Medicaid Services (CMS), 1
Champion, 145
Chatbots, 16
Chief complaint, 35–36
    principle, 43
Child and Adolescent Mental Health Services (CAMHS), 213–214
Childhood immunizations, timely delivery of, 32
Clarification phase, 173
Cleveland Clinic study, 58
Clinical decision support system (CDSS), 114
Clinical excellence, 52
Clinical outcomes, 41–42
CMS, *see* Centers for Medicare & Medicaid Services (CMS)
Communication principle, 45
Compassion, 36–37
Computer-aided nutrition/mixing, 114
Computerized physician order entry (CPOE), 114
Conducting focus groups, 91–93
Confidentiality, 30–31
    principle, 44, 46
Connect interdependent technologies, 195–196
Continuous data, 97
Correlation coefficient *(r)*, 181–182
CoxHealth, 5
CPOE, *see* Computerized physician order entry (CPOE)
Creativity phase, 173
Cybersecurity, 12

D

Daily life, 17
Data
    collection, 88
        methods, 89–90
    reliance on solid, 196
    security, 12
    stratifying, 94–95
    types of
        attribute or discrete data, 96–97
        variable or continuous data, 97
    variations, 95–96

Define, measure, analyze, improve, and control (DMAIC) model, 141
Deming cycle, 121
Deming, Edwards, 139
Digital health apps, 191–192
Digital transformation, 19
    digital health applications, 191–193
    employees, impact on, 193–194
    leadership, role of, 194–195
    refers, 190–191
    strategy, 195–196
Dignity principle, 44
Discrete data, 96–97
Disney attacks, 72–73
Distal touch, 21
Distraction, culture of, 81–83
DMAIC model, *see* Define, measure, analyze, improve, and control (DMAIC) model
Documents, 94
Donabedian, Avedis, 201
Drug interactions, 114

E

ED, *see* Emergency Department (ED); Emergency department (ED)
Effectiveness, 210
EHRs, *see* Electronic health records (EHRs)
Electronic health records (EHRs), 5, 106, 190
Electronic medical records (EMRs) system, 13–16
Electronic protected health information (ePHI), 200
Emergency Department (ED), 61
Emergency department (ED), 5
Empathy, 20–21, 84–85
    defined, 36
    principle, 44
Employee engagement/satisfaction, 64–65
EMRs system, *see* Electronic medical records (EMRs) system
ePHI, *see* Electronic protected health information (ePHI)
Equitability, 216–217
"Error-proofing," 113
Experiments, 94

F

Fee-for-service (FFS) model, 17
FFS model, *see* Fee-for-service (FFS) model
Field notes, 91
FIFO approach, *see* First-In First-Out (FIFO) approach
First-In First-Out (FIFO) approach, 131
Fishbone diagram, 178–182
Five S method, 119–121
    benefits of, 125
    planning for, 121–122
    steps for implementing, 122–124
Flow charts, 175–176
Focus group session, 91–93

G

"Gemba Walk," 57
Gold standard, 76–79
Green belts, 145

H

Hassle factor, 34–35, 56
    principle, 43
Haunted Mansion, 73
HCAHPS, *see* Hospital Consumer Assessment of Healthcare Providers and Systems (HCAHPS)
Health Affairs, 10, 64–65
Healthcare businesses, 193
Healthcare industry
    aging population in United States, 3–4
    behavioral, 10–12
    cost and sustainability, 1–3
    data and insights, 16–17
    data security, 12
    empathy and compassion, 19–22
    population health management, 7–8
    preventive care, 17–19
    price transparency, 8–10
    retail healthcare, 4–6
    technology and electronic medical records system, 13–16
    telemedicine and virtual healthcare, 6–7
    transition from volume-based, 22–23

Healthcare leaders' role, 84
Healthcare provider organizations, 14
Health Information Technology for Economic and Clinical Health (HITECH), 13
Health Insurance Portability and Accountability Act (HIPAA), 6, 200
Health plans, 66
Hemoglobin testing, 114–115
HIPAA, *see* Health Insurance Portability and Accountability Act (HIPAA)
Hire right staff, 64
Hispanic population, 4
HITECH, *see* Health Information Technology for Economic and Clinical Health (HITECH)
Home telemedicine unit (HTU), 211
Hospital billing error information, 149
Hospital Consumer Assessment of Healthcare Providers and Systems (HCAHPS), 66
    surveys, 54–57
    tactics and strategies for, 57–66
Hourly rounding, 59–61
HTU, *see* Home telemedicine unit (HTU)

I

IDEATel project, *see* Informatics for Diabetes and Education Telemedicine (IDEATel) project
Imai, Masaaki, 115
"Inadvertent error prevention.", 113
Infant abduction prevention, 113
Informatics for Diabetes and Education Telemedicine (IDEATel) project, 211
Information principle, 45
Inherent variation, 96
Institute of Medicine (IOM) model, 31, 205–206
Institutional Review Board (IRB), 128
Insurance Checker, 14
Insurance verification, 14
Integrated Services Digital Network (ISDN), 203
Interviews, 92–93
IOM model, *see* Institute of Medicine (IOM) model
IRB, *see* Institutional Review Board (IRB)

ISDN, *see* Integrated Services Digital
    Network (ISDN)
Ishikawa diagram, 178–182

J

*JAMA, see Journal of the American Medical
    Association (JAMA)*
Jidoka, 106
The Joint Commission (TJC), 62
Journal of General Internal Medicine, 36
*Journal of the American Medical Association
    (JAMA),* 41
Judging process stability, 162
Juran, J. M., 177

K

Kaizen, 115–116
    events, 116–119
Kanban, 130–132
    in hospitals and clinics, benefits of, 134
Knowledge management, 15

L

Lack of timeliness, 32
Leadership
    role of, 194–195
    rounding, 57–59
Lean management system
    five S method, 119–121
        benefits of, 125
        planning for, 121–122
        steps for implementing, 122–124
    Kaizen, 115–116
        events, 116–119
    Kanban, 130–132
        in hospitals and clinics, benefits of, 134
    poka-yoke, 113–115
    process, 104–107, 111–112, 135–136
    single-minute exchange of dies, 125–127
        healthcare applications, 127–129
    standardized and standard work, 134–135
        benefits of, 136
    tools and their applications, 107
    two-bin Kanban system, 132–134

value stream mapping, 107–109
    waste, defined, 110–111
Lean Six Sigma, 141
Long-term disability, 32
Lorenz, M.C., 177

M

Mammograms, 9
Master black belt, 145
Medical condition, defined, 29
Medical professionals, 192
Medical research, 17
Medicare Advantage plans, 41
Mental Health America (MHA), 11
MHA, *see* Mental Health America (MHA)
"Mistake-proofing," 113
Mobile health, 191
Moderator, role of, 92
Multi-voting, 174

N

National Conference of State Legislators
    (NCSL), 9
Natural language processing, 15
NCSL, *see* National Conference of State
    Legislators (NCSL)
Negligent adverse events, 140
New England Journal of Medicine, 40
Non-value-added activities, 111
NP-chart example, 150–152

O

OACT, *see* Office of the Actuary (OACT)
Observation, 90–91
OECD, *see* Organisation for Economic
    Co-operation and Development
    (OECD)
Office of the Actuary (OACT), 1
Ohno, Taiichi, 130
On-demand healthcare services, 5
Ongoing care, 17
Organisation for Economic Co-operation
    and Development (OECD), 3
Osborn, Alex F., 171

P

Pareto analysis, 177–178
Pareto, Vilfreo, 177
Participant observation, 90–91
Patient
    centeredness, defined, 18
    experience, 17
    identification/safety, 113–114
    medical condition, defined, 29
    privacy issues, 12
    safety, 32–33
        principle, 43–44
    stories, 64
    whiteboards, 62–63
Patient-centeredness
    process, 213
    structure, 212–213
P-chart
    example, 147
    procedure for constructing, 147–150
PCPs, *see* Primary care providers (PCPs)
PDSA cycle, *see* Plan-Do-Study-Act (PDSA)
        cycle
Personally identifiable information (PII), 200
Peters, Tom, 57
PHI, *see* Protected health information (PHI)
Physician-patient communication, 212
PII, *see* Personally identifiable
        information (PII)
Plan-Do-Study-Act (PDSA) cycle, 168–169
Poisson distribution, 146
Poka-yoke, 113–115
Population health management, 7–8
Post-discharge follow-up, 37
    calls, 62
    principle, 44
Precision hemoglobin testing, 114–115
Preventive care, 17–19
    services, 8
Price transparency, 8–10
    principle, 44
Price Waterhouse Coopers (PWC), 10
Primary care providers (PCPs), 5
Primary care services, 8
Privacy, 30–31
    principle, 46

Prospectively collected data, 90
Protected health information (PHI), 200
Purposeful (hourly) rounding, 59–61
PWC, *see* Price Waterhouse Coopers (PWC)

Q

Quality variables, in telemedicine, 218

R

Radio-frequency identification (RFID),
        88, 133
R-chart, procedure for constructing, 162–166
RDNs, *see* Registered dietitian
        nutritionists (RDNs)
Records, 94
Registered dietitian nutritionists (RDNs), 18
Registered nurses (RNs), 19
Reliance on solid data, 196
Remote Patient Education in a Telemedicine
        Environment (REPETE), 211
REPETE, *see* Remote Patient Education
        in a Telemedicine Environment
        (REPETE)
Respect principle, 44
Retail healthcare, 4–6
Retrospective data, 89–90
RFID, *see* Radio-frequency identification
        (RFID)
RNs, *see* Registered nurses (RNs)
Robotically mediated telesurgery, 216
Robotic process automation (RPA), 193
Roehrig, Charles, 10
RPA, *see* Robotic process automation (RPA)

S

SATCOM, *see* Satellite communication
        (SATCOM)
Satellite communication (SATCOM), 215
Scatter diagram, 179–181
Security, 30–31
    principle, 46
Seiketsu, 120
Seiri, 120
Seiso, 120

Seiton, 120
Semi-structured interviews, 93
Senior leadership education, 195
Sensitivity, 36–37
    principle, 44
Sentiment analysis, 15
Service excellence, 52
SHC, *see* Stanford Health Care (SHC)
Shingo, Shigeo, 125
Shitsuke, 120
"Siloed" care model, 22
Single-minute exchange of dies (SMED),
        125–127
    healthcare applications, 127–129
Six sigma
    attribute data chart
        categories, 146
        for non-conforming items, 146
        for non-conformities, 146–147
    brainstorming
        assessment phase, 174
        clarification phase, 173
        creativity phase, 173
    cause and effect diagrams, 178–182
    C-chart example, 154–156
    concepts of, 142
    control charts, 143
        for attribute data, 143–146
    control charts for variable data, 160–162
    defects, 142–143
    flow charts, 175–176
    judging process stability, 162
    multi-voting, 174
    NP-chart example, 150–152
    pareto analysis, 177–178
    P-chart
        example, 147
        procedure for constructing, 147–150
    process improvement tools, 168–170
    R-chart
        procedure for constructing, 162–166
    stable process, 160
    tools for gathering and analyzing
            data, 175
    tools for managing ideas, 170–171
    U-chart example, 156–159
    unstable process, 159–160

variable data, control charts for, 160–162
X-bar chart
    procedure for constructing, 167
X – R-chart, 162
X – S-chart, 167–168
SMED, *see* Single-minute exchange of dies
        (SMED)
Social determinants of health, 20
Social Security Numbers (SSNs), 200
SSNs, *see* Social Security Numbers (SSNs)
Stable process, 160
Staff training, 63–64
Standalone walk-in clinics, 4
Standardized/standard work, 134–135
    benefits of, 136
Stanford Health Care (SHC), 59
Starbucks, 73
Stirtz, Kevin, 73
Store-and-forward telemedicine, 213
Storefront clinics, 4
Stratifying data, 94–95
STRokE DOC, *see* Stroke Team Remote
        Evaluation using a Digital
        Observation Camera (STRokE DOC)
Stroke patients' mortality, 32
Stroke Team Remote Evaluation using
        a Digital Observation Camera
        (STRokE DOC), 211
Supplemental telemedicine services, 4
Surveys, 93–94

T

Team problem-solving process, 171
Telehealth, 191
Telemedicine
    process of care measures
        efficiency and process, 215–217
        implications for outcomes, 217–219
        Institute of Medicine (IOM) model,
            205–206
        quality measurement in, 206–215
    structure-related measures of
            quality, 204
Telemedicine healthcare, 6–7
Timeliness, 31–32
    principle, 46

and process, 214
and structure, 213–214
Timely antibiotic treatments, 32
Timely delivery of childhood
immunizations, 32
TJC, *see* The Joint Commission (TJC)
*To Err Is Human: Building a Safer Health
System,* 32
Total parenteral nutrition (TPN), 114
Toyoda, Sakichi, 129
Toyota Production System, 102, 120
TPN, *see* Total parenteral nutrition (TPN)
True cost principle, 45–46
Trust principle, 45
Two-bin Kanban system, 132–134
Type I muda, 111
Type II muda, 111

U

U-chart example, 156–159
Unstable process, 159–160
Urgent care clinics, 4

V

Value-based healthcare, 19
Value-based reimbursement (VBR) model,
22–24
Value proposition, 42–43
Value stream mapping (VSM), 107–109

Variable data, 97
control charts for, 160–162
Variation, 96
VBR model, *see* Value-based reimbursement
(VBR) model
Videotaping, 128
Virginia Mason Institute, 131
Virtual healthcare, 6–7
Visual cues, 21
VSM, *see* Value stream mapping (VSM)

W

Wall Street Journal Online, 57
Waste, defined, 110–111
Whiteboard templates, 63
"Whole person"
care for, 33–34
principle, 44–45
Wireless health, 191
Womack, Jim, 103

X

X-bar chart, procedure for constructing, 167
X – R-chart, 162
X – S-chart, 167–168

Z

Zocdoc app, 14

Printed in the United States
by Baker & Taylor Publisher Services